Transforming the Struggles of Tamars

Transforming the Struggles of Tamars

Single Women and Baptistic Communities

LINA ANDRONOVIENĖ

With a foreword by Parush R. Parushev

◥PICKWICK *Publications* · Eugene, Oregon

TRANSFORMING THE STRUGGLES OF TAMARS
Single Women and Baptistic Communities

Copyright © 2014 Lina Andronovienė. All rights reserved. Except for brief quotations in critical publications or reviews, no part of this book may be reproduced in any manner without prior written permission from the publisher. Write: Permissions, Wipf and Stock Publishers, 199 W. 8th Ave., Suite 3, Eugene, OR 97401.

Pickwick Publications
An Imprint of Wipf and Stock Publishers
199 W. 8th Ave., Suite 3
Eugene, OR 97401

www.wipfandstock.com

ISBN 13: 978-1-62564-108-3

Cataloging-in-Publication data:

Andronovienė, Lina.

   Transforming the struggles of Tamars : single women and baptistic communities / Lina Andronovienė ; with a foreword by Parush R. Parushev.

   xii + 288 p. ; 23 cm. Includes bibliographical references and index.

   ISBN 13: 978-1-62564-108-3

   1. Church work with single people. 2. Single women—Religious life. 3. Women in Christianity. 4. Christian women—Religious life. 5. Women in church work. I. Parushev, Parush R. II. Title.

BV639.S5 A526 2014

Manufactured in the U.S.A.

New Revised Standard Version Bible, copyright 1989, Division of Christian Education of the National Council of the Churches of Christ in the United States of America. Used by permission. All rights reserved.

*To my family in Lithuania,
who have faithfully shown me and many others
the reality of God's realm;*

*and to the people of the International Baptist Theological Seminary
in the Czech Republic (2001–2013), who have taught me
some of the most profound lessons about life
in Christian community*

Contents

Foreword by Parush R. Parushev   ix

Introduction   1

PART ONE: Involuntary Singleness: Socio-Ecclesial Maps

1. Churches and Single Women   15
2. Surface Theologies   38
3. Mirroring the Culture   61

PART TWO: Myths and Meanings: Exploring the Routes

4. Church, Family, and the Myths of Love   87
5. Convictions behind the Surface   115
6. The Fight of the Tamars: Feminist Interpretations   140

PART THREE: Costly Companionship: The Shape of the Journey

7. Community and Its Practices   167
8. I Have Called You Friends: A Theology of Friendship   201
9. The Grain That Dies: Creative Growth of Suffering-Love   224

Conclusion   253

Bibliography   259

Index   281

Foreword

WE TEND TO APPROACH reading a new book with some pre-understanding of the subject with which it deals. Our intuition, guided by our previous reading, often happens to be right not least because our selection of reading reflects our liking. My original understanding of the phenomenon of singleness was largely informed by dozens of books which I skimmed while shelving them as a book-consultant on the book-shelves of the Fuller Seminary bookstore—a California-based leading evangelical institution. Almost without exception those books were written for women in search for the right approach, or even technique, of securing a life-long partner. From that perspective, singleness is a transient and not particularly significant stage of life between adolescence and married life. Such an understanding is in line with the socially conservative evangelical theological focus on the family promoted by well-known radio broadcasters. Such a view of singleness will not resonate with the main concerns of this book. It belongs to the category of books that confronts the reader's prejudice and opens up a new perspective on the subject.

Whereas the book's clear focus is upon the challenges faced by single women struggling to find their place in life, and particularly in the life of baptistic communities largely in Europe, it narrates a much more complex story of the faith community's relationship with single persons crossing denominational, gender, regional and cultural boundaries. In this the title of the book promises less than the content delivers. The biblical metaphor and the deliberate address to the baptistic communities may suggest that the significance of this research is relevant only to certain sorts of Bible-believing evangelicals. The term *baptistic* refers to a particular way of being a church, usually referred to as pneumatological, Free Church or believer's church—a tradition of the adherents of the Radical Reformation which forms a separate ecclesial stream emphasizing discipleship and communal belonging. However, the concerns of this book go beyond the life within baptistic communities. The scope of the problem it addresses extends beyond the experience of a particular denomination; it appeals to any faith community as well as to any thick expression of human living which is called to evaluate the space it allows for the flourishing of a single person's life.

In contemporary living where sex and pairing for sensual pleasure is a habitual way of looking at one's life fulfilment the author asks: Can a deeper search for meaning be found elsewhere and with whom? In search for an answer Lithuanian scholar Dr. Lina Andronovienė presents a skilfully interwoven tapestry of insights and enquiries. From popular culture's amusement with the mythology of romantic love of the nuclear family "living happily ever after" to the worn-out pulpit clichés about God's plans for women being a happily married life; through some sharp but reductive feminist critical voices to the realistic assessment of a theology of happiness and friendship that takes into account suffering love, the kenotic aspect and communal character of human relationships leading to lasting and fulfilling friendships, in an almost encyclopaedic breadth, it seems she has considered all possible aspects of the subject.

If it would not have been for the clear focus of her work, the breadth of the themes and authors addressed might have produced a patchy treatment of the subject. Dr. Andronovienė is able to maintain the coherence of her work unchallenged. The structure and methodological setting of her argument makes a creative contribution to convictional theologizing. She proceeds from discerning the convictional grounds that have shaped the prevalent attitudes to singleness, to analyzing and assessing the reasons for their formation, and finally to critically investigating possible routes of transformation of conviction-sets by locating the issue of singleness in the holistic web of communal practices.

Building upon her first-hand observations and years of reflection on women's experience within baptistic tradition, Dr. Andronovienė creates a medium and vocabulary that enables her to relate that experience to a wider context. The strength of her research work lies in the masterful blend of experience and profound understanding of the contextual language of virtues and practices appropriated by this particular form of faith expression. Even if one opts for *doing* theology, as most of these communities indeed do, rather than constructing doctrinal schemes of how to do it, a convictional model or a map of the process for doing is still needed. The book is a rewarding attempt to expand the convictional language and insights of the baptistic tradition to embrace advanced conceptual thinking on human nature and human relationships. Dr. Andronovienė's penetrating analysis provides an excellent example of a much-needed link between the primary experiential life of faith communities and the well-developed conceptual vocabulary of secondary academic theological discourse. This is done in a readable and engaging way.

Dr. Andronovienė has accomplished a formidable task. In this book she has worked carefully on relating hard theological thinking with the experience of both an individual and an ecclesial community. While the premises of her work are contextually dependent, she has brought forth important issues for the whole Christian Church. I found her theological reflections refreshing and illuminating. One may not always agree with her assessment or follow her appropriation of a particular theological insight, but certainly her stimulating thought will leave indifferent no one concerned with the wellbeing of communities of faith.

Dr. Parush R. Parushev, Rector
International Baptist Theological Seminary
Prague, Czech Republic, September 2013

Introduction

A Story from of Old: Tamar

GENESIS 38 RELATES THE story of Tamar, the widow of Judah's son Er. Upon Er's death, Tamar's father-in-law asks his other son, Onan, to fulfill the duty of a brother-in-law and to ensure she has offspring, as law required. Onan, however, knows that if Tamar bears a son, it will significantly affect his own economic well-being. Thus he resorts to a technique of preventing her impregnation.

Consequently, Tamar remains childless. When Onan dies, she is promised by her father-in-law that when his youngest son, Shelah, grows up, she will be married to him. Time goes on, and Tamar realizes the promise has been purposefully forgotten. Finally, Tamar's mother-in-law dies, and Tamar hears that, after the time of mourning, her father-in-law is going up to Timnah to see his sheepshearers and to take part in local festivities there. She puts aside her widow's clothes, dresses up as a prostitute, puts a veil on her face, and takes a seat at the roadside at the entrance to Enaim. Her father-in-law approaches her and negotiates for her services, promising this prostitute a kid from his flock; however, she demands a deposit, and so Judah leaves his personal identification documents—signet, cord, and the staff.

Tamar keeps them safe, and soon knows that a new life is within her. Before long, her pregnancy becomes apparent to others. She is accused of playing the whore and brought out to her father-in-law who is ready to announce Tamar should be burnt alive for the shame she has brought on the family. However, Tamar stops the process by presenting the personal identification "documents" to this family court. "Take note, please, whose these are," she says; "it was the owner of these who made me pregnant." Then Judah utters, "She is more in the right than I, since I did not give her to my son Shelah."

The story of Tamar is powerful, mysterious, and uncomfortable. It speaks loudly about bodies and relationships; it causes embarrassment as we try to fathom and clumsily explain how this woman who "played the whore" and tricked her own father-in-law into incest is pronounced to be "more in the right" than the family patriarch. Some also wonder about how Judah's lot was different upon his confessing that it was he who slept with Tamar: it simply meant that she and the fruit of her womb would be allowed to live.

Inevitably, the text is hardly ever used for sermons or Bible studies or Sunday school classes, except perhaps to show how "imperfect" people can be the tools in God's plan or how Judah needed to be confronted with his own sin in order to repent. Biblical scholars have also been perplexed about the relationship of the story with the larger narrative of Genesis, often focusing on the problematics of that. Walter Brueggemann calls it a "peculiar," "enigmatic" chapter, "isolated in every way," and remarks that "it is difficult to know in what context it might be of value for theological exposition."[1]

However, some feminist, literary, and structuralist scholars have been genuinely interested in the unsettling nature of the story: "[Tamar], who had been dependent on the approaches of the men around her in regard to her sexual life, takes matters into her own hands."[2] Even from a soft US Evangelical perspective, Tamar's case can be seen as a "story of a woman who uses deception not to betray a man but to bring out the best in him."[3]

Tamar's obvious problem is the "lack of a willing and/or suitable man."[4] This book starts with this subject. The technical term for it is "singleness"; even more specifically, involuntary singleness, familiar to so many women today. The sin of Judah, on the other hand, is "[violating] her right to well-being and dignity in the community."[5] Tamar's story sadly mirrors the frequent encounter of neglect and disregard by those in the family (in the case of this book, represented by the faith

1. Brueggemann, *Genesis*, 307–8.
2. Bos, "Out of the Shadows," 45.
3. Schwartz and Kaplan, *Fruit of Her Hands*, 168.
4. Jackson, "Lot's Daughters and Tamar," 30.
5. Brueggemann, *Genesis*, 311.

community to which these women belong and which makes a theological claim of being their family) who have a considerable power to influence or change things.

Tamar's story is also a reminder that in the face of inaction of those with power and/or responsibility, Tamar needs to act on her own. Her actions may seem radical, although using the ready means she has—her body—is not unfamiliar to church life. Yet the fact of how lost the readers seem to be—both in the church and often in biblical/theological scholarship—when confronted with Tamar's story, also tells us something about Christian communities of faith.

Whatever else one might like to say about Judah, he should be given credit for owning up to his fault and for declaring that confession and recognition: "She is more in the right than I."[6] The fact that the story is placed within the larger narrative of Judah's life is also telling. It reflects the same hope which is expressed in this book: that the churches, who have become Tamar's family, can recognize their need to act according to their commitment claims, and that Tamar's story may awaken them to their own faults, hopefully before Tamar is driven to the point of resorting to anything as drastic as the events on the roadside at Enaim.

There are, of course, a number of differences in Tamar's original situation and the church life of today. For one thing, a single woman is not necessarily a dependent (although economically, socially, and culturally it is still often the case). Those with "authority" to change the lot of today's Tamars are not necessarily the males; the responsibility lies with the whole intentional community of faith, if it is to be serious about seeing itself as a family of God's people. The "solution," lies not necessarily with supplying such Tamars with spouses or heirs, even if the churches do play a role in matchmaking. The heart of the biblical Tamar's issue was the lack of status and the meaning of life, which in those times, for a woman, centered on producing a son.[7] For many single

---

6. This phrase sometimes is translated as "she is in the right, not I"; see, e.g., Wenham, *Genesis 16–50*, 370. One can also imagine some fear on Judah's behalf suspecting Tamar's direct or indirect responsibility for the deaths of his two sons, and therefore a scheme to "forget" the given promise (Bos, "Out of the Shadows," 44). Yet he does leave his seal, cord and staff in the hands of an unknown prostitute. As Bos, a feminist scholar, observes, he is "not a man to renege on his promises (!), at least in terms of the promise of a kid" (ibid., 46).

7. Thus, to be very precise, it is not a spouse which is Tamar's greatest goal, but a male heir (or two), as attested by the fact that the narrative does not say anything about

women in today's churches, the issue of the lack of status and the meaning of life are still at the heart of their pain, but the way to establish status and meaning is not necessarily a progeny.

On Terms and Presuppositions

Defining "Single"

The term "single" is becoming increasingly difficult to define, but I will mean by it those women *who consider themselves as single*. Some may have children, some may have been married and then divorced or separated; some may be widowed; still others may have never married. In many cases it will refer to women who are not in any kind of committed sexual relationship; however, the lines are blurred. Some of those who are legally single yet in a relationship (typically those who have a live-in partner) would not differ much from married women, whereas others (who do not see themselves as "attached" to their partner) would perceive themselves as single.[8]

Although the statistics can only be approximate, the overall tendency in the growth in numbers of single people throughout Western societies is striking. There is no doubt that significant shifts are taking place. It is "clear from the changes in marriage, divorce and cohabitation figures . . . that it is increasingly the case that most women experience periods of living alone at different stages in their adult lives."[9]

When it comes to churches, the majority of single people are women; this book will concentrate on them. Although there are certain similarities in the experience of singleness for men and women, the following chapters will illustrate that singleness is connected with the

---

Shelah taking Tamar as his wife after the birth of her and Judah's twins. Fuchs, *Sexual Politics in the Biblical Narrative*, 73.

8. In Western societies at large, cohabitation is increasingly gaining status comparable to that of marriage, even in countries which traditionally have seen themselves as the guardians of "traditional family values." (For one such example, see the summary of the results of the research into radical changes in partnership patterns in Lithuania, where it is now estimated that 80 percent of first partnerships start as cohabitation, in Stankūnienė and Maslauskaitė, "Lietuvos šeima.") As to how these numbers are reflected in the churches (and especially in the churches which are the focus of this book), it is difficult to ascertain: these are not the type of statistics eagerly collected or gladly shared. It would be safe to say, however, that the more conservative the congregation, the less inclined it would be to tolerate sexual relationships outside marriage.

9. Reynolds, *Single Woman*, 9.

issues of gender.[10] It seemed unhelpful, therefore, to include the study of single men in this work, except for an occasional point of contrast.

The focus of this book is "involuntary" singleness, rather than singleness by conscious choice, such as in the instance of the celibates. However, it has to be recognized that "choice" in this case is not a straightforward or fixed category. Single women may struggle in responding to the question of whether they are single by choice or not. How much is a reluctance to marry "just anyone"—an available option for many a single woman—a choice?

I will be looking at singleness both in society at large and in faith communities in particular. Moves from the first to the latter, and vice versa, will be indicated in the particular chapters. However, a few words must be said about the *intentional communities of faith* which are the focus of this book.

Defining "Baptistic"

While approaching the subject of involuntary singleness in its relationship to the church, I am primarily interested in a particular way of being a church which can be termed as baptistic, free church, or the believer's church—in other words, a tradition which follows in the footsteps of the Radical Reformation and has the task of the continuous transformation of the intentional community of disciples at its very core. It is not uncommon for these churches to be assigned to the Protestant "camp."[11] However, I side with those voices which treat this as a separate ecclesial stream in distinction from the accents which would be placed by other church forms, such as sacramental corporality in the Catholic, Orthodox, and high-church Protestant expressions, or the focus on the teaching of the Word in the bodies born in the Magisterial Reformation.[12] James Wm. McClendon, whose interpretation of the theological tradition of

---

10. The difference between men's and women's singleness is even starker in the church compared to the rest of society. As Linda Harding has put it, "In the church, a single man of thirty may be perceived as *going for God* while a single woman of the same age carries a feeling of *not having made it*." Harding, *Better Than or Equal To?* 27.

11. See, e.g., McGrath and Marks, "Protestantism—the Problem of Identity," 4.

12. For a concentrated exposition of such threefold ecclesial classification, see McClendon, *Doctrine*, 331–44; on a similar account using the imagery of the river and its streams, see Freeman et al., *Baptist Roots*, 1–4. Some other theologians have worked on similar categories too. For example, Lesslie Newbigin had suggested a "Pentecostal" designation alongside Catholicism and Protestantism. Newbigin, *Household of God*, 95.

baptistic (or in his words, "baptist") communities I employ, identifies the following marks of baptistic identity: the treatment of the Bible seen as trustful guidance for both faith and life in direct narrative link of the particular community with the communities of the past and the future still to come; the voluntary nature of committing to such a believing community; discipleship under the lordship of Christ as the indispensable requirement, or cost, of such commitment; the necessarily communal nature of such discipleship; and witness to the way of Christ, both by word and by deeds, as the way of life of such community.[13]

As my examples will demonstrate, the phenomenon of singleness would be encountered quite similarly in other ecclesial traditions too, especially with the increasing denominational migration (currently more expressed in the West than in the East, but even in the latter it is becoming a reality).[14] Just as in much of theological reflection, most of sociological research on issues such as gender tends to lump baptistic communities together with the other "Protestants"; this again is reflected in the sociological considerations I employ.

Nevertheless, although applicable and pertaining to a larger Christian tradition, this work is centered on the baptistic way of being the church. This is what I will primarily mean and refer to by my use of the term "church," unless specifically noted otherwise. Even more specifically, I will focus on the particular grouping called Baptists, who have been my community for most of my life. This delineation is not a rigid one and does not necessarily depend on the labels the churches apply to themselves. Instead, the distinction is made and the focus is kept on the basis of the *theological* baptistic identity, which often, but not always, overlaps with certain denominational names. Hence also the emphasis on the intentionality of such communities.[15] This is important for the

---

13. McClendon, *Ethics*, 17–34. For a related recasting of these same marks, see Parushev, "Doing Theology in a Baptist Way," 8–10.

14. Communities who have institutionalized celibacy would, to a degree, represent an exception, but, given the difference between the celibate (i.e., actively chosen, religious) calling and being involuntarily single, an apparent lack of theology of the latter can be observed. I am grateful to my colleague, Tim Noble, for this observation. See also the same concern explicated in an older writing of another Catholic, Francine Cardman, "Singleness and Spirituality."

15. At times these communities will be identical to the local church; on a number of other occasions, especially where there is a mixture of ecclesiologies, it may mean clusters within the church, whether the committed core or groups on the margins. I am writing out of my personal experience of encountering such communities, both in my

purposes of this work as, although the language of the church as the primary community (or "church as family") is familiar to all ecclesial traditions, it is particularly accentuated in churches such as Baptists, Pentecostals, and various Mennonite groups.[16] Such emphasis carries in itself a specific responsibility in the case of addressing the phenomenon of involuntary singleness—a responsibility which these churches often fail to take with appropriate seriousness.

On the Contextual/Regional Location

When I first embarked upon writing on the subject of singleness, I concentrated on the experience of singleness in post-Communist, and especially post-Soviet, Europe, and its baptistic churches. Even then, I received comments from those in the European West suggesting that my description was not dissimilar to their own church context. At that time, however, although Eastern Europe was already undergoing massive changes in its striving to "reintegrate into Europe," the shadow of the

---

childhood years at the Klaipeda Baptist church in Lithuania during the Soviet times, which possessed the features of strong intentional community, and more recently enjoying the blessing of the community at the International Baptist Theological Seminary which has become my second home. Following McClendon, *Doctrine*, 367, I would also allocate the base communities of Latin and Central America, theologically, to the "baptistic" stream. Anna L. Peterson underlines an important point in regard to both Amish (Anabaptist) and Salvadoran (progressive Catholic) "utopian communities": the kingdom of God is seen to have taken roots in the communities of God's people already. "These communities . . . represent the hope of learning, first, *that* it is possible not only to conceive of a different world but also to create one, to live and make a living by different rules. Second, these small communities help us see *how* they are possible: what they might require of us, what they might promise" (Peterson, *Seeds of the Kingdom*, 144–45). As an interesting side note to my argument, Peterson also maintains that the Roman Catholic and Anabaptist traditions have more resources for creating community life than, for example, the Protestant stream "because their basic unit is not the individual but the church or congregation" (106).

16. Another popular, although somewhat fuzzy, synonym I will employ is "evangelical"—a term widely used in regions such as much of the former USSR. It arises from its common everyday usage in the church to denote the same understanding of the voluntary nature of the church and the commitment that the participation in the life of the church requires. In much of Eastern Europe (but not in such countries where the "Evangelical" (German *Evangelische*) Lutherans or the Reformed are the state church), "evangelical" is applied to those churches which see themselves as independent from state support, ethnic sentiments, or geographical location. See, e.g., Grams and Parushev, *Towards an Understanding of European Baptist Identity*, 10. The same would apply to the experiences of the "low" Anglican church in Britain, for example, such as reflected in the work of the Evangelical Alliance.

Communist regimes throughout these countries was still a significant factor in shaping their context, encouraging me to limit the investigation to this specific milieu.[17]

In the last decade, however, cultural shifts in Eastern and Central Europe have accelerated to the extent that Eastern and Western Europe have become increasingly blurry categories in the socio-political language. The major factors facilitating such transition are those related to economics, global communication, and migration, especially as they play out in the European Union context. Thus, while certain contextual realities, such as greater appreciation of the communal dimension of life, typically characteristic of "Eastern Europe," may still be true, the speed with which the shifts are taking place suggest that the division is becoming increasingly artificial. My involvement in the life of (primarily, but not exclusively Baptist) churches in various parts of Europe have confirmed what I have been observing at close hand both in my home country of Lithuania, and at the International Baptist Theological Seminary in the Czech Republic. The way younger generations of Russian, Bulgarian or Hungarian evangelicals think and act has been significantly affected by their use of the Internet and, in numerous cases, by friends and/or family who live somewhere in the West and bring with them a "Western" outlook. This would also be true in relation to the resources that single and married people consult (especially the younger ones) regarding the issues explored here. The articles googled and the books looked at would be primarily coming from the "West," not to speak of the television programs and, even more, the pop songs which inhabit cafes, cars, and homes in both Eastern and Western Europe.

Thus, although the thrust of this book has grown out of Eastern and Central European realities, its examples across different contexts are not only legitimate but simply unavoidable in the mesh of human experience of the global village. Thus the scope of this work pertains to the part of the world which, for the lack of a better term, is referred to as "the West"—that is, regions and cultures nurtured by Western civilization, marked by the imprint of the classical cultures of Greece and Rome, the experience of Christendom, and the worldview shaped by Enlightenment philosophy.[18] It is in such understanding of the West that

17. Andronovienė, *Involuntarily Free*, 7–8.

18. Such definition should suffice for the purposes of this book, even though the definition of "the West" is by itself a focus of academic research and continuous debate.

another term, "culture," will be employed, even though it will be done with an understanding that within this Western culture, various subcultures and alternative cultures could be identified which may differ significantly from the general trends.

The Eastern boundaries of this "West" are fluid. The "European" part of Russia, for example, would be more "Western" than the remote Russian regions shaped by Buddhist or animist influences. On the other hand, many Russian speakers who migrated to Central Asia during the days of the Soviet Union, as well as their progeny, are still largely guided by the vision embodied by Western civilization even while living in Asian cultures. A few examples will be drawn from such contexts.

The category of the "West" allows for inclusion of some resources, examples and insights from North America, often with regard to their influence on the European context, through books, television programs, movies, Internet resources, etc. The influx of US material, both secular and Christian, is especially notable for the post-communist regions, both because of the way it is used by their media and, for churches, because of the activity of various Christian organizations which have translated and employed a variety of materials that originated in the United States. I hope to show that these reflect, illustrate, or in some cases even deepen the crisis relating to the issue of singleness.[19]

Thus, the regional focus of this work and the applications sought could be depicted as several concentric circles. The Eastern and Central European context has formed the core of my writing, especially in its early stages. The next, and perhaps the most prominent, circle includes a wider notion of "Europe," especially as exemplified by the European Union. The third circle would also encompass other regions considered to be "the West" in the sense described above.

For an example, see Abramsky, "Defining the Indefinable West."

19. One of the polarities used in contrasting "Europe" with "America" (meaning the United States) is the "secularity of Europe," sometimes even referred to as "Eurosecularity," over against the religiosity which is still seen as characterising the United States. See Berger et al., *Religious America, Secular Europe*, 11. I take the view that religiousness of human beings always finds a way of expression; whether it is addressed in religious terms or not is immaterial. Thus the current tendency toward secularism as exemplified in the development of the European Union does not mean the diminishing of things religious, but their morphing into other expressions—hence the careful attention to the "religion of culture," to be addressed in more detail in chap. 3.

Methodology, Argument, and Conversant Partners

For the overall structure, this book is most of all indebted to a Baptist theologian James Wm. McClendon Jr.[20] I follow his approach to theology which can be summarized as an effort to, first, describe, second, to interpret, and, third, to suggest appropriate ways for the transformation of, the convictions of a convictional community. This task also requires taking into account how these convictions cohere with each other, and how they relate to any other issues outside of the convictional set of that specific convictional community.[21]

I start, therefore, by seeking to establish the convictions bearing upon the issue of singleness that exist in the faith communities which are of special interest for this work. I then compare them to the convictions present in society at large, arguing that there is a direct relationship between the two which can, and, I claim, should be challenged. The information from which these convictions can be gleaned exists in a variety of forms: statistical data, in-house materials produced by churches, pieces of sociological research, and, not least, the media.

The discussion then moves to the theological exploration of the reasons that brought such a formation of the convictions of these believing communities, looking particularly at the way the theology of love and family has developed, and exploring its connections with the interpretations of happiness. I further this interpretative task by commencing a dialogue with one theological segment which has addressed the challenge which singleness presents for today's church: feminist theology.

I am then, third, in a position to propose the framework for a further focus in addressing the question which guides this book: How does the struggle faced by the female single members in the baptistic churches challenge current churchly ways of life and the theology expressed therein? Using some insights arising from postfoundational philosophical thought and the intersections between theology and science, I look at the implications of viewing a Christian community as an emergent structure which provides a home for practices leading to a positive change. I take an example of one such practice—friendship—and explore its implications for the transformation of the Christian

---

20. See esp. his *Ethics*, *Doctrine*, and *Witness*.

21. See McClendon, *Ethics*, 23. "Convictions" is a philosophical term referring to the persistent and largely unarticulated but strongly felt beliefs of communities which shape their identity. I will return to this concept in chap. 5, sec. 1.

community. I conclude with an exploration of a specific virtue—that of suffering-love—necessary for such transformation.

The way faith communities tend to react to singleness indicates a serious theological problem, or a clash of convictions. The clash is detrimental not only for single members of the churches, but also for faith communities as a whole. Conversely, a real, embodied affirmation of singleness as a valuable way of Christian life promises positive developments, not only for single Christians, but also for the life of the church. An avenue for such affirmation I propose is that of reframing the issue and adopting a larger perspective of communitarian life with its practices and virtues.

The selection of my conversant partners was governed by the interdisciplinary nature of the argument. I have benefited significantly from knowing some of these conversant partners personally, and am grateful for being able to test my questions and reflections in direct responses from them. I concentrate on resources in English, but also include some materials originating in other language contexts. A great part of what is found in non-English European languages on the subject of singleness in church life is actually translations from English; the scarcity of original material is a point of concern worthy of a separate study.[22]

The journey through this book has also turned out to be much more personal than I ever envisaged. It is my hope that my own experience of both singleness and marriage, even if not explicitly referred to in the following pages, adds something to the strength of the claim this book seeks to make.

---

22. Cf. critical observations in the same regard from a Lebanese perspective, in Shaw, "Ministry with Singles," 118.

PART ONE

Involuntary Singleness

Socio-Ecclesial Maps

1

Churches and Single Women

Introducing the Challenge

The church is filled with numerous Christian women who love God and who spend their spare time and energy doing voluntary work in their churches, but when it comes to finding a partner—despite their prayers and efforts—they draw a blank. This can fill them with anger, guilt and bitterness as they ask themselves what have they done wrong to cause God not to answer their prayers.[1]

THERE IS A POPULAR magazine published by a German-based evangelical mission organisation *Licht im Osten* (*Light in the East*) for Eastern Europe's evangelicals. The Russian version of the magazine, *Vera i Zhyzn* (*Faith and Life*), chose "loneliness" as its theme for the 2/2003 issue.[2] One of the articles was an anonymous letter written by a distressed single woman. Here are some of the excerpts.[3]

> Our church is a small one. Earlier there were some young sisters, but now they have families and are raising children. Now I'm the only one of this kind. I happen to come from another town, so I do not have my classmates and girlfriends, and I did not manage to acquire new friends through my time here. Women at my work

---

1. Dixon, "Why Are So Many Christian Women Single?"
2. The theme of the issue, however, could also be translated as "singleness." As in some other languages, the Russian "odinochestvo" represents both. The fact in itself is a telling one.
3. Unless indicated otherwise, all translations are mine.

place keep telling me: you need to get married, otherwise you'll always be only "auntie" for the kids, never a mum. Do you think that this is not painful to hear, that it does not pierce the soul? And then, so often their answer to any question is, "What problems do you have? You don't have kids, you don't have kittens..."

I sometimes think that if I were an invalid, or if I would be in the prison, or if I'd be a nun, then all would be clear: both my singleness and my prison-like life without relationships. But I am a normal human being... I will soon be 30, and I look ugly. So I can't expect to get married. But it's so difficult to live when you don't have anybody, when you're all alone–no family, no girlfriends. Alone at work, alone at church, alone at home as well...

Should I become a drug addict or start living licentiously? Then at least I won't be the only one, then at least my being rejected will have a reason...

But I do not want to hear the words of the brother preachers who are married and have lots of children. I don't want words fortified by Bible quotes. I don't want to hear words of encouragement that "all will be well with you also" uttered by the sisters who waited for long and finally gained family happiness. I do not want to hear the words of edification that first I need to worry about the things of the Lord, the words of old sisters who have grandchildren. I badly want to hear the words of an ordinary old sister from a small church who has never been married and doesn't have girlfriends, neither in the world nor in the church, just like me. How did you manage to live all these years, dear elderly sister? How did you cope with tears, with blaming yourself and with anger toward others?

The Lord gives comfort, I know it. That's what keeps me. If I had a chance to return back, [I would do the same again and would come to the Lord.] But for some reason, it makes me so sad.[4]

The letter was followed up by numerous responses from the readers of the magazine. Here is the summary of the leading themes:

- An acknowledgement of the lack of [proper] pastoral counselling, as pastors are not grasping the problem and do not have the needed skills to help involuntarily single people.
- Exhortations to find the joy of life by living in the presence of God, and by serving others: "Look around yourself: there are so many suffering and crying people! Both married and single

---

4. "Izpovedaniye."

feel unhappy because of loneliness. They all need the healing balm. Dear sister! Maybe there is a lonely old man or woman in need of help near you. Go to them."

- Response from those suffering similarly: "I was reading your letter and sobbing . . . God loves even us, ugly ones . . . I'm constantly in pain. But I console myself in prayer to our Jesus Christ. He knows all, including you and I . . . May the Lord protect us from envy."
- An offering of their service from a women's organisation in California: "We are the sisters you are looking for."[5]
- Some well-meaning advice from Seattle warning of the devil: "Currently, the devil has taken over your soul and mouth. He can kill, steal, and ruin . . . In the name of the Son of God, Jesus Christ, with the help of your parishioners (pastor, brothers and sisters), seek to cast away this devil of hatred from your life, and it will get better . . . [You have a talent, so don't let it go away], use it, and your time will be filled."
- Offer of psychological help by a professional psychologist.[6]

The editors of the magazine asked an older, always-single female to publicly respond to the letter. Here, again, are some extracts:

> Once I had this fleeting nagging thought: "Why is it that I, having such an array of positive qualities, am still on my own?" And I answered to myself, with a smile: "The one who'd be worthy of me hasn't been born yet, hasn't been born . . . again!" I am not frightened by the thoughts about the future. The Lord will take care of me, of this I am sure.
> . . . Since the time the Lord has made me busy by giving me a needed and loved work, I do not have time to be asking, "Why do I live?" I am immensely grateful to the Lord for exactly such lifestyle as I have . . . Of course, I also have some difficult moments, and even days. We are all human and experience low moments in health and in attitudes. But this is temporary, and it soon passes.

---

5. This response, as well as the one below, comes from one of the numerous Slavic-speaking Christian communities in the United States consisting mostly of those who have left the Soviet Union since the 1980s.

6. "Po sledam publikacii."

> After a storm and difficulties, calm, sunny weather descends on the soul. If you are with God, it cannot be any other way.
>
> I look at the brothers and sisters of my church and I rejoice that God has given me this family. Everybody has their problems, worries, at times difficulties, but it's enough for somebody to ask for help, and everybody will respond.
>
> What is the "beauty" which you talked about? "All at which you look with love is beautiful." Don't even start doubting that in the eyes of others you are beautiful . . .
>
> My wish for you is to understand that a lot depends only on you. Then you will not be celebrating your birthdays in tears and loneliness; even the children of others will be calling you mother; you will sing Christian songs with joy; you will not be falling into depression and isolation, and even more so, you will not be walking away from the church.[7]

This correspondence highlights the issue I want to start with: the presence of single women in the church and the church's reaction (or, rather, the lack or inappropriateness of it). The first letter is a desperate one indeed. Many single women would likely find it far (perhaps insultingly far) from describing their situation and attitudes. Yet the reaction it stirred is indicative of the church's unpreparedness to meet the challenge of increasing numbers of single people in its midst.

The second letter, put alongside the first, makes for a fairer picture of how singleness is experienced by female Christians. Yet, as admitted by the author of the letter, these single women are still facing difficult questions, still having low moments, and, as the following pages will indicate, are often left on their own to sort out their singleness, and may even be nagged and looked down upon by the very community of faith to which they belong.

In the following chapters, I hope to explore the church's response to the challenge of involuntary singleness, what it reveals about the church's own theology, and in what ways it can be transformed. The challenge of singleness goes beyond the "problem" of single women only, and the church's response is very detrimental to the health of the church as a whole. Indeed, the church risks losing these disillusioned women: "I've yet to meet [a single Christian] who hasn't a tale to tell about the poor way they've been treated by fellow believers because of their solo status. Equally, I am not surprised when I hear of yet another—

---

7. Belozerskaya, "Otvet moyey sestre."

invariably a thirtysomething female—who's left the church for that very same reason."[8] And it is not only thirtysomethings either:

> I am 47 yrs of age, never been married or had children. I am the daughter of a minister—so hence been brought in church for most of my life. I have always carried myself in a dignified fashion, dress well . . . I have a wonderful relationship with the Lord and everything else. But never been approached by a brother in the church in terms of marriage proposal.
>
> I was hoping to marry at least when I was in my thirties, settle down, have a child etc., and now everything I believed in and stood for has gone in the opposite direction. I am seeing someone who is not a christian at present, a very nice person who has a good heart and very caring—we are very good friends. Companionship means alot to me and he came at a time when I needed support and help.[9]

The reality of such single women leaving the church, with a non-believing partner or on their own but disillusioned by the church's inability or unwillingness to take singleness seriously, is a serious hazard for the health of the church. To retain these members and to be enriched by their contributions to community life, the church needs to think of expressions of respect and appropriate care. The church should also discuss the facilitation of the ways the single sisters might help each other: this exactly was the cry of the anonymous letter. It is also a question of justice, especially in a baptistic context, which very strongly affirms, at least in its spoken theology, the identity of the church understood as a family or an intentional community—in other words, a place of primary belonging for those who join it.

Moreover, singleness and its theology—both lived out and spoken out—make a difference to the faith community as a whole. Such theology is needed not just for the sake of the singles themselves, but for the sake of the church which needs its single people as some of its living prophets pointing to the vision of the Realm of God, over against many other tempting outlooks, some of which will be addressed in the following chapters.[10]

8. Ruhland, "All by Ourselves," 26.

9. Veronica, in response to the article by Dixon, "Why Are So Many Christian Women Single?"; language unedited.

10. Another comment needs to be added, lest the intent of this work is misunderstood. A similar letter to that of a single sister could have been written by a married one;

The Age of Singles. The Age of Women?

A very specific problem for Christian single women would seem to be the quantity and quality of Christian single men available.[11]

Singles in the Church

The last several decades have witnessed an unprecedented change in the make-up of both Western society and its churches, resulting in a very different, and still changing, picture in terms of people's marital status. I shall review the rapidly growing numbers of singles in society in chapter 3. I start, however, with the church.

Up-to-date information on singles in the church is surprisingly scarce, but 35 percent is an approximate figure offered frequently in the British context. A survey carried out back in 1992 by "Singularly Significant," a network under the auspices of the Evangelical Alliance, discovered that singles (over 18 years old) comprised 34.8 percent of the membership in the UK—"a finding which came as a surprise to many of the churches themselves!"[12] The percentage in inner-city churches was 42 percent.[13] The International Congregational Life Survey which in 2001 researched worshippers from Australia, New Zealand, England, and the United States, established the average at 34 percent.[14]

This number seems to be fairly representative across Europe, although by now 35 percent would be a minimalist estimate. I have been unable to access extensive up-to-date statistics for various regions; again, this is a telling fact. However, what follows next are brief profiles collected from various churches across Europe.[15] As illustrations, they

---

in fact, *Vera i Zhizn* has published such letters too. What is at stake here is a complex problem much bigger than the plight of the single sisters; they simply are the ones who often are in possession of a smaller number of role-masks and tasks to hide their longing for meaningful life.

11. Wilson, *Being Single*, 117.

12. Chilcraft, *One of Us*, 69. A summary of this report can be found in ibid., 69–77. A "grey" area in the survey were the cohabitees: some churches considered them as single whereas others assigned them to the "married" category (73). A later survey of Evangelical Alliance's Singularly Significant network suggested an average of "at least thirty-seven per cent" (Chilcraft, *One of Us*, 35); Chilcraft et al., *Single Issues*, 3.

13. "Single-Minded," 6.

14. Bruce et al., "International Survey of Congregations and Worshipers," 11.

15. Most of these numbers have been collected during the period of 2010–2011 and would reflect the statistics representing that time.

corroborate the claim that singles, with few exceptions, account for a significant portion of church membership.

- A Hungarian Baptist Church in Simleu Silvaniei, Romania: 80 members, out of which 35 (or 44 percent) are single.[16]
- Second Baptist Church in Prague, Czech Republic: out of 38 women and 22 men, 16 (thus, 27 percent) are single.[17]
- Another Baptist church in the United Kingdom, Wokingham: 273 members, out of which 101 are single, comprising 37 percent of membership.[18]
- Kohila Baptist Church in Estonia, one of the most secular countries in Europe: 176 members, 127 of whom are women and 49 men. 75, or 43 percent, are single.[19]
- Vilnius New Testament Baptist Church, Lithuania: 24 women and 17 men. Out of these, 12 (or 29 percent) are single.[20]
- Radiceva Street Baptist Church in Zagreb, Croatia: 119 men and 172 women. 112 of them, or 38 percent, are single.[21]
- "Familiekerk De Fakkel" in Utrecht, the Netherlands: 32 women and 26 men. 8 (or just below 14 percent) are single.[22]
- Skien Baptist Church, Norway: 279 members, out of which 250 are married and 29 (thus only 10 percent) are single.[23]
- Prohladny Baptist Church in Kabardino-Balkaria, Russia: 295 members, out of which 278, or 94 percent, are married.[24]

---

16. I am grateful to Lenard Kiraly for providing this information.
17. I thank Dr Lydie Kucova for providing these numbers.
18. This statistic has been provided for me by David Nixon, deacon of the church.
19. This information has been provided by Helle Liht, a member at Kohila. Five of those in the single category are under the age of eighteen, the standard minimum age for marriage in Estonia.
20. Statistics supplied by Irmantas Pinkoraitis, the pastor of the church.
21. Personal email correspondence with Enoh Šeba, member of the church.
22. Personal email correspondence with Marjon Pape, member of De Fakkel at the time of writing. Note that the name of the church is "Family Church."
23. Personal email correspondence with Jan Saethre, member of the church.
24. Personal email correspondence with Andrey Kravtsev, pastor of the church.

- Windsor Baptist Church in Belfast, Northern Ireland: out of a total of 178 of membership, 58 are single (that is, 27 percent).[25]

Although I do not claim any statistical significance of these anecdotal reports, there has been no discrimination of the data or exclusion of any responses I received. When it comes to proper sociological research, some interesting patterns emerge. A study which looked into the changes in church attendance and marriage, and the link between the two in five European countries where extensive statistical data was available, discovered that in the face of the declining numbers of both church attendees and marriages, there seems to be a link between church-going and being married. In other words, a church goer is more likely to be married compared to the proportion of the national average.[26] The authors of the study suggested that "it is reasonable to hypothesize that those who live outside conventional (married) family structures may wish to distance themselves from religious communities."[27] This observation is corroborated by church practitioners: "Local churches have always constructed their life around the nuclear family. Unseen by most, the number of single adults in the congregation has grown as the percentage of single people in society has grown. The church has not adapted to meet this change."[28] Yet even with the church's failure to embrace single people, their numbers among the church membership are likely to grow as single people increase among the population.

Women in the Church

In this context of the growing prominence of singles, another prominence is obvious. In the words of the editor of the aforementioned Russian-language magazine *Faith and Life*, "Many times I have been faced with the question: why is it that in all the [Eastern] Slavic churches there are more women than men—a substantial disproportion?"[29] Such

---

25. My thanks to Dorothy and David McMillan, members of the church, for supplying this information.

26. Williams et al., "Changing Patterns of Religious Affiliation," 173–82. The five countries explored were Great Britain, the Netherlands, Northern Ireland, Sweden, and Spain.

27. Ibid., 181.

28. Chilcraft, *One of Us*, 20.

29. Zorn, "Slovo redaktora."

disproportion is far from limited to the Eastern Slavic experience.[30] Throughout the Western context, with very few exceptions, men tend to comprize a minority in the churches; their participation in church activities is also more likely to be at a lesser level compared to that of women.[31] As can be observed empirically in many a church, with the increase of age, the unevenness in the ratio of single women to single men tends to increase greatly.[32] According to the "Singularly Significant" survey, from years 45 to 59, there are three women for one man. "This imbalance," says the survey, "is more pronounced in Baptist (70 percent : 30 percent) and Anglican (71 percent : 29 percent) than in the other denominations."[33]

This European reality also mirrors the situation elsewhere in the West,[34] and the phenomenon is not restricted to baptistic realities.[35] Occasionally (though still rarely, given how extensive this disproportion is), it results in a book or an article written by those in ministry, calling for a change in the way the church functions in order to be more appealing to men.[36] Another delicate aspect of this issue is the qualities of

30. The situation among Eastern Slavic churches may be especially expressive. As Constantine Prokhorov points out, during the 1960s–1980s it was not unusual for women to comprise up to 80 percent of the church membership among the Soviet Union's Evangelical Christians-Baptists. Prokhorov, "Russian Baptists and Orthodoxy," 15, 116–17.

31. See, e.g., the poll performed by Tearfund in the UK: Ashworth and Farthing, *Churchgoing in the UK*. Bruce et al. report an average of 67 percent of women among church-goers in England and 61 percent in the United States. Bruce et al., "International Survey of Congregations and Worshipers," 11.

32. Interestingly, although the church seems to be relatively unappealing to never-married or divorced women, the percentage of widows actively belonging to the church is high. See Woolever et al., "Gender Ratio in the Pews," 31.

33. Chilcraft, *One of Us*, 74.

34. For an example of an in-depth study of the typical profile of a female (Christian) worshipper from the North American context, see Woolever et al., "Gender Ratio in the Pews," 25–38.

35. For a sample ecumenical exploration, see World Council of Churches' *Living Letters*.

36. See the reflections of a (male) Russian pastor in Kontorovich, "Tochka zreniya"; for a female perspective based on popular psychology, see Mikula, "Pochemu v tserkvakh bol'she zhenshchin." Several online forums, including conversations among Christians that I came across on Facebook and Yahoo Answers, ask the same question, with suggestions typically revolving around men being "tougher" and less emotional compared with women who are seen as more easier to be impressed and needing less logical argumentation.

many of those men (single men especially) who *are* in the church, yet are often seen by women as "weak," "immature," "unattractive."[37] Still another perplexing issue is that of single men finding a spouse *outside* of Christian circles—and such spouse joining the faith community seems to be a more common experience than in the case of a woman finding a non-believing partner.[38]

Various questions have been asked and proposals made. Why is it that even those churches that are patriarchal and restrictive in regard to the role of women tend to attract more females than males? "The evidence ... is cumulative: in enquiry after enquiry, the predominance of women is not only affirmed, but striking."[39] Why do the changing conditions and freedoms increasingly available for women in the "modern" world not seem to affect their religiosity in the way it may be expected? Questions can be asked about the language used in relation to God,[40] the way the various church activities, including worship services, are organized, and the general "feminisation of the church,"[41] but so far none of the experiments of turning the church into a more "masculine" expression have produced any significant results.

37. "For the majority of single people (i.e., women) [the poor quality of available men in the church] may be the most pressing personal problem of all." Wilson, *Being Single*, 119.

38. I have not been able to find the statistics, but this is based on a number of conversations and personal observations of members of various churches. As one such male who has found a wife from outside the Christian community put it, "A certain familiarity ... in the church often makes girls less attractive ... A distance, or a certain tension, which at times is necessary for relationships between the sexes, is lost ... So although many women were seemingly available [for dating], the terminology of 'family' and perhaps communal life [as such] has become somewhat of a problem for me. For all of them are sisters, and incest is a serious matter ... [followed by a smiley]" (personal communication, 26 November 2002; personal details withheld for confidentiality reasons). Although it is outside the scope of the present discussion, the issue of healthy "tension" described above in the context of baptistic communities is a matter worthy of a serious reflection and appropriate action. I have briefly addressed the matchmaking role of the church in Andronovienė, "Involuntarily Free," 7–9.

39. Berger et al., *Religious America, Secular Europe?* 110.

40. I have touched upon the strongly feminine features of the Christian songs in an article, "As Songs Turn into Life," 129–41.

41. E.g., Podles, *The Church Impotent*; Murrow, *Why Men Hate Going to Church*. Murrow's suggestions in terms of the remedy would be significantly different from those developed in this work, focusing on the lost "masculinity" and therefore a need for strong pastoral leadership, reservation in regard to women in pastoral and other ministries as contributing to further haemorrhaging of the numbers of men, etc.

That may not be surprising given that the greater religiosity of women is a reality in other religions as well, prompting sociologists of religion to ask for the reasons of this "apparently 'universal' gender difference in religious commitment."[42] The puzzle remains, with no agreement reached regarding the nature of the gender and religion effect.[43] Rodney Stark has made one of the most startling suggestions that, alongside the considerably higher tendency toward criminal activity and, to a lesser degree, lack of responsibility in various areas of life, the lower level of religiosity in men cannot be explained primarily as a matter of socialisation, but instead points to the important role played by physiology.[44]

Exploring issues of this gender imbalance in detail or developing feasible strategies to achieve greater gender balance would be tasks for another book. My intention here is to accept this disproportion as a given, and to raise questions about how the churches respond to a significantly higher number of women in their midst, and the implications of this phenomenon in terms of their marital status. The issue is intensified for those Christian communities which practice homogamy, that is, marriage within the faith (and sometimes even only the same denomination).[45] The reasons may be clear for those single women who happen to find themselves in this reality, but they do not change the mat-

42. Miller and Stark, "Gender and Religiousness," 1399.

43. For an overview of the state of affairs within sociology in regard to the question of gender and (Christian) religion, cf. Berger et al., *Religious America, Secular Europe?* 109ff.; and the aforementioned article of Miller and Stark, "Gender and Religiousness," 1399–423. Cf. also Miller and Hoffman, "Risk and Religion," 63–75. For a theological take, see an older but still enlightening article by Walter, "Why Are Most Churchgoers Women?" 73–90.

44. Stark, "Physiology and Faith," 495–507. See, however, Carroll's critique of Stark's argument on the basis of a much larger male religiosity prior to nineteenth century, in "Give Me That Ol' Time Hormonal Religion," 275–78.

45. As one of the leaders of the Evangelical Christians-Baptists in the former Soviet Union, B. M. Zdorovets, recalls, the churches even practiced asking a public promise from young female baptismal candidates: "If an unbeliever makes an offer of marriage to you?"—"No, I have fallen in love with Jesus!" Zdorovets recognises a real sacrifice these young women were making by joining such "Baptist nunneries" with very few men available for marriage (Prokhorov, "'Living as Monks' and Fools," 156). As Prokhorov puts it, "In this way, Russian Baptists actually preordained the mass female monastic way of life" (ibid.). On the other hand, a number of women in these churches would get married to an unbeliever, sometimes with the full understanding that they would be excommunicated, yet hoping for (and usually receiving) reinstatement of their membership in a few years' time. Prokhorov, "Russian Baptists and Orthodoxy," 117. Cf. Aune, "Singleness and Secularization," 63.

ter. "You might understand that the world is fallen and often unfair, but that's still not the kind of answer that warms you on a lonely Saturday night. And if in your heart of hearts you still yearn to be married or have a family, this hard mystery lives, eats, and sleeps with you."[46]

There are good reasons for listening more to these single voices before moving to examine the response of the church. Here I offer four sketches of singleness as it is perceived by single women belonging to the church. As all sketches, they are true only to a degree; exceptions can always be found. They are gleaned from a range of writings by single Christian women, as well as from numerous personal conversations held over the years. They are not static; one sketch may interchange another. Yet they capture different perceptions women have about their life as singles.

Single Sketches

Temporary

> What are we doing with the single life God has given us? Are we using it for his glory and our good, or are we squandering it? Are we willing to align our will with his? If we're enjoying our singleness, let's rejoice. If we're not, we need to go humbly before God and state our cause. We can express our feelings, whatever they are—anger, hurt, disappointment or loneliness. Remember, he wants our honesty. He can handle it and will meet us there.[47]

The most prominent type of singleness is the one which is perceived to be a "temporary" state. This is the starting point of all young people which is expected to end sometime in their twenties or thirties, when the person marries, or realizes her singleness may be a more permanent state, thus moving to one (or more) of the remaining three categories.[48] Depending on the dating culture of the specific context, these young

---

46. Gilliam, *Revelations of a Single Woman*," 128.
47. McDonald, *And She Lived Happily Ever After*, 27.
48. Kaiser and Kashy suggested that, at least in the United States context, 95 percent of all adults who married were likely to do that by the time they were 36.2 years of age ("Contextual Nature and Function of Singlism," 122). Although the exact numbers are likely to differ in specific European contexts, there is a certain tipping point after which one is much less considered as "temporarily" single.

people may also be experiencing numerous episodes of moving from a "single stage" to that of "in a relationship."

Such singleness often comes with the sense of "preparation" (for "real" life which will follow, of course). Take, for example, an US Christian magazine called *Christian Single*—devoted to "purposeful single living, providing practical answers to the real-life needs of today's single adults, challenging them to intensify their faith and impact their community."[49] The November 2009 issue features on its cover articles on "101 Tips for Great Dates"; and "What's Next for Singles in the Church?" The editorial starts with the question:

> Do you ever feel like you're in limbo? Especially during the single season, it seems like we're somewhere between contentment with life and a deep longing for more.[50]

Consider also the following observation:

> In our society, marriage is the primary rite of passage into adulthood. It is when we marry that we typically set up our own home and are given the furnishings to make that possible. Since we have no analogous rite of passage for those who do not marry, many single people are treated as irresponsible adolescents well into middle life. Single adults are more likely to be addressed by their first names, even by small children, in settings where married people are addressed as Mr. or Mrs.[51]

One of the main aspects of this "temporary stage" is understood to be the issue of sexual chastity, as, in a considerable proportion of baptistic churches, the teaching would be clearly that sex is limited to marriage.[52] Insistence on this often proves to be a challenge; keeping on waiting for sex until marriage is not always a reality even in conservative circles, as indicated by an occasional hastily arranged wedding ceremony due to pregnancy. The tension over sexual matters, especially as intensified by the sexually aggressive popular culture which will be the topic

---

49. Arnault, "Living in the In-Between."
50. Ibid., 6.
51. Smit, *Loves Me, Loves Me Not*, 253.
52. This can be said not only about individual churches but also about Christian organisations, most notably True Love Waits (http://www.lifeway.com/tlw/), a ministry which seeks to "[challenge] teenagers and college students to make a commitment to sexual abstinence until marriage." Although American-based, it has also influenced churches and similar initiatives in Europe.

for chapter 3, has a significant impact on the faith development of young people, their perception of church discipline (that is, the "hierarchy of sins," in spite of the church's insistence there is no such hierarchy) and their view of the connection between the "realm of the church" and aspects of life which are outside it.[53] Given that most churches are generally embarrassed to talk about things pertaining to human sexuality and often do not even possess the language needed to enable such a conversation, these "temporary singles" are largely left to figure things out on their own. As time goes by, losing one's virginity for some becomes a sort of rite of passage they were denied by the absence of marriage: "My decision to opt out of virginity brought an immediate release from long-term mental anguish."[54]

Others stick with celibacy: "Do not stir up or awaken love until it is ready."[55] Yet for a number of these singles, celibate or not, there will come a point when it becomes clear that the stage is not as temporary as they had anticipated. After a longer or shorter struggle, they will either embrace it, or find it an impossible hurdle to overcome, and will start to actively look for a partner, possibly in a more hopeful setting than the church.

Singleness can also be perceived as a temporary stage by those who find themselves, in an unplanned or unexpected way, single by divorce or death, and it is to this experience of singleness that I turn next.

Unexpected

When one of us is suddenly one of them[56]

Even though many would prefer not to think about it, unexpected singleness will, at some point, be the lot for many women. Given the differ-

---

53. See, for instance, a helpful study of young women, mostly present or past members of Canadian baptistic churches, in Sharma, "When Young Women Say 'Yes,'" 71–82. One of the examples includes the acts of a sexually active young woman who alleviates the tension by cutting herself: "Secrecy is how [she] manages her shame and guilt amongst her church peers, while cutting is a way through which she manages her shame and guilt before God" (78). Another strategy of coping with the tension would be "disembodied sexuality" (79)—detaching oneself from one's sexual experience, assuming a passive role, and attempting to disengage from reflection on it.

54. Ruhland, "All by Ourselves," 29.

55. Song of Solomon 2:7b.

56. Clements, *Improvised Woman*, 87.

ences in life expectancy, for many of them it comes through the death of a spouse. Whether it is a long illness of the spouse or their sudden passing, it is likely to bring an unexpected disruption of personal identity in the social reality of ceasing to be a married woman.[57] Although such a loss can be extremely painful to come to terms with and it is recognized as a long-term stressor, it nevertheless carries with itself a certain air of dignity and invites a deserved sympathy. Widows, a well established biblical category and making up a considerable proportion of typical church membership, can count for some recognition of their loss in the early stages of bereavement, especially as expressed in the funeral service, which in a way can become a rite of passage into a new stage of life.[58] However, although showered by condolences and offers of help in the immediacy of her loss, a widow may soon find herself abandoned by her church community, and especially those with whom she used to share special bonds of friendship: unwittingly, she has become "a threat" to her coupled circle of friends.[59]

Another route into unexpected singleness—divorce or separation—makes the initial stage of grieving a rather different experience. It tends to exude attitudes of disappointment, speculations about who was the guilty party, and confusion about which label to assign to the divorcee, given that they are not "single" in the same way as those who have never been married or whose spouses have died. A woman abandoned by her first husband and then widowed after marrying a second time comments: "The first scenario is more painful."[60] Indeed, instead of memories to treasure, even while mourning their end, here one needs to deal with those memories in some other way—either by trying to blot them out or by learning, through pain, to accept the past with all the good that was in the marriage which has now been lost.[61]

---

57. See, e.g., Ajdacic-Gross et al., "Suicide after Bereavement," 673–76.

58. See, e.g., Fanestil, "Graveside Hope," 24–27.

59. Andronovienė, "Involuntarily Free," 10–11; the phenomenon of coupling will be discussed in more detail in chap. 3. In the words of a widow reflecting on the anguish arising from the sudden absence of physical contact, "people don't cuddle widows" (quoted in Cline, *Women, Celibacy and Passion*, 251).

60. Personal interview, 1 March 2009. Personal details withheld for confidentiality reasons.

61. For an account of one such struggle with involuntary divorce, see Croly, *Missing Being Mrs.*

Moreover, given the emphasis on Christian marriage as something at the very heart of the mission of the church, divorce in Christian circles often involves dishonour, regardless of whether the woman was the initiator or the recipient of the divorce.[62] In more conservative circles, especially in Eastern Europe, where divorce among the Evangelicals is still rare,[63] initiating the divorce would often be unimaginable, but even a wife who has been abandoned can face the shock of being shunned by her community, thus effectively losing both the spouse *and* the church. Divorce as such simply does not have a place in the theology of such a church; the woman is left to sort things out on her own. In some cases she may even be disciplined: "You would be told, 'If you were left by your husband, you must have done something wrong, or at least made a mistake; you must not have been in God's will in marrying this person.'"[64] Even in churches which would attempt to provide support, especially to those unexpectedly abandoned, those who have been judged to have worked hard in trying to save the marriage, or were the victims of a clearly abusive marriage, a dichotomy may remain between the members' good intentions and their instinctive detachment: "The people in church don't want their marriages threatened. If it can happen to me it can happen to them, you see . . . 'At least you have God with you,' they say, and their smile is self-satisfied and I close my mouth, suppress my emotions, raise my mask and return to a life alone."[65] Similar to the ex-

62. For an example of views which would be typical for a major proportion of European Baptists, see Briggs, "Divorce and Remarriage," 148.

63. Given the shame attached to divorce in communities which indeed knew very little of divorce during the times of the Communist regime, statistics are virtually impossible to get. However, my own exposure to the life of baptistic churches in various parts of Eastern Europe, as well as conversations on this topic with numerous church leaders, suggests that this is certainly a reality which is growing. See, e.g., Grams and Parushev, "Comparative Mapping," 41–60, which reports on the findings of the survey conducted among Baptists in various regions of Europe and Central Asia. Marital issues and, to a somewhat lesser extent, divorce are highlighted as major issues across the regions covered, and the article notes the lack of statistics which would indicate whether divorce in the churches is becoming more common (56). For the extended report of the survey, see Grams and Parushev, *Towards an Understanding of European Baptist Identity*.

64. Personal communication with a single woman from the Ukraine, 2 May 2009. For the sake of confidentiality, personal details are withheld.

65. Croly, *Missing Being Mrs*, 78. A sense of isolation and abandonment often accompanies the process of divorce not only in Christian, but also in secular contexts. "When a man and a woman divorce, many people tend to act as if they believe it might

perience of a widow, a divorcee may find herself abandoned, not because of the church's theology questioning the legitimacy of her new status or the circumstances of her loss, but because those who she thought were her friends now cannot cope with her being "partnerless." She is not invited anymore to dinners or outings; worse still, she may hear that those friend-couples now are entertaining her former husband and his new partner.[66]

However the unexpected singleness strikes, the experience is likely to have an immense impact on the woman's mental health, the potential of a whole range of negative emotions and a high risk of maladaptive behavior.[67] It may take a long time for the sense of abnormality to dissipate, and for the new marital status to become an integral part of a woman's identity. For some, it may remain a lament for life, captured in the following poetic "portrait."

Regretted

You see, I have been waiting
for God's Perfect Timing
for the Right Man
who never came
I have listened to
the Chorus of
Christian voices who kept saying
"God has the Right Man for you
Somewhere"
So I waited
and waited …[68]

---

be contagious … Despite the widespread acceptance of divorce in modern society, there remains something frightening at its core. It is as if married people are afraid that another's divorce will illuminate the cracks in their own relationships." Wallerstein and Blakeslee, *Second Chances*, 7–8.

66. Personal communication with a British pastor abandoned by her husband, 19 June 2009. For the sake of confidentiality, personal details are withheld.

67. For an overview of the studies of stress levels and the impact on mental health among the divorced and widowed, see, e.g., Spanish research conducted by Cardenal et al., "Impact on Personality Loss or Separation from Loved Ones," 267–92.

68. Keay, *Letters from a Solo Survivor*, 209–10. Reproduced by permission of Hodder & Stoughton.

The pain of not being married in some cases may be a very long, even a life long, experience. Such was the cry in the letter that opened this chapter. Albert Hsu calls these type of singles "disillusioned"—those who

> have unwillingly resigned themselves to the single life and are characterized by a hopeless or bitter spirit and feelings of despair and defeat. They may view their singleness as a punishment for some wrong they have committed, or they may raise a fist in anger against the powers that be, blaming God for inflicting an undesirable state upon them. Some see themselves as victims of fate. Others may just passively accept their lot in life as God's will.[69]

The motifs referred to above—reward for sin, the will of God, anger and rebellion against the injustice of singleness—will be explored later. For some, despair and a sense of defeat are the leading emotions of their life as singles. Aspects of this lament may seem (perhaps indeed may be, but who is to judge?) a self-imposed misery; black-tinted glasses of a sort. Wherever others may see freedom to make the decisions which can be bold and spontaneous, there is sorrow that nobody seems to care. The wide circle of friendship which is easier to maintain in the absence of the demands presented by a spouse's needs is seen as a *confirmation* of the absence of such a spouse, or as an impossibility—after all, how can a woman who did not manage to attract one single man hope to attract others, even if for friendship? An ability to decide over one's own finances may be supplanted by the longing to have someone to share that task with. As with many things and with many life situations, the issue of whether the glass is half full or half empty is an ambiguous one.

Few single women seem to have never experienced at least some periods of sadness, even if they are generally content with their state. Some days can be more difficult than others; regrets may be triggered by certain memories or occasions. One common trigger is the holiday season.

> Surviving the Commercial Calendar has become, for some of us, a major exercise. Christmas suffocated with tinsel and rampant commercialism; Valentine's Day followed . . . by Mother's Day. Then it's Easter, the time when some of us would actually like to celebrate more but that's usually pretty low key . . . When is

---

69. Hsu, *Single Issue*, 28.

it possible to take a break and not be reminded of all the gaps in our life?[70]

For some, such difficult times include weekends too: "Loneliness is the biggest problem I've found in being single. How do you describe loneliness? It's an absence; there's nothing *to* describe. Yet loneliness can be a dead weight inside you making even the simplest things difficult."[71]

Such sense of loneliness would often include the lack of physical intimacy, and/or sexual frustration—an area which not many dare to discuss openly, and for good reasons, as will become evident in the exploration of the church's reaction to things bodily in chapter 7. However, perhaps the most sensitive area, for some childless single women at least, is the various reminders of the absence of children. The letter quoted at the beginning of the chapter also contained the following lines:

> There has been a period in my life when I started hating all the children. I thank God that passed away quickly. That was the most difficult test for me, for I always loved children and had often had to baby-sit for someone. Now I love them even more, but when I look at them, tears gather in my eyes.[72]

Indeed, while some women do not find mothering as essential for their identity,[73] for others coming to terms with childlessness may be the most painful struggle in singleness. In many churches, becoming a single mother is not exactly the most acceptable act;[74] other barriers include legal or economic difficulties. The pressure for motherhood can often be

---

70. Keay, *Letters from a Solo Survivor*, 155. Reproduced by permission of Hodder & Stoughton.

71. Croly, *Missing Being Mrs*, 142; emphasis original.

72. "Izpovedaniye."

73. On voluntary childlessness, see Hird and Abshoff, "Women without Children," 347–66.

74. However, it does take place; and sometimes is accompanied by a surprising degree of understanding even in rather conservative settings. I was witnessing one such case in a rural Baptist church where a single female member explained to the congregation that, having realized that finding a husband was not likely, she still wanted a baby, and therefore was pregnant with one. Although officially excluded from church membership for a year (a discipline which would be expected in that church context), she was soon reinstalled and, indeed, resumed her role as a leader within that local congregation. In the words of another witness of that situation, "It was difficult to blame her." On the other hand, in more liberal settings (and in Western Europe more than in the East), intentional single motherhood, especially by adoption or artificial insemination, is becoming more prominent.

much stronger in the church, particularly the conservative communities where women do not exercise (visible) roles of leadership. In any case, we must start by acknowledging the pain and the right to lament of those for whom singleness has meant burying the dream of a child:

> Today I'll make my Eucharist . . .
> and pray
> for myself and all like me
> who bleed
> silently for
> their unborn children
> believing that the Best
> has yet to be.[75]

Taken On

> We single adults, I believe, should plunge into life in a whole-hearted and wholesome way and develop a unique style of being in the world.[76]

There are women who have always wanted to be single; there are also those for whom getting married or not did not matter much either way. Still for others, the preference for singleness has come after a time of struggle and anxiety about being single. Sometimes such acceptance of the single state as worth holding onto and enjoying comes after long years of struggle. In the words of one author who was abandoned after twenty years of marriage and spent many subsequent years trying to find a way to "fit in,"

> Only in recent years have I come to some sort of peace with the circumstances of my life. Now retired and a grandmother, I can contemplate with pleasure and gratitude a serene life filled with family activities, creative pursuits, and volunteer opportunities. In short, I have finally come to accept the life I have so reluctantly led.[77]

Some of these single women strive to create a healthy and fulfilled life; some others, especially if they have been hurt in relationships, shy

---

75. Keay, *Letters from a Solo Survivor*, 212. Reproduced by permission of Hodder & Stoughton.

76. Sheridan, *Unwilling Celibates*, 53.

77. Ibid., 2.

away from deeper friendships and turn to work, ministry or some other activity which can serve as a sort of distraction.[78] Their growing numbers make their status increasingly normative, although they may still feel singled out, especially in the church context. The aforementioned magazine, *Christian Single*, has been in print for thirty years, but November 2009 was its last issue. The reason was not the lack of single people in churches; instead, "it seems we singles don't really want to be singled out anymore"—a trend which has been reflected in the "continual decline in [the magazine's] subscription base."[79] Whereas it is perhaps not surprising why a magazine of such nature would fail to attract enough subscribers, its existence points to the body of resources available (and indeed effectively used) by single people worldwide. Most of these resources, however, come from the secular corners of society, with very little being done by the churches. Chapter 2 will begin probing as to why this is the case, and Part Two will explore this issue in more detail.

Many single women may not even be able to say whether they have embraced their singleness as a thoroughly positive thing: not dissimilarly to those who are married, these women would feel completely happy about their state on some days, yet wishing things were different on some other. Indeed, many—including those who are otherwise content with their single status—would talk about times of isolation or loneliness, often felt more acutely in the church. Nevertheless, even such difficult moments can be welcome in the totality of the single experience, for they stand as challenging reminders of the search for meaningfulness and integrated life.

Making sense of one's singleness is a constant motif. Connally Gilliam, a single author in her thirties, describes a conversation with an older friend who explained her experience of unwanted singleness as a prophetic suffering: "You see, your generation is experiencing the fallout of a culture profoundly confused about who God is and therefore about what it is to be human and what it is to love. Your relational disappointments and suffering are, sadly, emblematic of the age." After the initial embarrassment and an attempt to convey the message of "all is OK with me," Gilliam recognized the deep truth of these words:

---

78. As Sheridan comments, such a constricting focus of life is a danger for any lifestyle, yet she sees single people as particularly vulnerable due to the lack of a framework which would force one to divide attention among various areas of life. Ibid., 22.

79. Arnault, "Living in the In-Between," 6.

What now? How then should I live? I wasn't sure what living prophetically meant (images of wild-haired, wide-eyed, angry men came to mind), but I knew at minimum it meant living in the truth. It meant admitting that the confusion plaguing me (and so many of the men and women around me) was real and not easily navigated. It meant owning my unmet desires and the related disappointment. And it also meant holding on to and holding up the goodness and the realness of God in the midst of it.[80]

The journey for meaning-making implies a context of community. This is not just any community (for many of them enjoy strong and deep friendships, are fulfilled in their work, and have plenty of social life), but a community which may be called the church—except that many a time the social reality called the church may not correspond to that deep belonging which these women are seeking. However, sharing in a community where meaning-making is possible marks the stories of many single women who find their own lives as overall happy and fulfilled: an "*intentional* community, one in which I and other like-minded people overtly expressed our mutual commitment to one another in a conscious and deliberate way."[81] "For single people," the same author observes, "the presence or absence of a small intentional community may be the single most important factor in their lives, and a critical matter of survival."[82] The quest for such community will form much of the core of this book as well.

Alongside an opening account of the issue and the numbers, I have presented four sketches of single women who are living out their Christian convictions. As all sketches, they are rough; much more could be said about the particular experiences and differences among those who have never been married; those who have been rejected by their partner; those who buried an abusive husband and experienced a mixture of relief and guilt for feeling such relief; those widowed in young age; and of those in

---

80. Gilliam, *Revelations of a Single Woman*, 130–31.

81. Sheridan, *Unwilling Celibates*, 106. Coming from a Catholic background, Sheridan uses various synonyms to describe such a community: "small church, base church, small Christian community, faith-sharing, or intentional Christian community movement" (ibid.).

82. Ibid., 113.

a long-term intimate partnership that never materialized into marriage. These profiles point to the fact that the category of "single woman" is highly imprecise. An argument could be made that as a category, it is not a useful one, except that this category is continuously imposed as an opposite of the married status, and therefore it is still a reality that these women have to live with.

These sketches were also begging profound questions. What can singleness teach as a preparation for marriage? How can the painful experiences of unexpected or unplanned singleness be redeemed? And, can a genuine and transformative Christian community be found which would welcome the singles? Every one of these questions should be answered by the churches. After all, they claim to be the place where the good news of redemption is preached and the true meaning of life is discerned. It is to this community I turn next, including, but not limited to, the words and ideas it offers to those who approach it.

2

Surface Theologies

The Culture of the Church

There is no doubt that for many single people their biggest problem is the rest of the church.[1]

LOOKING AT THE COMMUNITY of faith to which singles belong will be of utmost importance for several reasons. In order to speak about faith (or, to use a more neutral language, religion) and its social expressions, it is not sufficient to explore the collection of propositional statements deemed to form its doctrinal core. Nor would it be adequate to restrict the discussion to the experiences seen to form the basis for the external characteristics of an institution such as a church. As George Lindbeck argued, religion represents an entire culture, rather than merely either the cognitive or emotive aspects of particular religious sensibilities.[2] It is a particular way of seeing, and interpreting, the world: a worldview. In terms of seeing a church as a culture[3] which reflects a particular interpretive scheme for making sense of the world, it extends to various areas of life—not only to things which happen during the

---

1. Wilkinson-Hayes and Mortimore, *Belonging*, 44.
2. Lindbeck, *Nature of Doctrine*, passim.
3. "Culture" here stands for the basic cultural anthropological understanding of the whole of a form of life. In such an understanding, different aspects of a particular culture all represent material for interpretation, as meaning-making takes place in all of them rather than in one particular sphere of life.

main worship service, but, among other things, to Christian music, magazines, books, and other forms of media.

Any culture wanting to evaluate and learn something about itself will benefit from studying the process of induction necessary for a newcomer or an outsider wishing to become a part of it. "To become a Christian involves learning the story of Jesus well enough to interpret and experience one's world in its terms," claims Lindbeck.[4] The propositional and narrative aspects will, no doubt, be important in this learning process, especially for baptistic churches which see themselves as centered around the Scriptures. Lindbeck proposes that the Scriptures indeed become formative as a community of faith learns to adopt the stance taken by the Bible as *the* interpretation of its current realities. Later I will investigate how faithful the church seems to be to the scriptural authority in its teaching about singleness.

However, "acculturation" cannot be achieved if it is limited to the level of explicit teaching. One must consider the formative role of the practices which the church sees as essential to its function: it is through these practices that faith would be internalized.[5] Thus, as the case of a newcomer to the church would reveal, becoming a Christian will involve distinct patterns of behaviour and feelings. Contrary to the experiential-expressive model of religion which sees the "inner" realities, such as religious feelings, to be primary to their "outward" expression in religious language and rituals, Lindbeck insists that "the humanly real . . . is not constructed from below upward or from the inner to the outer, but from the outer to the inner, and from above downward."[6]

Why is this important? My argument is that the present approach to singleness in the Christian context cannot be remedied only by introducing "more of the right teaching" on singleness. Becoming a Christian and joining a church involves acquiring a particular worldview for interpreting oneself, others, and the world around. More will be said about the dynamics of such a worldview in chapter 5, but here I wish to highlight the need to look beyond the doctrinal dimension to the actual practices of the churches. Indeed, as Lindbeck puts it,

---

4. Lindbeck, *Nature of Doctrine*, 20. The concept of downward causation and its repercussions, albeit from a different angle, will be taken up again in chap. 7.

5. The nature and the role of interrelated practices will be specifically explored in chap. 7.

6. Lindbeck, *Nature of Doctrine*, 48.

> to become religious . . . is to interiorize a set of skills by practice and training. One learns how to feel, act, and think in conformity with a religious tradition that is, in its inner structure, far richer and more subtle than can be explicitly articulated. The primary knowledge is not *about* the religion, not *that* religion teaches such and such, but rather *how* to be religious in such and such ways. Sometimes explicitly formulated statements of the beliefs or behavioral norms of a religion may be helpful in the learning process, but by no means always. Ritual, prayer, and example are normally much more important.[7]

Thus a worldview is formed in a way which often goes unnoticed. This is important to bear in mind as I turn to the next section, which notes certain things that are being explicitly said about singleness in the church.[8]

Professed Theologies of Singleness

> There is a very different attitude to the singles in the churches: for some they are the objects of compassion, for others—the hunters for a husband, and for the majority they actually do not exist . . . Sometimes they are blamed that it is their fault in being single because they do not behave right, they do not look right, they say things that are not right, they do not pray right.[9]

Exploring the Field

The fact that singleness is becoming a serious issue for the church is reflected by a body of literature targeting popular Christian readership. Much of this literature would argue that singleness still receives shockingly little attention.[10] Both East and West, the results of browsing of the

---

7. Ibid., 21.

8. The ideas reported below are usually meant to apply to both genders, yet, given the gender imbalance in most congregations, in practice would be directed primarily to women.

9. Vershina, "Gift I Would Like to Return," 12.

10. For the readers interested in following up some of the popular resources on singleness, I provide a brief list of those I found significant. One of the books emerged out of the concern of the Evangelical Alliance and its Consultation on Singleness, led by Steve Chilcraft (*One of Us*). Designed as a practical reflection directed primarily toward the church in Europe rather than single people themselves, it challenged the church to take singleness seriously. The Alliance's Singularly Significant network has produced booklets primarily for use within a Bible study or similar group (e.g., Chilcraft et al.,

available resources would be similar to Hsu's description of a standard Christian bookshop: it would have "a wealth of titles on marriage and on parenting, children and family issues, but only a handful of books about singleness. Some of these are geared for 'single-again' divorcees or widows. Of the remainder, many are about 'how to find the right partner.'"[11]

My own interpretation of prevalent attitudes toward singleness most likely to be encountered in the context of the church suggests three broad categories: ignoring the problem (singles overlooked); "looking over" to the singles as a peculiar class (singles taught); and taking singleness as a reality to be appreciated with sensitivity and consciously or intuitively incorporated into the larger network of the churchly practices (singles welcomed).

Singles Overlooked

"Single people have been largely ignored, marginalized and uncatered for in much of our church life. This has not been conscious neglect. It was never intended to imply rejection. But often that has been the unfortunate result of our conduct."[12] Such statements would be confirmed

---

Single Issues). Another work which has received considerable publicity was published in the United States and later in the United Kingdom. Al Hsu *(The Single Issue)* addresses mostly single people themselves, though with study questions carefully designed to fit both married and single readers. Hsu takes issue with the way singleness is (mis)treated in the church, the shallowness of community relationships, and is concerned about the high status of the contemporary family as the "biblical model."

On the subject of single Christian women specifically, one may note Kristin Aune, who explored the perception and experience of singleness among British evangelicals in *Single Women: Challenge to the Church?* Based on the author's academic work but written for a popular churchgoing public, it argued that "the sheer number [of single women in the church] makes it necessary for them and for the rest of the church to think through the issues they face" (xi). In 2005 another helpful work appeared, also on the British scene (Wilson, *Being Single: Insights for Tomorrow's Church*). Both Wilson and Aune, directing their argument primarily to the church, feature actual interviews with single people which illustrate their enormous disappointment with the church's response (or lack of it) to their needs.

At the time of writing, I have not been able to find any noteworthy original resource on singleness in the church available in other European languages. (As noted earlier, Perry Shaw, offering an article on single Christians in Lebanon, also notes the absence of materials for a non-Western context, and, as most other authors, bemoans the lack of depth in the existing British and American Christian publications on singleness. "Ministry with Singles," 116–18.)

11. Hsu, *Single Issue*, 9.

12. Calver, foreword to Chilcraft, *One of Us*, 12.

by too many to list or count.[13] Some would even go further to say such neglect at times seems to be somewhat conscious, stemming out of the perception of a single lifestyle as a threat to the currently fragile institution of the family and to personal happiness: "The church with no understanding can ignore singles because the singleness of others is a reminder that the same dreaded fate may come their way."[14]

The aptness of words such as "overlooking," "ignoring," or "neglect" can be difficult to assess. Yet the message coming both from single people (especially women) themselves and articles and books on singleness is straightforward. Singles often feel invisible and insignificant: "All church activities are in a way, not always on purpose, focused on couples and families and the way they experience life."[15] Language is a powerful illustrator of this, such as in referring to one's spouse as "one's other half" (what does it make a single person?).[16] Then there are all the rites of passage, such as marriage and marriage anniversaries and the blessing of the infants—"but there's really nothing that we do to celebrate any of the events in a single person's life."[17] Instead, "individuals who are married with children enjoy a privileged status while those who are not are easily rendered invisible and voiceless."[18]

Such oversight or neglect can take almost cruel forms. "My biggest gripe was being asked to babysit by people who seemed to expect that I had a duty to serve in this way. If I was ever invited round for a meal, it was with the children. This gave me a sense that you only really became an adult when you are married, whatever your age."[19] An obviously different treatment of a single woman compared to those who belong to the "family club," sadly, is an experience a number of single women I have encountered, as in the following observation:

---

13. For just a few examples, see, e.g., Deshpande, *Singled Out of One in the Body*, 3; or Goering and Krause, "Odd Wo/Man Out," 211–30.

14. Patterson, "Singles and the Church," 49.

15. Personal communication with a single woman from the Netherlands, 5 April 2011. For the sake of confidentiality, personal details are withheld.

16. Harding, *Better Than or Equal To?* 47.

17. Response of an interviewee. Goering and Krause, "Odd Wo/Man Out," 217.

18. Ibid., 213.

19. Bridget, 43 years old, in Aune, *Single Women*, 27. As noted by Sheen Gillies, "Marriage seems to be the unspoken rite of passage to maturity and to the ability to be stable and cope with responsibility" (Gillies, "Relationships and Sexuality," in Chilcraft, *One of Us*, 164).

> Growing older, with no obvious gifts or skills to offer, and being a relative stranger to some churches, I have experienced the sensation of being "invisible." People pass by you in church on their way to speak to their friends, and look through you . . . People seem to have their backs to the door and operate as a social club to themselves.[20]

Singles Taught

Some communities do realize there is a problem, and respond by focusing on the teaching on singleness. How far this teaching still needs to go is illustrated by the insistence of a Russian pastor: "We all need to agree that a single person is not a second-rate member of the church."[21] Or, as John Howard Yoder suggested nearly forty years ago, "it needs to be taught as normative Christian truth that singleness is the first normal state for every Christian . . . There exists no Christian imperative to become married as soon as one can, or to prefer marriage over singleness as a more whole or wholesome situation."[22]

In order to emphasize that a single person is not a second-rate member of the community, the notion of singleness as a gift comes in handy: "Singleness is not a curse, but a gift from God."[23] Positively, such a line helps to redeem some of the negative connotations associated with singleness, providing an explanation for their being different. "Whether by conscious decision, i.e., 'voluntary singleness' as part of God's calling, or by gradual realisation and acceptance of God's will, the gift of celibacy is available."[24] It is down to the single person to recognize, accept and develop the gift,[25] even if it is felt to be "an unwanted gift, because our society associates singleness with failure or even punishment."[26]

However, the problem of the exact nature of God's will and the "return policy" on this gift[27] is not resolved so easily. If singleness is seen to be a special gift, then it applies only to some single Christians, leaving a

20. Moira, 57 years old, in Aune, *Single Women*, 43.
21. Pirogov, "Stradayushchim."
22. Yoder, *Singleness in Ethical and Pastoral Perspective*, 3–4.
23. Pirogov, "Stradayushchim."
24. Harding, *Better Than or Equal To?* 35–36.
25. Ibid., 35.
26. Ibid., 34.
27. Virden, *If Singleness Is a Gift*.

struggling single person on shaky ground: do they or do they not possess this gift?[28] The prevailing church attitude would often suggest that those who are not especially despairing to marry are seen to possess such a gift—mistaking "the gift of singleness with healthy self-identity."[29]

As to the way this gift is to be used, it is often directly associated with serving God and God's church. Here one may expect notable differences depending on how a particular church perceives the role of women in ministry. Those which exclude women from most pastoral, teaching and leading positions, would naturally see them serving with ministries such as music or children's work.[30] For those churches which uphold the view of equal gifting for ministry for both genders, the options are wider. However, there are still complaints that

> any evangelical promotion of singleness as "a gift" was contradicted by a notable lack of singles being given prominent church roles. For example, never before had there been so many graduate Christian women, yet, at events such as Spring Harvest, a woman's selection as a speaker was largely dependent on her husband's leadership position.[31]

Such a complaint points back to the lurking, yet rarely verbalized, assumption that singleness unavoidably is linked with the lack of maturity and authority.[32] "It is a sad fact that today, many evangelical churches would not permit John the Baptist, Paul or Jesus Himself even to lead a house group because they are not married (they would probably ban Peter too, as he spends too little time with this family!)."[33] This would certainly be true in regard to male ministers, who are typically

---

28. Hsu, *Single Issue*, 61. Hsu's own response to this is to always consider one's present marital status as a gift—for this day or for however long the status may last.

29. Ibid., 57.

30. Even while remaining in the background, such active single women could be the actual pillars of the congregation; cf. Prokhorov, "Russian Baptists and Orthodoxy," 270–71, on the vital role of single women and their church ministry in the Russian Baptist context.

31. Ruhland, "All by Ourselves," 28.

32. In many ways, this is an unsurprising consequence of the Reformation's rejection of the idea of the calling to the religious life over against marriage, and calls for an appreciation of the Orthodox or Catholic practice of consecrated celibacy.

33. Chilcraft, *One of Us*, 121. Cf. "Single-Minded: Single People in the Church." This is also corroborated by the research done by Aune, "Singleness and Secularization," 60.

expected to be married.³⁴ Where the situation is likely to be different is in the case of a female minister, for those churches who do recognize female leadership.³⁵

The Bible, particularly the New Testament, portrays a number of single people, many of whom are women, even if their status is not always clarified. Yet addresses featuring such single people, such as Jeremiah, Mary Magdalene, or Martha and Mary, do not seem to be common. Perhaps it is because the preacher is more often than not male, and therefore likely finds it easier to identify with another male; or because the biblical material on any of those women is comparatively scarce—it can be more challenging to discuss a less fully developed character. It may be for this reason that sermons on Martha and Mary, an otherwise popular sermon theme, still lack sufficient detail and depth to make them come alive as single women, even though Mary sitting at Jesus' feet is a powerful image that could easily be used to show the single-heartedness of devotion to God. Jesus is often appealed to as a single role model, but here one needs to jump through tricky hoops in working out what could be applied from the life of the One who the church confesses to have been without sin. Moreover, the model of Jesus should suggest a much more communitarian life which "is far more close-knit than the churches that most of us attend. Jesus is both surrounded by friends yet has time to himself. Even the Son of God needs regular human companionship and intimacy but it is notably balanced with him finding space alone to think and pray."³⁶

---

34. Wilson, *Being Single*, 155; Andronovienė, *Involuntarily Free*, 27–28. In the observation of a Canadian Mennonite, Gareth Brandt, "None of the contemporary evangelical men's books I've surveyed even mention singleness as an option for men." *Under Construction*, 112.

35. Cf. Beasley-Murray, *Power for God's Sake*, 27. It would be preferred that such a minister be single, as that would make her more available for the needs of the congregation. However, even for those churches which embrace women in ministry, a single status may still be associated with the lack of life experience and maturity. Comments conveying such understanding are often spoken behind the single woman's back, but sometimes are offered directly to her face: "There were . . . people . . . in the church who put down any problems that I had to the fact that I was single, and if only I could get a man, and people said this, you know, if you had somebody, then you wouldn't have these problems . . . It was awful for me . . . I suppose I was more challenging later on. I said, 'Well, why? You know? Why would it be different?'" (A single woman with a leadership role in a Baptist church in southern England, reported by Wilson in *Being Single*, 136).

36. Ruhland, "All by Ourselves," 29.

Teaching about singleness is likely to revolve around a couple of key scriptural references.[37] One of them is Matthew 19:3–12, which underscores the challenge of living in marriage and explains three different ways in which people can be single: some are born "this way"; some are single because of circumstances or people; and those who have chosen it "because of the kingdom of heaven."[38] This affirms singleness, but often implies special heroism, especially in the case of those who "have made themselves eunuchs for the sake of the kingdom of heaven." Such heroes may be missionaries and other great people of God, but surely not one third of a typical church membership.

As with the Gospels in general, however, these references retreat to the background in order to give the limelight to the Pauline corpus.[39] Thus another reference employed in the church's explicit teaching on singleness is Paul's ideas recorded in 1 Corinthians 7. Although exegetically this chapter expresses a strong preference for singleness, it is not necessarily conveyed this way. Listeners are often reminded of the context for Corinth as a city of great sexual promiscuity and therefore a reason for Paul to urge the believers to remain pure by remaining single.[40] As to applying the same concern in today's context, listeners are unlikely to be advised to stay single in order to be spared distress. "Stay as you are" is more likely to be used to urge one not to seek separation from one's wife if one finds himself to be married already. Paul's remark that "if you marry, you do not sin" is never forgotten too, even though

---

37. Here I will not engage with biblical scholarship in detail; my purpose rather is to describe the contours of habitual church teaching on singleness, which normally would revolve around the two texts I reflect on below: Matt 19:3–12 and 1 Cor 7. For an example of how these resources are used with the most positive intent, see Chilcraft et al., *Single Issues*, 7–10.

38. E.g., Harding, *Better Than or Equal To?* 32.

39. Limelight on Paul can be empirically observed in many churches, including those of a baptistic type. I would also corroborate this claim by having participated, now for a number of years, in the discussions at the Practice of Ministry seminars at the International Baptist Theological Seminary, where students come from a variety of geographical and denominational contexts and commonly confirm the centrality of Paul for the preaching ministry in their home churches. This would not be unique to Europe. Glen Stassen has observed that on one occasion, listening to the (Southern Baptist Convention) preachers for two full days, he did not hear even one sermon from the Gospels (Nordenhaug Lectures 2011, International Baptist Theological Seminary, 31 October, 2011).

40. E.g., Harding, *Better Than or Equal To?* 33–34.

Paul's view of marriage seems to be bluntly based on inability to practice self-control.⁴¹

The advantages of singleness outlined by Paul in the same chapter seem to fail to appeal to or correspond with today's realities. Being free from anxieties seems to be hardly true of a single life, when living on one's own means more responsibility for all the household chores alone or having to take care of elderly relatives. Using Paul's encouragement regarding the possibilities of a single person to serve the Lord exclusively can acquire a rather insensitive interpretation when it is assumed that singles *ought to* take upon themselves considerably more tasks in the church *because* they are single and "have time," whereas family folk must have time to spend with the family.⁴²

Another way in which singleness is addressed is in relation to the church's teaching on marriage. The way this takes place is often a few words on singleness being tagged on to (a much more extensive) teaching on marriage. Even worse, for some churches, singleness will make sense only as the temporary stage discussed in chapter 1: "We had a series on Song of Songs, which covered the subjects of marriage and sex, but without much reference to singleness (except in the form: 'If you're not married, this is how it will be when you are . . .')."⁴³

The absence of marriage in heaven (based on Matt 22:30) is commonly recognized, but if it is not further explored, it can produce a contrary ambition—if the earth is the only place where marriage can be experienced, then one may understandably desire to get the experience while one can.⁴⁴ Using the imagery of earthly marriage, it is sometimes suggested that single women can look up to God to fulfill all their needs and be their true Husband.⁴⁵ The analogy becomes difficult if it were

---

41. Some would point out the difference between struggling with desire (which is likely to be there in all cases) and the struggle which has resulted in one being unable to resist sexual temptation. Thus, the latter case would be a strong one for marrying. Aune, *Single Women*, 112.

42. E.g., Wilson, *Being Single*, 139–45.

43. Aune, *Single Women*, 48.

44. Such an understanding is intrinsically connected with the deeply ingrained conviction that marriage is a highly desirable thing, which will be further explored in the last section of this chapter. Interestingly, it also clashes with a belief that heaven is the best possible state, and provides an example of how our "surface theology" may differ from our deepest loyalties and interests (themes to be developed in chap. 5).

45. Or, in another version, to have "an affair with God"! Murrow, *Why Men Hate Going to Church*, 137.

accompanied by an equally serious suggestion that a single man should look up to God as his true Wife.

More conservative communities would also tend to be concerned that their single people remain celibate. Teaching on single believers' sexuality in those cases can be summarized in one word: "Don't." Any further discussion on how one's sexuality could or should affect one's everyday life is very sparse.[46] The desired result seems to be an asexual human being who, in case of entering marriage at some point, would swiftly become a sensual and passionate lover. It is no wonder that such settings become a breeding ground for early and swift marriages.[47] Such tendencies are noted and criticized by some voices: "There is something dangerous in the extreme where any Christian community's ethics effectively turns marriage into little more than the proper place for legalised lust."[48]

However, even in the case of those communities which do not insist on celibacy for singles or increasingly turn a blind eye to actual practices of church members, it seems indeed the case that "the Church doesn't know what it would teach."[49] Such silence suggests the avoidance of discussing not only explicitly sexual urges, but also their connection with the desire for emotional intimacy and deeply fulfilling relationships.[50] As I will argue later, there may be good reasons for sexual issues not to be at the forefront of the church's agenda, but the absence of the recognition of sexual struggles or frustrations is notable.

Some teaching on singleness takes place through specialized groups, such as singles' ministries. They might take the shape of a meeting for the bereaved, single parents, age-related groups, or smaller groups of singles joining with a similar one in another church.[51] In general, such groups tend to be much more popular in the United States of America than Europe.[52] However, what often does exist in the European context

---

46. Aune, *Single Women*, 71–79.

47. Wilson, *Being Single*, 128; Vershina, "Gift I Would Like to Return," 11.

48. Wilson, *Being Single*, 128. At the same time, "whether many single Christians actually live celibate lives is worth pondering" (ibid., 57): a euphemistic way to say a lot is going on, mostly unaccounted for, unless it bursts into some sort of "scandal."

49. Ibid., 125.

50. Harding, *Better Than or Equal To?* 67.

51. E.g., "Single-Minded: Single People in the Church," 14.

52. Wilson, *Being Single*, 59.

is the so-called "youth group" of the church which would often cater primarily (and in some contexts, exclusively) for single people (admittedly, the young ones). In some cases, these may be the only social groups in a church that a single person has a right to frequent—as in the example of a woman whose engagement was broken, and immediately after it was suggested she transfer into the singles' group.[53] It is in reaction to such attitudes and actions that some have argued that "the greatest need for single people is to be accepted by and integrated into the community of the church, and groups specially for them do not contribute to this."[54]

Singles' ministries are commonly seen as the place for finding a spouse. At times the church may also actively support or promote Christian dating agencies and websites aimed either solely at a "soul-mate search," or expanding the repertoire to include friendship.[55] In the tongue-in-cheek words of Kathy Keay,

> It all seems quite sensible really. After all, we're members of a religious minority group, required to live a Peculiar Lifestyle. The churches have no Eligible and Available men left and life is so busy that there's not much time or energy to engage in Serious Socialising outside your Own Immediate Circle. The fun part is making up your own advert about yourself and what you require from the Mythical Man.[56]

Some are not very enthused. "If this is the Church's *only* response to dating problems, then we should be worried about the kind of Church we will have in the next fifty years, let alone the kind of relationships we will have."[57]

Not surprisingly, preoccupation with matching the singles can trigger a rebellion against all singles' ministries: "*Single people are not a special breed—they are first and foremost people who happen to be single today.*"[58] Indeed, "the very act of being identified as "single" by their churches in a bid to respond to their needs had left them alienated.

---

53. Reported by Wilson in *Being Single*, 133.

54. "Single-Minded: Single People in the Church," 4–5.

55. Wilson, *Being Single*, 115. On the experience of single British evangelical women in regard to dating agencies, see Aune, *Single Women*, 68–71.

56. *Letters from a Solo Survivor*, 149. Reproduced by permission of Hodder & Stoughton.

57. Wilson, *Being Single*, 115.

58. Harding, *Better Than or Equal To?* 28; emphasis original.

By definition, this posited them as somehow apart from the married "norm."[59] As the last section of this chapter will argue, at the core of this perception of the "norm" is a persuasion that singleness *per se* is a sad and problematic state. Even seemingly good intentions to point to the goodness of the single state may be an unwitting demonstration of a convictional clash between what we would like to say, what we feel is right, and what we actually convey:

> Whether singles will feel welcome to the church depends on us, who have families and are well-to-do. Is it not us who have to help them to feel warmth and care? How to do it? We could at least once invite to our quiet family hearth those who have got weary in their search of love and fellowship. If God Himself brings into His house those who are lonely (Ps 67:7), will we stay indifferent and turn away from the *unmarried, sick and old*?[60]

Are there models of true welcome, rather than pity? To this I turn in the next section.

Singles Welcomed

The difficulty with noting cases of churches welcoming singles is that they are harder to pinpoint and identify. An explicit theology of singleness may not be verbalized; rather, such welcoming attitude can be more easily discerned by observing the life of such communities, seeing them discern intuitively the time and place for singleness to be highlighted and affirmed, yet most of the time, providing support by simply living as a rich community consisting of various people in diverse situations. Here I aim to highlight some measures taken, and also point to the measures desired by those concerned about the issue.

An acknowledgment of the need to welcome singles serves as the first positive sign that at least some churches and groups may be prepared to change. "Single Christians are routinely advised to look to Jesus as the single role model, but his is more a model for community living, and it is far more close-knit than the churches that most of us attend."[61] It is only when the church seriously explores genuine and appropriate community expressions that the teachings regarding the Christian

---

59. Ruhland, "All by Ourselves," 28.
60. Pirogov, "Stradayushchim"; emphasis mine.
61. Ruhland, "All by Ourselves," 29.

single life reviewed earlier begin to gain validity. For the churches that insist on the celibacy of the unmarried, it is only such "fellowship of men and women in Christ," as Philip Turner claims, that becomes "the word beyond 'no'" when the church speaks to its single people about chastity.[62]

The Recommendations produced by the Evangelical Alliance Consultation on Singleness[63] include suggestions aimed at affirming and supporting single life in all its seasons, including providing "[opportunities] for exploring alternative models of community living . . . Economic pressure," the document continues, "acting against this, particularly for younger single people, must be tackled, e.g., through new methods of housing provision."[64] It argues against isolation of single people and instead calls for the integration of people through practices of hospitality and discipleship. It also begins to address issues of language, such as so-called "family services."[65] Others have also picked up the importance of changing the language from phrases such as "never married" to "always single," so that the persons' identity is described by what they are rather than by what they are not.[66]

These Recommendations have been included in a resource book published by the Baptist Union of Great Britain, which provides further suggestions on how single and married people can share in the lives of each other in the context of the community of Christ's disciples.[67] Practical suggestions are made, starting with the simple exercise of finding out the numbers of single people in one's congregation. It also includes worship resources, acknowledging the role worship plays in the formation of convictions.

One aspect of such welcoming community would be appreciation for the gifts that each person, single or married, can bring into the church: "What the church must offer for a single person is not a partner, but ministry."[68] Going against the implicit belief explored earlier that

---

62. Turner, "Sex and the Single Life," 20.

63. "Recommendations of the Evangelical Alliance Consultation on Singleness," November 1987, in Chilcraft, *One of Us*, 211–13.

64. Ibid., 211.

65. Ibid., 211–12.

66. Patterson, "Singles and the Church," 46.

67. See Wilkinson-Hayes and Mortimore, *Belonging*, 48 for the reprint of Recommendations.

68. Pirogov, "Stradayushchim."

singleness is somehow related to immaturity and the lack of experience, such actions can be seen, at least partially, in the numbers of those who are exercising leadership roles in the community. It is encouraging when a single person can remark, "Very important committees always have single people on them. I'm always impressed that there's a single person's voice";[69] or "I am respected, if I may say so. I am trusted. I feel good in the church."[70]

There are also particular times to note one's single status, such as during the time of transition from marriage to singleness. Whereas the challenges associated with entering into matrimony are commonly acknowledged and accompanied by offers (or even requirements) of premarital counselling, it is virtually unheard-of to have any counselling offered to newly single people, either by death of a partner or divorce, except by professional psychologists. It is perhaps assumed that they know what to do because they have been single before; the radical extent of the change to which a newly single person has to adjust is rarely recognized. Yet some intentional communities of faith do recognize it and offer help. At times it is left to other singles in the community to deal with it. A recently widowed woman recalls how her singles group "helped me through the transition from being married to widowed because they were just there for me. On a Saturday night the phone would ring and it would be them saying, 'let's go out to a movie or out for pizza'. The church really came through for me."[71]

Another area where some churches show more initiative than others is creating single-sex groups for discussing more personal/intimate issues, as well as mentoring arrangements.[72] In an atmosphere where marital status is deemed insignificant, single-sex groups, alongside all-community activities, contribute to the health not only of individual members, but of the community as a whole. It is in such an environment that it becomes possible to say: "Thank God for singleness—for tomorrow you may be married! Thank God for marriage—for tomorrow you may be single!"[73]

69. Remark of an interviewee in Goering and Krause, "Odd Wo/Man Out," 226.

70. Personal communication with a single woman from Lithuania, 19 April, 2011. For the sake of confidentiality, personal details are withheld.

71. Patterson, "Singles and the Church," 48.

72. Cf. recommendations for churches in Aune, *Single Women*, 135–36.

73. Harding, *Better Than or Equal To?* 43.

Regrettably, cases of welcome and affirmation are frequently drowned in a sea of complaints about suffering in silence, of neglect or suspicion. There is an obvious clash between those occasions when the church feels obliged to affirm singleness as a fulfilling way of life in God's will, and the enormous emphasis put on the institution of marriage as the source of a happy, fulfilled and good life. These adjectives—"happy," "fulfilled," "good"—are common in the discussion, though much less frequently analysed from a theological point of view. Thus the next section explores this theological contradiction by looking at how the church struggles to connect singleness and (Christian) happiness.

God's Will and Happiness

> During a prayer at church celebrating wedding anniversaries, the person praying says a special prayer for all the people that are still single and lonely. (True story)[74]

In the Christian context, "happiness" can be an uneasy term. David K. Naugle, a Baptist theologian, remarks that on occasions, "both leaders and laity . . . throw a wet blanket on the idea of a happy life as a legitimate spiritual concern. Ask a group of veteran Christians if they want to be happy, and many of them are reluctant to answer positively out of fear of appearing unspiritual, even if they secretly desire it."[75] When happiness is discussed, it is likely to be related to God and God's will, or God's desire for a particular human being. This has already been surfacing in the discussion on the extent of "being called to singleness." Depending on a particular understanding of God, anthropology, and other related issues, there can be different variants of how these two—the will of God and one's happiness—are related. However, attention must be paid not only to the examples of explicit and intentional teaching by way of sermons, Bible studies or seminars, but also testimonies, well-meant advice, songs, gossipy comments on the lives of others, and other elements making up the complex fabric of first-order theology. How is the message about the will of God and its relation to happiness broadcast in a typical evangelical church context?

---

74. Acuff, "Surviving Church as a Single."
75. Naugle, *Reordered Love, Reordered Lives*, 12.

God, Marriage, and Family

The most widely expressed version focuses on the notion of blessing and rewards for being obedient to God's will. The charismatic movements such as Word of Faith, Full Gospel, and other expressions of prosperity gospel which swept across Europe a few decades ago, frequently provide an ultimate example of such a view, but certainly they are not the only examples. After all, it makes a lot of sense to suggest and to believe that God desires the best for his children. Job notwithstanding, there are plenty of biblical narratives confirming that God desires the best for his followers.

The real issue here, however, is what is understood to be "the best." The "staple" elements, for a female believer especially, almost invariably seemt to include a successful ("happy") marriage, problem-free children, and an overall comfortable life, such as economic blessings. Such a view is, at times, defended on biblical and/or theological grounds. Hsu comments on how God's will is recurrently understood to be in favor of marriage, quoting Gen 2:18: "God's design is for all to marry."[76] At times this is combined with the idea that God has chosen a particular individual to be one's marital partner. The task of the believer then becomes clear: "I just have to find that person."[77] Indeed, what Ronald Rolheiser observed about American culture is often true throughout the West: "No possibility of real happiness is seen outside [marriage]."[78] As noted by one young woman, "Being single I have been taught so many times how I should pray for my future husband: fasting, a special way of prayers and persistency of prayers were included. Sometimes it seemed that the better God is given an explanation of what He is supposed to do and who He is supposed to send the faster and better a result will follow!"[79]

A deeply ingrained belief that marriage brings happiness in the way singleness cannot is present even in the most well intended teachings on singleness. The culture of evangelical churches nearly univocally suggest that "marriage and motherhood equals 'success' for a female; singleness branded her a failure."[80] Such an attitude and behaviour betray a deep-

---

76. Hsu, *Single Issue*, 72.
77. Ibid., 73.
78. Rolheiser, *Forgotten among the Lilies*, 51.
79. Vershina, "Gift I Would Like to Return," 26.
80. Langton, "Woman's Worth," 8; see also Harding, *Better Than or Equal To?* 27.

seated conviction that, despite what Paul may have had to say about singleness and marriage, it is much nicer to be in the latter position. The words of a Pentecostal pastor express it well:

> It is better; it's Paul isn't it, that says it's better to be single um so um, so I think it probably is. But then having said that I think it's really good it's just fun—it's great to be married um, and I think it's a natural thing and I think, you know, you'd expect for most people to get married in the end.[81]

Whether explicit or not, such notions contain a disconcerting echo of what Sheron Patterson terms "marriage elitism"—a view "that married people are better than single people."[82] Family is seen to function as "a primary normative, meaning-making framework,"[83] even with the occasional attempts to affirm singleness as an option: "Never mind how much we intone that singleness is great, the general attitude is that marriage is better."[84] "Better" in this case also means "more pleasurable": "the path to ultimate adulthood joy,"[85] which singles are denied.

> In retrospect, it's not that anyone overtly declared to me there was no joy to be had as a single, celibate woman. It's just that like many of us, I secretly believed that the *deepest drafts* are to be drunk only by those invited to a joy party. And the only people invited to that party are those walking in the marriage/sex/kids shoes. Too bad for me or anyone else stuck wearing these unsought single shoes.[86]

The triad of "marriage/sex/kids" is still very much the one assumed under such "Christian version of happiness," in contrast with much of contemporary society, which expects not so much marriage as "*any* kind of a sexual relationship."[87] As observed from a Mennonite context, "To some extent we have bought the idea that unless one has experiences of

---

81. Quoted in Aune, "Singleness and Secularization," 63.
82. Patterson, "Singles and the Church," 55.
83. Goering and Krause, "Odd Wo/Man Out," 212.
84. Winner, "Solitary Refinement," 36.
85. Gilliam, *Revelations of a Single Woman*, 136.
86. Ibid., 137.
87. One of the respondents in Wilson, *Being Single*, 110. Cf. also Chilcraft et al., *Single Issues*, 5: "Outside the church, people think you're strange because you are not having sexual relationships. Inside the church, you're labelled strange because you're not married."

sexual intercourse, one is not a whole person. We say we don't believe the messages on billboards, in magazines, and on television, promising that we will find happiness and completeness when we give in to our sexual urges; yet these images seep into our consciousness."[88]

Thus, if marriage is seen to be an obligatory part of the "happiness package," singleness almost automatically comes to represent the "unhappiness package." "Another woman recounts, 'I have a vivid memory of sitting in my church some years ago, listening to my pastor pray for "the sick, the lonely, the shut-in, the single." He was completely baffled when I told him this made me angry.'"[89] No wonder, then, that most of those who end up "involuntarily free" found such outcome to be contrary to the "Christian scenario":

> Every Good Christian is expected somewhere between the ages of eighteen and twenty-five to Meet and Marry, Raise a Family and become Leading Lights in their Local Church . . . We're left wondering, if God makes marriages in Heaven, why on Earth hasn't He made one for us? This is not an unreasonable question, and there is no shortage of pre-packaged good advice. "Have Faith," you are told, "God will Provide." "Ask and you will Receive!" So you ask (after you've looked around, that is), and your Mum asks and all your aunties ask and all your best friends and pet gerbils ask, "Ple-e-ase God," and just occasionally faith rises and you believe that it won't be long now until the Man/Woman of your Dreams (or rather of God's Choice), comes along. Time passes, and no one comes along, so you repeat the whole scenario again, praying with more faith, believing, hoping this time it'll work. It's a bit like putting your money into a Divine Fruit Machine; you keep putting your money in, getting change, putting more money in, and praying like mad, but those little old fruits never line up! What happens then? The money and your faith run out.[90]

Thus, some singles "conclude that they have failed if the promise does not become a reality, others blame God for not answering their prayer."[91] Some resort to even more prayer and Christian growth as a way to "con-

---

88. Steinmann, "Singleness and Sexuality," n.p.

89. Smit, *Loves Me, Loves Me Not*, 254.

90. Keay, *Letters from a Solo Survivor*, 128–29. Reproduced by permission of Hodder & Stoughton.

91. Harding, *Better Than or Equal To?* 27.

vince" God to grant them a partner,[92] while others give up their wholehearted commitment to the Christian way or at least to the church.

The notion of family also represents another facet of happiness which is generally unavailable for single Christians: the experience of motherhood. Mary Grey contends that although there have been strong voices contesting and deconstructing this doctrine, "motherhood is still the official ecclesial discourse for women,"[93] both biologically as well as socially.[94] Within various contexts, women are still being seen as saved through childbearing (including the still existing literal interpretation within some conservative enclaves in the territory of the former Soviet Union[95]). For some of those denied such an opportunity, the struggle may be hard indeed: "Coping with the stigma of being childless, as well as not being married, can be intolerable for some women. Motherhood is so powerfully associated with being a true woman that some single women today are deliberately choosing to have children."[96] Even in traditionally conservative settings, where such actions would not be approved and the single mother could be excluded from membership, privately people might acknowledge that they "do understand" these single mothers: "If I did have a child out of wedlock, it wouldn't have been from a lack of desire to do it the Proper Way, and I suspect some people might even sigh with relief, wondering why I'd never married and glad to know I was Normal after all."[97]

God's Will and Happiness: Alternative Views

Is there anything to counter-balance this dominant perception of a Christian woman's happiness as intrinsically linked to marriage and childbearing? There are some attempts. One of them would be pointing out the benefits of a single life in contrast to the challenges of a married

---

92. "If I love God enough, maybe he'll give me a spouse." Hsu, *Single Issue*, 125.

93. Grey, *Wisdom of Fools*, 35.

94. Ibid., 33.

95. Coming from that part of the world, I have personally encountered such a view, with the appropriate quotation from 1 Tim 2:11–15, on a number of occasions, even if it is becoming considerably rare.

96. Harding, *Better Than or Equal To?* 79–80.

97. Keay, *Letters from a Solo Survivor*, 66–67. Reproduced by permission of Hodder & Stoughton.

life. In this case, the "goodness" of the single status is essentially about having more goods of various sorts at one's personal disposal:

- "I can watch whatever TV show I want and listen to whatever music I desire."
- "I don't have to cook or clean house if I don't want to."
- "I don't have to try to please someone all the time."[98]

Even when true, these aspects of a single life can hardly be sufficient to constitute the value of life in singleness. There are, however, other attempts to affirm singleness as a Christian way of life, and they require a look at the issue of happiness from another angle. For example, there is an approach which could be termed "living for the future," based on the understanding of the fleeting nature of this life and the importance of "storing up one's treasures in heaven" (Matt 6:20). In other words, it is a recognition that one's life here may not be as good as others', but being a Christian in any case will turn out to be a gain in the future life. It does leave open the question, however, of why some Christians seem to be in a better position by also having the opportunity to experience marriage before the time for heaven comes.

Another approach is an insistence that happiness and God's will may not have anything or much in common."[99] Such an understanding is preached with a conviction that "God isn't concerned about happiness, but rather about holiness. To God, your character matters, not your comfort or convenience."[100] Directly opposing the tenets of the prosperity gospel, such a view takes the command of Jesus to deny oneself very seriously as the task of consciously resisting personal desires, and recognizing that they may be distorted and thus leading us away from being faithful disciples. However, such disregard for happiness seems to be devoid of life and Spirit and can be easily used to demean or control others.[101]

The last approach I highlight is one which suggests that the problem lies not with one's life which does not seem to correspond to the

---

98. McDonald, *And She Lived Happily Ever After*, 25.

99. For consideration of the roots of such a theological stance, see, e.g., Thatcher, "Religion, Family Form and the Question of Happiness," 149–52.

100. Naugle, *Reordered Love, Reordered Lives*, 12.

101. Naugle again: "Christianity, many think, is a dehumanizing and life-denyying . . . religion. Believers are straight-laced, sober, and sad" (ibid.).

common understanding of happiness, but precisely with the perception of happiness within a Christian framework. Together with this prevailing view, it confirms that God desires our utmost happiness, but contests the belief that the present understanding of happiness is the right one. In other words, it underscores a need to discover a different way of being happy, of "relearning" happiness.[102] It also suggests that much of modern Christianity has been avoiding the notion of denying oneself or becoming a grain which falls into the soil and dies. As I will explore in the following chapters, for such a view of happiness, the notion of a meaningful life will be an important term.

This chapter started with framing the issue of singleness in the notion of the church as a culture, which goes beyond the doctrinal aspects frequently seen to make up the "core" of the Christian faith. The culture of the church provides those who participate in its form of life with a comprehensive interpretive web of practices and beliefs. It necessarily borrows and adapts aspects of the surrounding culture(s). Such borrowing becomes especially extensive when the cultural dimension of religion is missed, ignored, or denied. Understanding how such sinterchange take place requires, among other things, the need to look at how the doctrine claimed to be taught is actually embodied in the way a church leads its life.

The next task of this chapter, therefore, was to identify the dominant patterns of the church's treatment of singleness. These appeared in three categories. The first one dealt with the overall sense of many single believers of being ignored or overlooked. The second category dealt with the teaching which the churches provide about singleness. I reflected on the biblical materials used, the teaching regarding the sexual dimension of life, and the ministry opportunities both by and for singles. Finally I reviewed the wished-for and real cases where singles are genuinely valued.

---

102. A number of authors on Christian spirituality would point to the error of the present perception of happiness in today's church. In terms of relating this issue to that of singleness, the authors who are celibate would offer specific thoughts on de-learning the world's happiness. See, for instance, Rolheiser, *Forgotten among the Lilies*.

The last section of the chapter explored how the church relates God's will to happiness and to marriage. As the following chapters will suggest, these currently dominant motifs of happiness closely resemble the way in which happiness is popularly perceived in society at large. There is ample evidence for the prevailing conviction that typical Christian happiness involves marriage, which almost inevitably deems singleness as a much less attractive way of life. Several alternative views of God's will and singleness were also reviewed. One of them is an attempt to highlight a positive side of singleness: the lack of the problems of married life. Another viewpoint recommends concentrating on the future, that is, the fullness of God's Kingdom, and considering the discomforts of this life as insignificant in that perspective. Yet another approach contests the link between happiness and God's will, happiness being a "worldly" preoccupation. Still another stance—the one I find most hopeful—questions not the link between God's will and happiness, but the church's current convictions about happiness.

3

Mirroring the Culture

The Gods of the Culture

By THE ASSOCIATED PRESS, February 14, 2007

ROME (AP) Archaeologists working on the eve of Valentine's Day carefully began digging up the bones of a prehistoric couple on Tuesday, hoping to keep their 5,000-year-old embrace undisturbed forever...

The pair, buried between 5,000 and 6,000 years ago in the late Neolithic period, are believed to be a man and a woman who died young...

The burial was unearthed on the outskirts of Mantua during construction work. The site is 25 miles south of Verona, the city where Shakespeare set the story of "Romeo and Juliet," and the discovery fuelled musings in the media about prehistoric love.[1]

T HE PREVIOUS CHAPTER BEGAN with the claim that religion is always expressed as a culture, embodied in a particular narrative, the language of which gives it its shape and movement. However, the same can be said the other way around. Not only does religion always have a cultural form, but culture also possesses a religious dimension; or, as Paul Tillich puts it, culture is inevitably religious.[2] Religion in this sense is understood as the inescapable orientation of life toward something, whatever that "something" may be. Tillich came up with a helpful term,

---

1. Ariel, "Ancient Lovers to Be Kept Together," n.p.
2. Tillich, *Systematic Theology*, 3:248.

"ultimate reality," reflecting the same notion of life-orientation.³ To further this insight, I follow the line developed by McClendon in his applied theology of culture—an insistence that one is to make sense of "many cultures, many religions, many [rivalling] 'gods.'"⁴

To introduce a concept of "religion" or "gods" in some way can seem insulting in relation to those who subscribe to a secular or explicitly atheistic culture. However, as noted above, "gods" and religion in the way I use the terms here are not meant to denote an explicitly religious devotion or confession. Indeed, there are other ways to express culture's ideological dimension (such as employing the language of convictions, explored in chap. 5). Nevertheless, as the argument of this book is directed toward a religious community, the language of "gods" is fitting at this point, as it also exposes how readily (even if unconsciously) some of these gods are idolatrously incorporated into the culture of the church.⁵

The usage of "gods" to signify something to which homage is paid and for which time and efforts are spent has old roots. "Love is a mighty god," Phaedrus and Socrates remarked many centuries ago.⁶ Romantic love indeed seems to be one of the mightiest gods, even inside the community of believers, but it is by far not the only god high in the pantheon of today's Western society. In the same way as the people of God in the Old Testament were challenged in their times, "today we have a new range of gods: technology, achievement, money, appearance, power."⁷ Peter Vardy suggests that one god which seems to rule "above all other gods today, is the great god of sex. Many people worship at its altar and, even if they do not, 'tolerance' of every perspective means that the priority of sex in society is widely accepted and few challenge it."⁸

---

3. Tillich, *Biblical Religion and the Search for Ultimate Reality*.

4. McClendon, *Witness*, 97. McClendon starts with Tillich, but finds his theology of correlation insufficient for developing fully-fledged "trajectory" of a theology of culture, and turns to two other theologians: Julian Hart (specifically his *Christian Critique of American Culture*) and John Howard Yoder in his many works, but especially *The Politics of Jesus*. For an overview of this "theological trajectory" of McClendon, see his chap. 1, "What Is Theology of Culture?" in *Witness*, 17–58. Cf. Parushev and Andronovienė, "McClendon's Concept of Mission as Witness," 247–64.

5. For an insightful treatment of the proper role these gods can—and should—play in human life when properly aligned under the sovereignty of God, see Wink's trilogy *The Powers: Naming the Powers; Unmasking the Powers; Engaging the Powers*.

6. Phaedrus and Socrates in Plato, *Symposium*.

7. Vardy, *Puzzle of Sex*, 165.

8. Ibid.

A theology of culture as outlined above will be specifically applied in section 3.3, which explores varying views toward happiness. As in the previous chapter, the notion of happiness will once again emerge as important. Different pictures of happiness will be explored to see what kind of gods they point to, and how they shape the desires of the people—the "worshippers." Before such exploration, however, something more substantial needs to be said about singles in today's society and how singleness in society is met with different kinds of theologies of a sort—in other words, different interpretations of what it should, or could, mean in today's still extensively "coupled" world.

Minority Taking Over: Singleness in Today's Society

"Why in the whole world a single woman is a normal thing, and in our country [Russia] it's considered shameful?"[9]

Definitions and Numbers

As already noted, "singleness" is a rather complicated category. It "has different meanings which offer different subject positions for women, for instance: 'celibate,' 'solitary,' 'independent,' 'desperate for a man' or 'powerful.' . . . Singleness is thus open to constant rereading and reinterpretation."[10] In 2006, the Census Bureau of the United States announced the fact that for the first time in modern history, married people have been outnumbered by unmarried ones, making up only 49.7 percent of the country's population.[11] Of course, this did not mean that the 50.3 percent of households were "pure" singles—more than 5 percent among them were opposite-sex partners sharing a household, and one would also have to take into account the romantic relationships (whether heterosexual or homosexual) that a significant proportion would likely be sharing—but there was a clear acknowledgment that this change and its "potential social and economic implications [were] profound."[12]

9. Ogloblina, "Nepolnotsennaya zhenshchina?"
10. Reynolds, *Single Woman*, 13.
11. Roberts, "It's Official: To Be Married Means to Be Outnumbered."
12. Ibid. The numbers of same-sex partners sharing a household were under 1 percent, although in reality they were likely to be higher given the reluctance of many gay partners to identify themselves as such (ibid.).

This change is not unique to the United States. The numbers of single persons, in various age groups and in various Western countries, keep increasing; "the trend is unmistakable."[13] High numbers of single women are especially notable in older age: "More than 50% of all women aged 65 or more lived alone in half of the [European Union] Member States for which data are available."[14] Higher numbers certainly have something to do with lower life expectancy for men, but that does not take account of the whole picture. The overall trend toward a growing number of single-person households is reflected throughout the European Union.[15] The country in which I am writing, the Czech Republic, at the moment has one of the highest divorce rates in Europe, and the number of marriages is the lowest it has ever been—so much so that the question is asked, "does the institution of marriage have a future in this country?"[16] Outside of the EU, the 2010 census in Russia indicated an overall decrease of the currently married population, although, interestingly, the number of always singles has also decreased.[17] There are voices suggesting that "the institution of marriage as such over the last few years is becoming a thing of the past."[18]

However, the above statistical data also points to the confusing nature of defining "singleness." The largest "culprit" in creating a vast grey area is the number of those who cohabit.[19] Where do they belong? Some

---

13. Roberts, "51% of Women Are Now Living without Spouse." Britain's Office for National Statistics continues to report the growing number of single people and the decline in the numbers of those who are married. The category of the latter, for example, has declined from 50 percent in 1978 to 40 percent in 2008, whereas the number of single people (which does not include the widowed and divorced) has grown to 47 percent in 2008. Office for National Statistics, "Population Estimates by Marital Status." On an overview of the way changes in women's lives are reflected in changing family patterns in Europe and the United States, see Marler, "Religious Change in the West," in Aune et al., "Women and Religion in the West," 24–34.

14. Eurostat, *Life of Men and Women in Europe*.

15. Eurostat, *Demography Report 2010*, 70; Eurostat, "8 March 2011: International Women's Day." Variations in particular member states are diverse, but the growth of the numbers of unmarried persons is noticeable in all.

16. Lazarova, "Have Young Czechs Given Up on Marriage?"

17. For an overview, see "Ob itogah."

18. Zhebit, "Odin doma."

19. See, e.g., the demographic data collected by the Statistical Office of the European Union, Eurostat, such as in *Europe in Figures—Eurostat Yearbook 2010*, chap. 2, "Population."

of them will consider themselves, in effect, as married, while for others their single legal status will be an important way to describe their own identity.[20]

One of the ways to identify those who are "really single" has been to concentrate on the phenomenon of "single households." Although it is a helpful indicator which, alongside others, points to the growing numbers of single people in society over against those who marry, it is also not entirely accurate. Those who share some sort of love/sexual relationship may have different arrangements ranging from spending most of the time together to seeing each other only occasionally. On the other hand, a number of single people, especially in Eastern Europe, live with their family, due to economic reasons or personal choice.[21] There are also people sharing households and indeed lives without a romantic or family relationship: something two of such women have termed a relationship with a "non-romantic, significant other (an NRSO)."[22]

Any research related to issues such as "marital status" must keep in mind these various complications and the tension between the categories. As observed by E. Kay Trimberger, whose academic work focused on singleness studies:

> What I discovered challenged the strict demarcation between single and coupled women. Instead, I found a continuum, with many ways to exist between being a married, cohabiting couple and an individual residing by herself. But I simultaneously observed that the cultural rhetoric developing after the mid-1990s more strictly categorizes women as married or as single/divorced and sees these two types of women as rivals and threats to each other. On the one hand, defenders of marriage denigrate the lives of single and divorced women. On the other hand, those who extol the virtues of single life disparage marriage. Both sides try

---

20. For an illustration of the complexities of defining "single" for the purposes of research in a Hungarian context (and the growth of numbers of singles), see Utasi, "Independent, Never Married People in Their Thirties," 75–103. On singleness as a social category and the debate as to who should be included in it, see Reynolds, *Single Woman*, 17–18.

21. See, e.g., Vershina, "Gift I Would Like to Return," 23–24.

22. Trimberger, *New Single Woman*, 222ff. For a personal account of such a relationship, see, e.g., an article featuring two such women in Holden and Kendall, First Person, November 21, 2008. Noting that they "live in a relationship that has no name," they describe the nature of that relationship as that of partnership and friendship—a theme to be picked up in chap. 8.

to claim cohabiters as belonging in their camp—either as the equivalent of married people or as having rejected marriage and identified themselves as single.[23]

In wading through such tangles, this chapter concentrates on those women who *consider themselves single*. This allows for some fluctuations and variations inside this group, but helps to retain the focus on the growing population of those who identify themselves as single.

Singleness in Theologies of Culture

The growing numbers of single people are finally recognized by the media and businesses who are adjusting their services to cater to this expanding market. Thus, for example, www.unmarriedamerica.org introduces itself as "an information service for America's 112 million unmarried adults—who head up a majority of the nation's households. Our services focus on your interests as employees, consumers, taxpayers, and voters, regardless of your household size or family structure."[24] In Europe, there is also an increasing realisation that "in the future, single households will be the most important consumer group not only because of their rapidly rising number but also because they are leading the way in changing consumer lifestyles."[25] A recent documentary entitled "Generace Singles" by a Czech director, Jana Počtová, suggests this is already happening. Following the life of six singles for a year, the film aims to raise an awareness of the growing number of singles in the country and reveal the complexity of single life in the desires and experiences of the singles themselves as well as the reactions of others.[26]

To this I may add a personal example. While recently shopping for glassware in Prague, I noticed a box with a collection of six different glasses for six kinds of drinks. The picture on the box was of a Buddha-like woman, holding a glass in each of her six hands. The primary target group of this consumer item was clear.

Significant changes may be ahead not only in the area of marketing, but also language, where different linguistic examples, even when they are anecdotal, reflect the varying attitudes to be found. On the one hand,

23. Trimberger, *New Single Woman*, 203.
24. www.unmarriedamerica.org.
25. Hodgson, "One Person Households."
26. Počtová, *Generace Singles*.

the word "single" is often perceived as possessing negative connotations. In English, "single" in the literal sense would suggest "a person's isolation from all close relationships."[27] For several Indo-European languages, such as Russian or Lithuanian, the same word has been used for both "single" and "lonely." On the other hand, some languages, such as Czech, have the term "free" to legally describe the status of a woman who is not married, denoting a different and significantly more positive attitude toward singleness as freedom from routine and sacrifice of one's personal interests and desires.[28] The notion of "free" certainly seems to be coming to the fore in the face of the growth of the numbers of single women and successful models of a single lifestyle, and suggests singleness as an increasingly more acceptable, and at times even desirable, option. The role of the media should also be acknowledged, as is exemplified by television programmes such as *Friends* or *Sex and the City*, which have enjoyed great popularity in much of the West.[29]

However, a closer look at language suggests that marriage remains the constant point of reference. In a number of languages, singleness is primarily used to describe the state of being "unmarried"—which, given that the single state comes before a possible married state, is rather interesting: "why aren't married people called unsingle?"[30] Byrne and Carr propose that "although demographic patterns and other major social changes are creating an historical and social context where singles may lead lives that are as rich and fulfilling as married persons, cultural values and attitudes still blithely endorse and perpetuate the Ideology of Marriage and Family."[31] A number of authors note the lingering presence of discrimination in economic and social terms.[32] Perhaps one of

27. Clark and Graham, "Do Relationship Researchers Neglect Singles?" 135.

28. However, this is still primarily a legal category which therefore is seen as too narrow. The same would be true of the Slovak language; hence an increasing adoption of the English "singles." Drotován and Bleha, "Analýza fenoménu singles," 62–81.

29. It ought to be noted that the portrayal of singleness in *Friends*, *Sex and the City*, and many others is still as a temporary phase. Even while "happily single," virtually everybody seems to be in the search of a partner, and eventually finds one.

30. DePaulo and Morris, "Singles in Society and in Science," 58.

31. Byrne and Carr, "Caught in the Cultural Lag." Reference to "the Ideology of Marriage and Family" is taken from the thesis of DePaulo and Morris.

32. On the likelihood of the at-risk-of-poverty situation for single adults living on their own or with dependants compared to those whose household comprises of several adults, see Eurostat's publication, *Europe in Figures—Eurostat Yearbook 2010*, chap. 6, "Living Conditions and Welfare," 11. On the considerably lesser number of single pro-

the most noticeable examples would be the family discounts offered by medical clinics, sports facilities, entertainment centers, travel agencies and the like.

> How long would married people put up with their experiences, and how long would it take social scientists to include them as members of a stigmatized group, if their lives included the following:
>
> - Every time you get married, you have to give expensive presents to single people.
>
> - When you travel with your spouse, you have to pay more than when you travel alone.
>
> - When you tell people you are married, they tilt their heads and say things like, "aaaawwww" or "don't worry honey, your turn to divorce will come."
>
> - You get paid less than single people for the same work.
>
> - Single people can add another adult to their health care plan; you can't. [...]
>
> - When you browse the bookstores, you see shelves bursting with titles such as "If I'm So Wonderful, Why Am I Still Married," and "How to Ditch Your Husband After Age 35 Using What I Learned at Harvard Business School."
>
> - Moreover, no one thinks there is anything wrong with any of this.[33]

---

fessors in higher education institutions compared to the national average, see Wilson, "Singular Mistreatment," and the numerous responses in letters to the editor, *Chronicle of Higher Education*, June 11, 2004. An article by DePaulo and Morris, "Singles in Society and in Science," 57–83, has led to a series of commentaries on the question of whether and how far singles are prejudiced against married people in the US context. Various reactions, most of which have fully or partially supported the claims made by DePaulo and Morris that singles are consistently discriminated against, appear as "Singles in Society and in Science," 84–141. On an overview of the results of research comparing the experiences of discrimination at various social and institutional levels in the American context, see especially the article by Byrne and Carr, "Caught in the Cultural Lag," 87. Even though there may be reservations about the comprehensiveness of such research, it is clear that it reflects general tendencies sufficiently accurately.

33. DePaulo and Morris, "Should Singles and the Scholars Who Study Them Make Their Mark," 145–46; followed up by "Singles in Society and in Science," 84–141. While acknowledging that such discrimination cannot be compared to much more serious cases of persecution and abuse, DePaulo and Morris note: "We bet our annual salaries that married citizens would scream bloody murder if these kinds of things routinely happened to them" ("Should Singles and the Scholars Who Study Them," 146).

DePaulo and Morris also draw attention to a high degree of stereotyping and unchecked assumptions in science.[34] One of the consequences of such firmly held assumptions in science has been the consistent portrayal of single persons as necessarily less happy, even when a significant amount of research suggests this is not necessarily the case.[35] Marriage is often assumed to provide for quality relationships (a key factor in a person's well-being) better than a single lifestyle, yet such an assumption is taken for granted. What is often ignored is the fact that single people (women in particular) tend to maintain more, not less, significant and deep relationships, such as sibling ties or intimate friendships, which contribute to a person's well-being.[36] Yet singles are persistently evaluated more negatively than married people—even by single people themselves.[37] Given the persistence of such a message, even a woman for whom her marital status is not a dominant feature of describing herself, is constantly reminded of her singleness as she engages in various practices of daily life. "The available ways of representing singleness seem likely to shape how women on their own make sense of, and talk about, what they do."[38] How then do single women perceive themselves?

Previously I have explored four major perceived "types" of singles: "spinster," "single mum," "widow" and the "new kind of woman," the one who is actively creating meaning and satisfaction in life without marital ties.[39] Of course, such "types" can only serve as caricatures outlining the way different kinds of singleness are perceived by culture and single women themselves. Alternatively, one may speak of "the lonely

---

34. DePaulo and Morris, "Singles in Society and in Science," 65–80. DePaulo has also produced a compilation of academic research on singleness at http://belladepaulo.com/singles-research-and-writing.

35. This applies particularly to the way single people who are well into the "marrying age" are perceived as necessarily less happy and less attractive in terms of their personality traits. See DePaulo and Morris, "Singles in Society and in Science," 65–80.

36. "It is not that single people have larger social networks than married people; they do not... What they may have, though, is intentional communities." DePaulo and Morris, "Singles in Society and in Science," 72. Another important reminder of DePaulo and Morris is the difference in the "bouncing back" of women after divorce depending on how much of the (previous) friendship network is available to them after divorce (72, quoting an earlier research; cf. Kalmijn and van Groenou, "Differential Effects of Divorce on Social Integration," 455–76).

37. DePaulo and Morris, "Singles in Society and in Science," 62.

38. Reynolds, *Single Woman*, 15.

39. Andronovienė, *Involuntarily Free*, 13–16.

spinster; the swinger; the available woman; the social network activist; the dangerous divorcee; the family helper; the fiercely independent battler; the self-reliant coper."[40] These pictures of single women have been suggested by Reynolds in her investigation of single identities. Reynolds has discerned certain common ways singleness was approached by the participants of her research. These reoccurring themes can be summarized thus:

- Singleness signifying a personality problem
- Singleness resulting in exclusion from a significant section of social life
- Singleness allowing to exercise a much greater deal of freedom compared to the married life
- Singleness as an avenue for success and growth.[41]

Reynolds notes that most of her interviewees employed all four motifs: a striking example of a high degree of ambivalence when the subject of singleness is approached.[42] This ambivalence and ambiguity is an important feature to bear in mind. Reynolds' work illustrates how many of the participants of her research both confess a desire to find a partner and claim to lead happy lives without such a partner.[43] Even while celebrating all the different possibilities of a single life, a woman may admit that, should there come an appropriate opportunity, she would choose to become coupled.[44]

> On a day-to-day basis, what does it mean to live alone now? How do we gauge the balance between privacy and loneliness, solitude and unfettered anxiety, vulnerability and independence? For some women the relationship between home and comfort is obvious. For others, the experience is one of complex and constantly shifting contradictions, varying from day to day, sometimes from hour to hour, just the way one expects the light does in a well-known room.[45]

---

40. Reynolds, *Single Woman*, 19.
41. Ibid., 49ff.
42. Ibid., 60.
43. See, e.g., discussion in ibid., 66–70.
44. Ibid., 69–73.
45. Clements, *Improvised Woman*, 200.

Such ambiguity may be seen as inconsistency or even a lack of integrity in recognising the extent of the struggle within a single life, but it also points to the recognition that any state of life, whether marital status, career, or geographical location, represents certain limitations which at times would be regretted even in the context of an overall satisfaction with life. The question is more about the degree of such ambiguities.

The set of the motifs, or the "interpretative repertoires," suggested by Reynolds, does not only employ contradictory evaluations of a single state of life; it also represents a degree of inconsistency in that the first of the four seems to deal with the explanation of singleness—"something must be wrong with the woman if she has not been able to find a spouse"—whereas the other three seem to be dealing with consequences, both *de facto* and possible ones. For my purposes, I propose to consider a slightly altered set of dominant motifs in perceiving *and* representing singleness which reflect a continuum of the outlook on single life. As in Reynold's research, a possibility of embracing several motifs at the same time points to their coexistence in construing the meaning of singleness by one and the same individual. These motifs can be expressed thus: a tragedy in the world of unfairness; a calling or necessity; and an avenue to flourishing. Comments are offered on each of them below.

It Is an Unfair World. There may be different interpretations for the reasons of such unfairness—whether a "personal problem," unfortunate circumstances, lack of luck, or the cold reality of uneven numbers of women and men seeking marriage. However, in the context of marriage as a frequently dominating motif for human life, it is likely to force a single woman to ask the question, at least occasionally, as to whether her single status has something to do with personal deficiencies of some sort.[46]

Whether it is the personality faults or accidental factors that are seen to be the reason for one's singleness, this motif largely perceives singleness as an undesirable state and in contrast to the bliss of married life. "This sense of strong binary, a separated geography of two unrelated states, is a commonplace feature of the broader discourse of singleness. In this repertoire, typically, one of these spaces, coupledom,

---

46 Reynolds, *Single Woman*, 63.

is constructed as privileged, and the other, singleness, as excluded, lacking and disadvantaged."[47]

An Aspiration Higher than Marriage. Here singleness is accepted as a possible or necessary piece of the parcel of a specific calling of one's life. An example would be a particularly demanding career. It ought to be noted, however, first, that a career is rarely seen as incompatible with family life for men; and, second, that a successful career of a single woman can also be interpreted both as her solution of her singleness and as the reason. The motif has become easier to adopt with the diminishing significance of marriage, where the choice between "having a family" and a desired path of career or calling is less painful than before.[48]

Others may feel the necessity to stay single for ideological reasons, such as represented in some tracks of the feminist thought. Marriage can be seen either as an irrelevant factor or indeed a symbol of injustice toward women and therefore a matter of active opposition: "In reality we will hardly meet a woman who does not experience if not physical or sexual, then economic or psychological violence in her family. . . Most women burn their talents, dreams and hopes to be happy on the altar of the family."[49]

An Avenue to Flourishing. On the opposite end of the continuum from a sense of tragedy and unfairness is the recognition of singleness as either a preferred or utterly satisfactory lifestyle. This motif can be discerned in a growing body of literature exploring singleness which asks "whether remaining or returning to being single can be a preferred option rather than a problem to be endured."[50] It is strengthened by the less-than-happy experiences of marriages, where the newly found freedom and space, or "intimacy with solitude is precisely what may predispose [such women] not to enter into a new relationship."[51]

Although gaining prominence recently, such an approach has been sported by some single women during the times when singleness

---

47. Ibid., 55.
48. Pillsworth and Haselton, "Evolution of Coupling," 102.
49. "Mitai apie santuoką arba nutekėjimo laimė."
50. Reynolds, *Single Woman*, 97.
51. Clements, *Improvised Woman*, 201.

was seen as a decidedly "tragic" option. Marjorie Hillis gained massive popularity by suggesting, back in 1936, that

> there is a technique about living alone successfully, as there is about doing anything really well. Whether you view your one-woman ménage as Doom or Adventure, and whether you are twenty-six or sixty-six, you need a plan, if you are going to make the best of it.
> The best can be very nice indeed.[52]

These very different approaches to singleness are also strongly influenced by the dominant message about happiness broadcast by today's culture—a theme of the last section of this chapter.

Happiness in the Eyes of the Culture

What makes women happy? Self help, surgery, sex? Money, power, career? The options for women now are endless. But has too much choice killed off contentment?[53]

Recent decades have witnessed an unprecedented growth in interest in happiness. The growing output of research and popular writing devoted to happiness is also marked by a variety of meanings attached to the concept. Some would concentrate on the objective reality or quality of life that can be quantified and evaluated as less or more "happy," while others would focus on subjective factors such as moods, perceptions, and feelings. The question of happiness is also linked to the meaning of one's life: "We care a great deal, as that common death-bed question

---

52. Hillis, *Live Alone and Like It*, 14. Working out "a plan," as suggested by Hillis, is an important element of this motif which frequently recognizes that, in contrast to marriage which seems to come with ready moulds, satisfying single life requires conscious efforts and possibly even resistance to certain unhelpful moulds and stereotypes. Trimberger describes the efforts that single women make in order to create an alternative to family life (which may include collective households, or being in a sexual relationship while retaining separate households). Her focus is on those women who settled on pursuing a happy life of living on one's own. See esp. Trimberger, *New Single Woman*, chap. 3, "Crafting Singular Lives." Her recommended support system consists of the following: "(1) fulfilling work, (2) connections to the next generation, (3) a home, (4) intimate relationships with a network of friends and extended family, (5) a community, and (6) acceptance of our sexuality whether we have an active sex life or are celibate" (ibid., 65 and ff.).

53. Bedell, "What Makes Women Happy?" n.p.

attests, whether we have had a good life."⁵⁴ Different understandings of happiness will be discussed later, but my interest here is to look at a cluster of terms related to a positive experience or positive evaluation of life, whether it be termed "quality of life," "life satisfaction," "subjective wellbeing," "goodness of life," "fulfillment," "flourishing," or "happiness."⁵⁵ What is of special concern is what kind of major themes, or motifs, are reflected (and reinforced) in the ways the culture tends to portray sources of happiness.

The interest in happiness has been growing alongside economic standards, often accompanied by a question as to whether greater wealth should be expected to increase levels of happiness.⁵⁶ The lives of women, even in the poorest countries in the West, has changed radically. However, levels of happiness do not seem to have a straightforward relationship to economic development and the extent of personal freedom. On the contrary, people in affluent countries today seem to be less, not more, happy.⁵⁷ Among the suggested culprits are developments such as the spreading of individualism which has ruptured the fabric of societies and communities;⁵⁸ the increasing demands on what counts as a sufficiently "happy" life; or the very fact that people now have time to reflect on happiness as opposed to having to put all their energies into surviving.⁵⁹ Thus various initiatives have emerged which encourage a change in the way the development of well-being is measured. The Happy Planet Index 2.0, prepared by the New Economics Foundation, for example, encourages a "radical departure from our current obsession with GDP"

---

54. Griffin, "What Do Happiness Studies Study?" 141.

55. The research on happiness, or well-being, generally divides into two streams on the basis for their preference for either objective or subjective emphasis in measuring well-being. A short overview, including the problems with each of the approaches, can be found in Forgeard et al., "Doing the Right Thing," 79–106.

56. For an overview of literature devoted to the relationship between economics and happiness, see Steedman, "Economic Theory and Happiness," 23–41.

57. For one of the most prominent holders of this view, see Layard, *Happiness: Lessons from a New Science*. See also Eaton and Eswaran, "Well-Being and Affluence," 1088–104. See also Stevenson and Wolfers, "Paradox of Declining Female Happiness," 190–225.

58. Eaton and Eswaran point out to what they term "community" or "social leisure" as a crucial factor in the promotion of well-being, habitually ignored by economists. "Well-Being and Affluence," 1098–102.

59. Cf. Layard, *Happiness: Lessons from a New Science*, 546.

as the indicator of human satisfaction with life[60] and, in its *Charter for a Happy Planet*, advocates "a new narrative of progress"[61] which would include such factors as life expectancy and ecological efficiency.

Greater attention is also being paid to the question, *what* is it that makes people happy (and therefore, their lives good)? This has been witnessed by the massive industry of self-help materials as well as an interest in academia. Much of it is related to a specific turn in the field of psychology, commonly known as positive psychology.[62] Although a comparatively contained "corner" of psychology, it serves as a good illustration of the general interest in and expectations of happiness. Positive psychology has greatly contributed to an understanding, and indeed insistence, that there exist different ways to be happy.[63] The idea gets repeated in popular culture, including considerations about singleness and marriage: "Each person's happiness is a very individual matter. A possession of a spouse doesn't guarantee anything."[64]

Yet here comes the paradox. Despite the seeming variety of paths to happiness, society, and women in particular, seem to be strongly shaped by one single motif of happiness and fulfillment. This motif, although undergoing considerable change, still centers around coupledom. To

60. New Economics Foundation, "Happy Planet Index 2.0," 3.

61. Ibid., 6. The same spirit marks the next report of the Foundation prepared by Michaelson et al., *National Accounts of Wellbeing*.

62. Positive psychology is interested in what contributes, from the psychological point of view, to healthy and positive experience of life. An interest in such "psychology of happiness" largely arose out of frustration of the preoccupation of standard psychologies with the anomalous and pathological. An impressive number of the books written by positive psychologists for the general public have become bestsellers and been translated into various languages, then followed up by references and quotations in the popular media (perhaps especially notably magazines). Thus, although quotations from positive psychology here will mostly come from the English language originals, it must be borne in mind that their effect is much wider.

63. Cf. the title of the popular work of Martin E. P. Seligman: *Authentic Happiness: Using the New Positive Psychology to Realize Your Potential for Lasting Fulfillment*.

64. "Kodėl mes norime ištekėti?" Almost any periodical geared to women is bound to have something on happiness. At the time of writing this chapter, I picked up the current issue of *Red*, a British monthly publication. Sure enough, it had "17 pages of inspiration and advice from the world's top happiness gurus. Contentment begins now." The editor of these seventeen pages expresses hope that the reader will "find one thing (hopefully many more) that will make you live a little happier" (Moss, "Real Happiness Starts Here," 155). As in most of popular reflections on happiness, there is little discussion about the criteria of choosing these ways except the need to find the ones "which will work for you."

this I turn next, suggesting that it mirrors the icons of the good, fulfilled, happy Christian life seen earlier.

The Standard of Coupledom

In March 2007, Lithuanian society was shaken by a tragic news story: the murder of two boys, aged 8 and 12, by their 35-year-old mother who was promptly charged and sentenced to life imprisonment. Whatever the actual motives of the murder (and they seem to involve, according to the mother, her deep unhappiness in her marriage due to her husband's alcohol abuse and the hopes to find a better husband by reducing the number of her children from five to three), it is the ensuing attention to the father, who was left raising the couple's remaining three children, which is illustrative for my purposes here.[65] The man was flooded by letters from women of various ages, widows and divorcees. "All letters are similar: the women briefly describe themselves, present their condolences in regard to the family tragedy, offer some compliments, and suggest a contact by short text messaging."[66]

Tragedies such as this often trigger the above reaction, but they also illustrate the eagerness of the women searching for a marriage partner. As Vivasvan Soni suggests, marriage is very much seen as "[inaugurating] the time of consummation, satisfaction, and fulfillment: the time of happiness itself."[67] No matter how often it goes wrong, the happiness-is-marriage motif is still very resilient: "Each normal woman dreams to get married to a good man who would love and respect her and would carry her on his arms."[68]

It may be observed that given the plummeting number of marriages, there must be a shift occurring in the culture which places an emphasis on factors other than marriage as the conditions for happiness. Indeed, the focal point is no longer the form or the length of marriage, but the perception of the necessity of a romantic and sexual relationship, or "being a couple," that is needed for one's happiness as a woman. "The dominant cultural storyline for the lives of women is one of marriage

---

65. The story was, not surprisingly, widely covered by the media, including a monograph on the media coverage of the tragedy (Ežerskytė, "R. Parafinavičius").

66. "Geidžiamas vienišius," 2.

67. Soni, *Mourning Happiness*, 268.

68. From an article in a popular Lithuanian news portal. "Kodėl mes norime ištekėti?"

and family relationships."[69] Predominantly interpreted through the lens of a soul mate as the basis of forming a couple, these relationships easily break down when they cease to be centered on the romantic/sexual aspect, but can be quickly replaced by a fresh search for a new soul mate.

Such an understanding of what is necessary for life to be good assumes such sexual and romantic partnerships to be highly surpassing any other type of relationship, and shapes certain "habits of the mind" not only for individual people, but also for the researchers and, of course, the media.[70] Public policies are based on such presumptions and regulate life patterns in a certain way, and scientists conduct their research based on the assumption of the primacy and unquestionable desirability of marriage or coupledom, therefore finding it in the results of the studies they carry out.[71] While the importance of meaningful, lasting relationships is certainly confirmed by different kinds of surveys and studies carried out in different contexts, marital or similar sexual relationships are often assumed to be the sum-total or the epitome of such lasting relationships.[72] The extent of this ideology can be tremendously powerful: consider the message little girls absorb "from the time they receive their first Barbie doll and start asking for a matching Ken."[73]

That such an understanding of happiness is a prevalent one may not be surprising. What may be more puzzling is why this view is held so adamantly to the extent that single people—even seemingly happy single people—are regularly viewed with suspicion or pity, and why

---

69. Reynolds, *Single Woman*, 74.

70. Consider, for example, the statement popularised by Layard: "People generally become happier as a result of marriage." Layard, *Happines*, 1060. He explains: "The main benefits of marriage or cohabitation are obvious: you give each other love and comfort; you share resources, gaining economies of scale; you help each other. Married people also have better sex lives . . . Furthermore, married people are healthier and live longer" (1071).

71. DePaulo and Morris, "Singles in Society and in Science," 57–83. DePaulo and Morris (writing specifically regarding American society) see this as a result of what they call the "Ideology of Marriage and Family"—the ideology which "has gone largely unrecognized and uncontested" (58). DePaulo and Morris point to, and provide critique for, an assumed bias in much of social science that there is a direct link between marriage and happiness (65–80). This article solicited a number of responses from different sub-fields of research which appeared in the same issue ("Singles in Society and in Science" 84–141). I will refer to these responses on several occasions in this chapter.

72. DePaulo and Morris, "Singles in Society and in Science," 71.

73. Smit, *Loves Me, Loves Me Not*, 164.

this motif does not seem to tolerate alternative ones. If a single woman appears happy, "she [must nevertheless be] unhappy. Although you wouldn't tell that just by looking. She's full of the joy of life (most often), she's beautiful and smart."[74] If a single person appears to be happy, it becomes a challenge to the ideology holding that a romantic relationship is necessary for a fulfilled, happy life.[75] Such a challenge may meet severe resistance, especially because the presence of a single person also serves as a reminder of the possibility for anybody to become single at any point of their life.[76] The "ideology of coupledom" provides a helpful concentration on the standard way to happiness.

Alternatives?

The "standard," however, is not entirely without contest. The above prescription for happiness and the meaning of life increasingly clashes with the growing number of people who do not conform. Alternative variants of a satisfying life are being increasingly suggested, from within academic books in positive psychology to glossy magazines and TV programmes, and although they may still be largely perceived as "complementary" or "alternative" (i.e., in relation to marriage or other type of sexual relationship as *the* most important thing) options, they come with a recognition that there are other possibilities. As many "happiness gurus" are quick to point out, there are different routes to happiness, even if they are less prominent than the happiness-in-coupledom motif. Here I suggest two significant variants of the "hermeneutics of happiness" specifically in relation to women.

The first one, *motherhood*, shares a close, but not absolutely necessary, link with the coupledom motif, and in some ways can be seen as forming one larger "satisfaction domain," functioning as a single motif: "We are not free from our nature and almost all of us dream about one and the same thing: a beloved next to us and healthy and smart children."[77] There is an expectation that the happiness of a sexual partnership will become a gate into happiness of motherhood, but the link has been weakened by increasing numbers of single mothers. This

---

74. "Kodėl mes norime ištekėti?"
75. Kaiser and Kashy, "Contextual Nature and Function of Singlism," 125.
76. Paterson, "Singles and the Church," 49.
77. Ogloblina, "Nepolnotsennaya zhenshchina?"

is even more so in the case of those single mothers who happen to be celebrities and therefore function as role models for a considerable part of society. Indeed, nowadays motherhood has gained a certain "fashionability," as evident from the attention of the media directed to the progeny (whether adopted or biological) of various celebrities.[78]

This version of fulfillment is propped up by various explanations, from the still-lingering modern ideal of mothering as the essence of a woman's identity[79] to the pop-versions of classical psychoanalysis' interpretation of "penis deprivation" which is naturally resolved as a woman becomes a mother.[80] In some cases, and especially after a major disappointment in coupledom as a source of the bliss of happiness, motherhood becomes the major motif of fulfilled life: "Through this modern rite of female passage a modern woman is left with few doubts about her primary identity. She may be a wife, consort, helpmeet, and lover, but she is above all a mother."[81] The happiness-in-motherhood motif may be stronger in the Eastern (post-socialist) parts of Europe, but it is common throughout the Western world.[82]

Yet the prominence of the role of woman-as-mother has a price: in order to be a happy mother, one is supposed to be a good—indeed, an *ideal*, mother. The job description for this role is frighteningly

78. Consider, for example, the centrality of the search for happiness by the main character of a popular television series *Ally McBeal* and her eventual choice to center her life around motherhood (in her case, also foregoing a romantic relationship as an implication). Mckee, "Views on Happiness in the Television Series *Ally McBeal*," 385–411.

79. For an insightful overview of the development of the practice of "mothering" and how sharply it differs from pre-modern realities, see Gillis, *World of Their Own Making*, chap. 8, 152–78. Gillis notes that in pre-modern times, the care now associated almost exclusively with a mother's love was given to children in several alternative ways, such as wet-nursing (not only for the upper class but for working mothers too), adoption by relatives of various sorts, or indeed by those not related, or by the child being presented to the church. "Anyone who mothered was called 'Mother,' regardless of biology . . . Mothering knew no age, race, or gender boundaries" (ibid., 155). Indeed, "until the nineteenth century, nurturing capacity was thought of as an acquired talent more than as a sex-specific natural quality" (ibid., 157).

80. It could, of course, be argued that this is a reductive version which does not do justice to the scope of Freudian psychoanalysis in terms of gender. See Graham, *Words Made Flesh*, 71–72.

81. Gillis, *World of Their Own Making*, 158.

82. Rokven, Josja, et al. "Family"; Margolis and Myrskylä, "Global Perspective on Happiness and Fertility," 45–46.

demanding,[83] reflecting what Gillis considers to be a "contemporary notion that individual mothers are wholly responsible for the physical, spiritual, and emotional well-being of their children."[84]

> Unable to accept their own humanity and the shortcomings this inevitably entails, many women feel a disconnection between the idealized motherhood they are expected to live up to and the realities of everyday mothering. Modern culture has thus added yet another task to mother's work: representing herself to herself and to others as something she can never completely be. Never before has this cultural imperative taken up so much space and time in women's lives. Never have mothers been so burdened by motherhood.[85]

It is at least partly in reaction to such an idea of motherhood burdened by high expectations that a growing number of women are opting for voluntary childlessness.[86]

When both of the above paths into a good life are found wanting, attention often turns to some form of *personal development*. With its encouragement to celebrate different ways of shaping one's identity, it does not necessarily rule out the first two paths—finding a partner and having a child—yet it does suggest that other ways are possible.[87] "A woman must first find happiness within herself and only then decide whether she needs a man or not, whether she needs children."[88] Expressions of personal development are countless indeed: from the trendiness of practising yoga or joining a local book-reader's club, through the whole health, beauty and diet industry, to time management, or career ambitions.[89] Such development can be seen as very "spiritual" or very "down

---

83. For a summary of research on the effects of childbearing (and their changes with age) on women, see Margolis and Myrskylä, "Global Perspective on Happiness and Fertility," 30.

84. Gillis, *World of Their Own Making*, 156.

85. Ibid., 178.

86. Hird and Abshoff, "Women without Children," 347–66. For an example of an expression of a consciously chosen child-free state, see Hymas, "GINK Manifesto."

87. Gillis, *World of Their Own Making*, 233. One important area in which such efforts are evident is the reconstruction of the way old age is viewed—or "reimagined." Gillis notes that women have demonstrated more creativity in shaping these new identities of an old person. Ibid., 234.

88. Ogloblina, "Nepolnotsennaya zhenshchina?"

89. Kotter-Grühn et al. also note the vagueness often accompanying this motif

to earth." The more "spiritual" ambitions tend to relate to goals, such as becoming more at peace with oneself and the world. As Layard recaps, "Through education and practice, it is possible to improve your inner life—to accept yourself better and to feel more for others. In most of us there is a deep positive force, which can be liberated if we can overcome our negative thoughts."[90] However, "working on oneself" can also be about perfecting one's body. The latter—the necessity of gaining, or at least coming closer to, the "right" body image—often forms one of the key links to the well-being of women particularly.[91] It can also be intrinsically linked to the first motif: once one's body is more beautiful, the hope is to attract a partner and therefore to maximize one's chances for happiness.

Is the "trio" of the motifs reviewed above sufficiently accurate in reflecting the way happiness is commonly interpreted? After all, there are so many approaches taken by sociologists that the task of "proving" the above becomes either very easy (one could simply choose those studies which are in agreement with one's gut feeling) or very difficult (its difficulty lies in relating these motifs to the mass of research on happiness, life satisfaction, or well-being which has mushroomed in recent decades). At the very least, the motifs reviewed so far could be arranged differently. Both romantic/sexual partnership and motherhood can be seen as representing one single motif of "family," a life domain receiving a great deal of attention from happiness researchers. It may be expanded further into what sociologists refer to as the domain of relational goods or social capital in general, therefore including the role of social networks in general and friendships in particular.[92] They could also be

---

which may not contain any concrete images or goals, but often may be expressed in terms of a desire to learn to love oneself or to find ways of self-actualization. "What Is It We Are Longing For?" 428–37.

90. Layard, *Happiness*, 3405.

91. See an overview of issues related to the media images of the "ideal female body" in Polivy and Herman, "Sociocultural Idealization of Thin Female Body Shapes," 1–6.

92. There is a substantial body of sociological research on the importance of friendships as reported by the subjects for their personal well-being, (e.g., Demir and Özdemir, "Friendship, Need Satisfaction and Happiness," 243–59), but it is typically accompanied by an acknowledgement that in the case of existing romantic/family relationships, the importance of friendships seems to diminish. See, e.g., Plagnol, "Subjective Well-Being over the Life Course," 754–55. The importance of friendships, however, is gaining increasingly greater attention from different fields of study. I will turn to this theme in chap. 8.

followed by other motifs, such as money/pleasure,[93] health[94] or spiritual affiliation[95] (and indeed an insight that a happy life necessarily involves a balance between different sources of happiness).[96]

However, I have sought to account for the fact that whatever other motifs may be around, at the present time none of them seem to be so pervasive as the coupledom/partnership/family motif in terms of people's (and researchers'?) *perceptions* of happiness. Why is this so, in spite of the insistence on various sources of fulfillment? One answer would be that this is simply how things are; that happiness, to a great extent, truly lies in romantic and sexual partnership.[97] Yet a brief overview provided here, and further considerations later, suggest that things are not that simple, and that today's Western culture may indeed be under a deep enthralment of a very mighty god of coupledom.[98]

If it is not the case, if happiness is to be found—"stumbled upon"[99] —through a variety means, as many happiness writers would suggest, why is the motif of coupledom so pervasive? At least part of the answer is to do with the fact that our desires—our "life longings"—do not arise in a vacuum. They are often shaped by what other people want, or what other people have, no matter how many times we may be encouraged to search for that "authentic happiness" that would be truly best for us. Thus the pervasiveness of the coupledom motif is hardly surprising given how important marriage (or some other variant of coupledom) is considered to be for happiness. Human beings end up still looking for

---

93. On the economic and leisure satisfaction in terms of gender differences, see, e.g., a Danish study by Bonke et al., "Time and Money," 113–31.

94. The importance of this motif usually grows with age, as health deteriorates. Kotter-Grühn et al., "What Is It We Are Longing For?" 435. For an overview of studies on self-reported health and happiness and their implications for public policy, see Graham, "Happiness And Health," 72–87.

95. See, e.g., Wills, "Spirituality and Subjective Well-Being," 49–69.

96. E.g., Sirgy and Wu, "Pleasant Life," 183–96. A commonly suggested triad of "satisfaction domains" is marriage, economic well-being, and health (see, e.g., Plagnol, "Subjective Well-Being over the Life Course," 753ff.). Layard, a highly popular happiness economist, suggests seven factors which have a real influence on happiness: family relationships, income, work, friendships and community, health, personal freedom and personal values. Layard, *Happiness*, location 981.

97. E.g., Zimmermann and Easterlin, "Happily Ever After," 511–28.

98. Lucas et al., "Reexamining Adaptation," 527–39.

99. *Stumbling on Happiness* is a title of an international bestseller by Daniel Gilbert, challenging the human ability to accurately predict happiness determinants.

confirmation that they are on the right road to happiness and have the right tools for it. They cannot do without a larger framework—stories, signposts, communities of reference—and in the current milieu, this is often serviced not only by what others around seem to desire, but also by the popular media (perhaps most notably, the advertising industry).

This chapter explored the currents of contemporary Western culture that are, subversively or explicitly, reflected in the church's view toward singleness. The first section addressed the inescapable religiousness of culture (which therefore could be expected to be a constant source of clashes with the convictions proper to the Christian Way). I then looked at the ways in which singles function in today's society. On the one hand, there is an unprecedented growth of their numbers. On the other hand, the levels of economic and social discrimination point to the extent to which being single has been "a largely unnoticed social stigma."[100] As some would put it, such a strong emphasis on marriage, in fact, functions as an ideology which holds that in getting a partner, "true happiness and deep meaningfulness are part of the package. To people who are happily single, the ideology holds out the myth that in marriage and family there is a level of happiness and completeness that a single person cannot even fathom."[101] I then explored three attitudes of singles toward their marital status: singleness as a negative and undesirable state; as a calling or necessity in relation to some larger purpose of one's life; and as a life of freedom and growth superior to that of marriage.

The last section of this chapter considered how goodness of life and happiness is perceived by the societies in which the churches live. I surveyed the recent growth in the interest in happiness studies which explore different routes to happiness, but which nevertheless seem to be dominated by one factor—coupledom (or, more broadly, family)—as *the* requirement for happiness. Certainly this requirement is not the only one; I have pointed to two others which play a major role in the lives of women in particular: the experience of motherhood, and self-development in the broad sense of the term. Yet both of these still pale in comparison to the attention given to romantic love and coupledom

---

100. Williams and Nida, "Obliviously Ostracizing Singles," 127.
101. DePaulo and Morris, "Singles in Society and in Science," 77.

as a source of happiness. As Trimberger notes, "Because romantic love plays such a central role in contemporary culture, moving beyond the soul-mate ideal as the standard for personal happiness necessitates developing an alternative vision."[102] So far, such vision has failed to emerge, both within the culture at large and, as chapter 2 pointed out, within the church. Indeed, "it remains that the church of today has colluded massively with a notion of happiness in marriage which, because ill-defined, draws promiscuously (as it were) on strands of culture within and beyond the church."[103]

---

102. Trimberger, *New Single Woman*, 17.
103. Brown, "Happiness Isn't Working," 79.

PART TWO

Myths and Meanings

Exploring the Routes

4

Church, Family, and the Myths of Love

Crisis in the Families

Families of church members are breaking down . . . this is a tragedy.[1]

Turning to a discussion on marriage and the family may be a surprising one: after all, it is the challenge of singleness that this book seeks to address. However, I have already indicated a tight relationship between the two issues of singleness and marriage. Not only this is so because the understanding, or theology, of marriage is intricately connected to that of single life, but also because the crisis in which the institution and the practice of the family[2] is presently found is understood to be related to the challenges faced by the church as a whole and thus, by implication, by its singles as well.

Earlier I already listed some of the symptoms and the extent of the "family crisis," reflected in the dwindling number of marriages, a

---

1. Sergey Zolotarevskyi, regional deputy Chairman of the Russian Union of Evangelical Christians-Baptists, "Nasha propoved."

2. "Family" in this case refers to the nuclear model comprising of a heterosexual couple and, if there is such, their progeny. While I appreciate the differences between the terms "marriage," "coupledom" and "family," they are used more or less interchangeably for the purposes of this chapter, reflecting a contrast to single life. "Marriage and family"—a common title of many a college course and a common way to speak of a coupledom-based lifestyle—can be seen as constituting one broad practice. Of course, the boundaries are not neat; a single parent family can still be called a family, but it is usually perceived as a distortion of the "ideal type."

high number of divorces and the ease with which they can be obtained.[3] Indeed, the contemporary family is no longer easy to describe. It is more complex in its relationships than a nuclear model of father, mother and two children, as indicated by terms such as "blended," "binuclear," or "stepfamilies."[4] The departure from the nuclear model, often termed "the traditional family," has given rise to the urge to fight for so-called family values. The aforementioned opponents of the "ideology of Marriage and Family," DePaulo and Morris, suggest that the very way family values are defended signifies the deep crisis which that model is undergoing.[5] In this crisis, however, the notion of coupledom continues to play a central role:

> Marriage as an institution may seem to be on the rocks, but romantic love has never been more valued than right now. The conjugal has become the standard for all relations, the premarital as well as the marital, the homosexual as well as the heterosexual. Children play at it, and teenagers practice it. Establishing a romantic relationship with another person, of different or same sex, is the sign of adulthood in modern Western culture. Yet all of this is a recent development, for it was not really until the [nineteenth] century that the perfect couple assumed a central place in the Western imagination.[6]

I will return to the reasons for this development later, but it is worthwhile noting that the role that romantic relationships play is seen by

---

3. Wallerstein noted more than twenty years ago: "How little we really know about the world we have created in the last twenty years—a world in which marriage is freely terminable at any time, for the first time in our history" (Wallerstein and Blakeslee, *Second Chances*, 297). Although considerable study has been carried out in the meantime, there is still a need to come to terms with the long-term impact of the "culture of divorce" on Western society. Europe has experienced no less change in what has been called "the traditional family." A recent decision of the Constitutional Court of the Republic of Lithuania, for example, overturned an earlier decree of the Lithuanian Parliament which limited the concept of family to that comprised of married persons on the grounds that such limitation is unconstitutional. See also Eurostat, "Marriage and Divorce Statistics" (2011); United Nations Statistics Division, "Marriage and Divorce."

4. Balswick and Balswick, *The Family*, 324. The realities of such contemporary families are taken up by the media, such as in the sitcom *Modern Family*, featuring a "traditional" nuclear family the relations of which include a gay couple with an adopted daughter, and a father married to a much younger second wife, who together raise her son from the first marriage.

5. DePaulo and Morris, "Singles in Society and in Science," 60.

6. Gillis, *World of Their Own Making*, 133.

some to be a direct reason for the present crisis: the expectations of such relationships in terms of romantic experience are simply too high. This has led some voices to suggest that "some marriages break up not because people expected too little from marriage, but because they have expected too much."[7] Stripped of many other functions it played previously, marriage ends up depending on whether such romantic bond contributes to the individual happiness of the partners—however that happiness is perceived.[8] These perceptions of happiness and the role of coupledom and family have made their way into the life of the churches on a large scale.

As the crisis in the family affects singleness as well, this is already a reason for a substantial discussion of marriage and family. Moreover, such a discussion is essential because of another issue: the way the churches view themselves. As the numbers of churchgoers decline in many parts of the West, this decline has often been associated with the challenges to the institution of the family. Thus, "the family is now not only atomized, broken off from any comprehensive institution that might give it content and purpose, but is made the very foundation of all order and morality."[9] Church and the traditional family are understood to be inseparable in the eyes of many, both in the church and outside it.[10] The question becomes pressing when the communities of faith experience a decline in membership and at the same time have to face difficult issues relating to the divorces of their own members. Different churches fare differently, many of them acknowledging the effects of the crumbling of the familial structures, others considering themselves as the bastions of family values that are no longer upheld in their societies, but all of them are bound to feel a considerable threat by the crisis which the family is undergoing.[11]

7. May, "Four Mischievous Theories of Sex," 195.
8. Rougemont, *Love in the Western World*, 280.
9. Clapp, "From Family Values to Family Virtues," 191.
10. Rodney Clapp has observed that in the American evangelical experience, it is "the survival of the traditional family, capitalism and the United States of America" that are tightly connected (and defended together). See his landmark *Families at the Crossroads*, 11.
11. Thus, in 1994, the General Council of the Baptist World Alliance issued a resolution admitting that "family life is under threat in all cultures" (BWA Information Service, "BWA Reflection on the Family"). Such an understanding would also be true for Eastern European evangelicals. See, e.g., Grams and Parushev, *Towards an*

When churches react by putting a lot of effort into emphasising the importance of the institution of the family as a necessary element of keeping the church going and growing, such efforts easily lead to a disregard of the growing numbers of singles, and an unverbalized perception of singleness as a threat to the institution of marriage (and, by extension, the church itself). Although a focus on the family is understandable in the light of the present pressures it faces, such attention to upholding "family values" in fact puts the family under more strain. It is encouraging to see some contemporary baptistic reactions which go against the stream of focusing on "family values" as such and recognize the wider questions which need to be asked. For example, a resource published by the Baptist Union of Great Britain, recognizing the crisis befalling the institution of the family, also acknowledges its cultural setting and makes it clear that

> if the church were wise in faith rather than anxious to prove itself it would investigate the invitation [to support "traditional family values"] before it responded to it. It would try to avoid acting on theologically simplistic diagnoses . . . Given that we are swimming, possibly drowning, in a society disordered from above as well as from below, by respectable power as well as by criminal deviance, by intellectual confusion as well as by malevolence, it is foolish to expect that the family can rescue us.[12]

The next section turns to the question of how the present perceptions of coupledom and family as a center of both church life and happiness have come to be.

How Did We Get Here?

> Look at how often it is stated from the pulpits, "If you are feeling lonely, you should start a family." Preachers explain: "It is not good for a person to be alone"![13]

Understanding of European Baptist Identity. For all of the regions, marital issues were indicated as representing a key concern among moral challenges. An unprecedented rise of divorce within the church has been especially shocking in post-Communist contexts which have previously known very little of this problem.

12. Wilkinson-Hayes and Mortimore, *Belonging*, 25.
13. Pirogov, "Stradayushchim."

Church, Family, and the Myths of Love 91

The model which the proponents of family values long to see return, and which is often assumed to represent a God-given order for Christians, cannot be defended as one directly drawn from the Bible. Should one investigate its roots, they would be found much less in the Bible than in the making of modernity, especially in the circumstances created by the Industrial Revolution and the views consolidated within the Victorian outlook.[14] As such, this model can be seen to represent a bourgeois relic which, quite understandably, is crumbling in the present, significantly different, context.[15]

What is significant about this model is that in contrast to pre-modern times, the role of the family was no longer an economically productive unit, but a locus of commodities such as emotional pleasure and prestige. Surely, the lives of many families were far from prestigious—one only needs to recall the poor quality of life of the working classes during the worst period of industrialisation—but the model, solidified in middle-class family life, was to become an icon to strive to resemble. "It now seemed that family was perpetually on display . . . Family became a kind of performance, demanding just the right language, dress, and etiquette."[16] The idea of performance could be recognized in the perceptions and expectations of how a "happy family" must look like and behave. Posed family photographs, once available, have become literal reflections of such "pictures."[17]

The changes in the perception of the role of the wife are particularly significant. While in pre-modern times, the work of both husband and wife was directed at maintaining the economic productivity of their unit, within the new model, the wife's domestic work was seen to be an integral part of her role in "[creating] the rituals, myths, and images on which the newly enchanted world of family had come to depend."[18] This has largely remained largely the woman's role even with the shift from wife as a homemaker to wife at the workplace that took place at a later

---

14. Although the "Victorian outlook" would be specific only to particular contexts, the image and the practice of the family which was formed during the mid-1800s has affected the West as a whole. For the tracing of the development of this "Victorian model," see Ruether, *Christianity and the Making of the Modern Family*, and Gillis, *World of Their Own Making*.

15. Clapp, *Families at the Crossroads*, 11.

16. Gillis, *World of Their Own Making*, 76.

17. Cf. ibid., 78.

18. Ibid., 77.

stage. Even as an equal bread-winner, or even in the case of being the sole bread-winner with an unemployed husband, the woman is likely to be seen as the major contributor to the "making of the family" in the sense of its identity and sub-practices.

As these changes took place in the shadow of growing individualism and secularism, the family began to take over the function previously performed by the community and religion.[19] The religious dimension is especially striking: "What religious and communal rituals, images, and symbols had previously provided, these household gods and goddesses would now be responsible for."[20] (Compare this with the notion of family as a "miniature church" or "domestic church.") It is no wonder that Clapp terms such family model "sentimental": "It serves as haven and oasis, emotional stabilizer and battery-charger for its members. It demands that spouses and children love and trust one another, that they intensely enjoy being together."[21] This is not to mean that the families in pre-modern times could not love and trust one another, but that such love and trust was now stripped of other ties that previously bound members of the extended family and their community. Various substitutions have been employed to consolidate a sense of "our family," such as household objects which now were primarily marked not by economic, but by sentimental value. The introduction of domestic animals as members of the family is likely to reflect the same need.[22]

The pressure of maintaining this family model has become an even greater challenge by the fact that the duration of marriage grew significantly due to the increased life expectancy of the partners, with couples able to spend much more time together, both raising their children and also after the children left home.[23] It was now possible to reduce the family to the permanent elements of such a family—the spouses. "The contemporary couple, in scientific theory as well as in the cultural imagination, is the ultimate all-in-one solution."[24] One can also see why

---

19. Gillis, *World of Their Own Making*, 72. A secular person himself, Gillis' work provides a very helpful overview of the development of the institution of the family, paying particular attention to its interplay with the religious convictions accompanying and shaping it.

20. Ibid., 72.

21. Clapp, *Families at the Crossroads*, 13.

22. Gillis, *World of Their Own Making*, 75–76.

23. Whitehead and Whitehead, "Meaning of Marriage," 129.

24. DePaulo and Morris, "Singles in Society and in Science," 76.

relating as couples has become an important element in maintaining the model.²⁵

Exploring such assumptions lead to the acknowledgment, in the words of Diogenes Allen, of the "unrealistic expectations [which] make it impossible for the institution of marriage to provide the blessings it *can* offer." He continues:

> We expect our spouse to be a friend, indeed, to be our best friend. This may happen, but is it a requirement of marriage? In our confusion over the nature of friendship, we ask a spouse to be something we do not ask of friends. A spouse is to take an interest in everything a husband or wife does, but this contradicts the nature of friendship, which is based on freedom. As if this were not enough, parents are also required to participate in their children's interests. Then, on top of all this, marriage is supposed to allow us to realize our potential, enable us to grow, and not cut us off from any of life's interesting and desirable experiences. Is it surprising that people are disappointed with their marriages when their expectations are so demanding and contradictory?²⁶

In contrast, marriage in premodern times was primarily a pragmatic business. "As long as love was multivalent and could find refuge in a variety of other relationships, getting married was a relatively straightforward practical matter."²⁷ Those who did not get married had a role nevertheless. With the home being the center of production, a pair of hands was helpful whether those were the hands of a married woman or a "spinster" doing the work of spinning.²⁸ The home was a place where relationships were aligned just as much around economic activities as

---

25. "That's the way married people socialize, by and large: with other couples. Do I wish I were invited? Not as a single woman, I don't. People deal with single women like people who have some kind of disease. They're polite and everything, but there's some way in which they're afraid of single women." Andrea H, in Clements, *Improvised Woman*, 88. The experience may be different for someone who belonged to such a coupled world but was ejected as a result of a divorce or widowhood: "Soon I realized that I had to put away any hope of belonging to the coupled society in the town. Not only was I excluded from their gatherings, but the wives were cautious about developing friendships. I didn't blame them; when I was married, I knew few divorced women and those I did know were not included in our social life. But it was a bitter pill to swallow when I realized that I was on the other side now and simply did not 'belong' anymore." Sheridan, *Unwilling Celibates*, 16.

26. Allen, *Love*, 97.

27. Gillis, *World of Their Own Making*, 150.

28. MacIntyre, *After Virtue*, 240.

around personal affections. There was comparatively little separation between the family and the larger community, which also included associations such as lay confraternities centered on deeper spirituality, mutual practical assistance, or a common project.[29]

Yet if marriage and the family have changed so much over the past few centuries, there is hope that they may also survive the current challenges. Indeed, as Carolyn Osiek notes, "The family is a very strong social structure, strong precisely because it is so flexible."[30] Thus I turn next to the key period of changes to understanding and practice of family: the experience of early Christians.

What Can Be Biblical about Family

What would be the shape and function of the "biblical family" that the churches should, or at least could, support and encourage? There is a danger of answering this question simplistically, by naively attempting to jump from the realities of today to those of biblical times. However, drawing from the Bible and aligning the present with biblical stories is a natural practice, especially for the hermeneutical vision of baptistic faith communities which are the focus of this book; what matters is that it would be done with what Barton calls "creative fidelity" to the Scriptures.[31] What follows is an offer of a few theological accents which I find crucial to the present discussion.

First of all, there is no way of keeping "the biblical family model" in the singular. A "model" could refer to Adam and Eve, or Abraham, Sarah and Hagar, or Solomon and his wives and concubines. In the Old Testament world, with very few exceptions, marriage is simply assumed. At times polygamous, marriage was a covenant between two usually related families, where the preferences of the spouses-to-be would rarely

---

29. It is also notable that women participated in confraternities more or less in the same numbers as men. Lynch, *Individuals, Families, and Communities in Europe*, 95.

30. Osiek, "Family in Early Christianity," 24.

31. McClendon speaks of such "creative fidelity" as "the baptist vision"—i.e., a hermeneutical approach of a community constantly and dynamically identifying itself with God's people (both past and future) found in the scriptural narrative (*Ethics*, 31–35). Barton also notes that both uncritically applying the texts to the realities of today so that they confirm what is already believed, and the scholar's tendency to demonstrate the enormous differences between the ancient world and that of today, may be equally unfaithful to the spirit of the New Testament. Barton, "Living as Families in the Light of the New Testament," 130–31.

play a major role.³² Its purpose is expressly having progeny, sons being preferable to daughters, the key component of the goods of the practice in ensuring the survival of the family's name, especially in the light of the "hesitant belief" in afterlife.³³ In this context, the greatest tragedy was a woman's barrenness.

Yet Jesus' life and teaching on marriage and singleness, followed by that of Paul, brought a radical change by subverting the existing role of the family. Such teaching made sense only in the light of the broader vision of the realm of God³⁴ and was particularly shaped in the context of the resurrection of Jesus which, as Clapp puts it, "brought about nothing less than epochal shift for marriage and singleness."³⁵ With words such as, "Who are my mother and my brothers?" (Mark 3:33), Jesus redefines family by unequivocally announcing the community of faith to constitute the primary family. Jesus' answer to the Sadducees regarding marriage after the resurrection suggests that heaven "is the formation of a new *politeia*, a new earthly order of society already displacing the old. In it, family ties cannot be the *last* word, for God is forming a new, heavenly family for the age to come."³⁶ It is no surprise, then, that in that sense the stance of Jesus seems to be "antifamily."³⁷ It was nothing short of being iconoclastic, challenging the order understood to be the best that society had and deeply cherished.³⁸ Instead, "a new basis for intimacy and mutual support is established. This new family loyalty must even take priority over traditional ones, for those who give them up will receive them a hundredfold."³⁹ The promise of "a hundredfold" implies the positive value of the family as something desirable and leaves one

---

32. Mackin, "Primitive Christian Understanding of Marriage," 23.

33. Ibid., 24.

34. I prefer "the realm of God" over against the patriarchic connotations of the "kingdom of God." Even though the latter is a biblical phrase, the "kingdom" language often communicates meanings very different from what Beasley-Murray, following other biblical scholars, terms "a dynamic activity of God." Beasley-Murray, *Jesus and the Kingdom of God*, 74.

35. Clapp, *Families at the Crossroads*, 89.

36. McClendon, *Doctrine*, 87–88.

37. Cf. Ruether, *Christianity and the Making of the Modern Family*, 3.

38. Cahill, "Christian Social Perspective on the Family," 164.

39. Osiek, "New Testament and the Family," 7.

with the stunning prospect, given that the family or household that one was being called to forego, was a numerous group already.[40]

The "new family" of the disciples of Jesus was juxtaposed to a familial structure which involved the whole household, people, and property that in most cases was under the headship of a male elder, combined with the moral authority of parents regardless of the age of children. (Note how differently passages exhorting the children to obey their parents are interpreted today!)[41] Instead, as Galatians 4:7 puts it, all believers, "whether male or female, and of whatever ethnic and legal identity, are given the status of sons in the household, that is, heirs to the estate."[42] Allegiance to Christ meant leaving one's structure of life and identity and joining an alternative support system. No wonder that Christian churches were seen to be in direct confrontation with the established system. Such confrontation is even more striking in the light of the general imperial policy requiring all Roman citizens to be married.[43] Inevitably, many early Christians were married, but the practice of celibacy was most clearly displaying the eschatological motif of the Christian story.

This is not to mean that there was no eschatological meaning in marriage as redefined by New Testament teaching and practices. A key element of that meaning lies in the very renunciation of the primacy of family bonds in order to live a life of loyalty much broader than one's own clan. Alongside Jesus' descriptions of God as merciful Father, rather different from the patriarchal figure of the *paterfamilias*, there emerges

---

40. This would be the case both in regard to the Jewish extended family and the pagan *paterfamilias*. As Osiek notes, "Households and family units [in the Roman world of early Christianity] included children, slaves, unmarried relatives, and often freedmen and freedwomen or other renters of shop or residential property." Osiek, "Family in Early Christianity," 11.

41. Osiek, "New Testament and the Family," 2. It is worth noting that, judging from surviving documentation, divorce was rather common both in Jewish as well as Greco-Roman systems. Ibid., 4.

42. Ibid., 5.

43. Emperor Augustus had issued a decree requiring all female citizens (except Vestal Virgins) between the ages of 20 and 50, and every male citizen between the ages of 25 and 60, to be married, with penalties for the unmarried as a way to battle low birth rates. Widows were given two or three years to remarry after the death of their husband. The sanctions on the unmarried were revoked only by Constantine in AD 320. See, e.g., Grubbs, *Women and the Law in the Roman Empire*, 83–87; 103–4.

a picture of a new family ready for the already coming realm of God.[44] Such a vision enabled early Christians to function in the context of households—extended family structures—yet engage in a continuous conversion of the features not compatible with Christian identity.[45] This vision is also relevant for the resolution of present family issues, urging not a return to a family of biblical times, but to the future into which God leads: "In the light of the coming of God the full meaning of life together in families past and present lies in the future."[46]

Thus, aligning with the vision and practice of what the realm of God entails provides a meaningful context for the life of marriage and family. What is striking is that such a relegation of marriage and biological family enriches it rather than weakens it. Otherwise, "any family that attempts to be the world for itself in fact creates a stunted, shrunken world."[47] The push to exert even more efforts and time for the family is not only counterproductive, but also deeply anti-Christian; nothing short of idolatry.[48] As Hauerwas and Willimon put it,

> Marriage is subservient to discipleship. Our marriages are ultimately significant only as a means of supporting each of us in our ministry, including the ministries of childrearing, conversion of the young, protection of the old. We think marriage is a place where Christians are able to be truthful with one another because marriage is more determinative than their immediate feelings.[49]

Such a conviction has been embodied time and again by those Christians who did lose their closest family because of their response to the call to become part of the community of disciples. Those parts of Europe which have experienced the suppression of Christian faith by the communist regimes offer numerous stories of the experiences of real embrace of the

---

44. Cahill, "Christian Social Perspective on the Family," 166.

45. "On the other hand," notes Cahill, "particularly because more revolutionary challenges to family and class were part of the memory of the risen Jesus from the beginning, one might well maintain that the house communities could have and should have been even more radical in reconfiguring the domestic order." Ibid., 169.

46. Barton, "Living as Families," 132.

47. Clapp, *Families at the Crossroads*, 86.

48. "Idolatry of family" has been named by authors such as Fishburn, *Confronting the Idolatry of Family*.

49. Hauerwas and Willimon, *Where Resident Aliens Live*, 86.

church as the *first family*, at times in the context of the opposition and betrayal of blood relations.[50]

Much more could be said about an appropriate theology of family for today. One would need to reflect on the Ephesians passage on the calling for spousal relationships to reflect the love between Christ and the church (5:25–32).[51] The relationship of a "nuclear" family, in whatever shape, with the whole of the believing community also needs to be thought through further.[52] That, however, would be a different project; and such projects are undertaken in their own right.[53] My purpose was to provide a context in which contemporary issues of marriage and family could be addressed, especially in relation to singleness. As Wilson helpfully notes, "it seems many churches need to ponder whether they are predominantly institutions *for* families or communities that operate *as* a family, with all kinds of members. Until this happens, many churches will have no idea what 'to do with' its single members."[54]

Thus, if there is one motif that can be called a "biblical teaching on the family," it is that the family—whatever its shape—"must look outward and be part of something greater than itself. Only then will it achieve its end in fostering the most basic qualities of faith, hope, and love. These are the family values worth striving for."[55] Yet, rather than employing the vague language of *values*, a better use can be made of faith, hope and love, all of which have a long-standing tradition as the theological *virtues*. These virtues are developed as "the real-world embodiment of our discipleship in all of our dealings and relationships, first and foremost

---

50. It is worthwhile to remember also the deep conviction of "church as first family" of the early Anabaptists; see Roth, "Family, Community and Discipleship in the Anabaptist-Mennonite Tradition," 147–52.

51. On the passage's reflection of the vision of the "new humanity" in Christ, see Gombis, "Radically New Humanity," 317–30.

52. The role of the communal in supporting family structures is recognised to be of great importance in the various fields of academia. Consider the remark by the anthropologist Margaret Mead: "There is no society in the world where people have stayed married without enormous community pressure to do so." Reported in Wallerstein and Blakeslee, *Second Chances*, 297.

53. I have already referred to Clapp, *Families at the Crossroads*, written for the general Christian public but echoing insights from theologians such as Stanley Hauerwas and James Wm. McClendon. McCarthy's *Sex and Love in the Home* would be another example.

54. Wilson, *Being Single*, 59–60; emphasis original.

55. Osiek, "Family in Early Christianity," 24.

in that body we call the church, and second in our families."[56] Of course, it will take more than these three virtues to make family a blessing. One may think about the importance of hospitality—arguably a key virtue for marriage and family practice—or forgiveness. The discussion of how these and other virtues can be embodied would lead to a consideration of the practices in which they take shape, and the tradition which calls for such practices and makes them meaningful—the tasks I turn to in chapter 7.

Yet one of these virtues—love—has been seen to belong to the core of what today's marriage and family—however defined—is supposed to be. "Love" is also a key word for describing human happiness, used in a variety of ways with a confusing variety of meanings. The discussion that follows focuses on the way the meaning of "love" has been impacted by two powerful myths regarding its nature and function in marriage or an alternative arrangement.

The Guiding Myths of Love

> We are fundamentally shaped by our loves and deformed by their distortions.[57]

One way to discuss the theme of love would be to turn to the Greek words for love, especially in expounding on the differences and the interplay of *eros* and *agape*. At the height of modernity, with its drive, among other things, to determine the meaning of every single word in an utterance, such an approach has been especially popularized by the now classical work of a Swedish theologian, Anders Nygren and his 1932 book *Agape and Eros*.[58] Nygren's proposal generated a lot of reaction and, becoming a modern classic of theology, made its way to the pulpits and into the churchly literature elaborating on this distinction between (divine) *agape* and (human—by implication, defective) *eros*.

---

56. Lee, *Beyond Family Values*, 13–14. See Lee's exploration of the virtues of faith, hope and love, ibid., 143–228.

57. Rolheiser, *Forgotten among the Lilies*, 3.

58. Interestingly enough, Nygren bypassed any discussion of the *philia*, friend-love, or mutual love, and instead worked on the contrast between the selfishness of *eros* and the total selflessness of the divine *agape*.

Yet while *agape* is considered as something to be unquestionably prized, can *eros* really count as its antipode? Such approach to the theology of love requires extensive acrobatics in reasoning. My own language, Lithuanian, has only one word for love—*meilė*; a number of other languages, English included, also seem to have difficulties with distinguishing the Greek shades. Unless the Greeks had a higher moral development and more evolved practice of love than most of us, perhaps the types of love might not be so easily or uniformly distinguishable. Life and love just do not seem to be able to be separated into such neat compartments of "this love" and "that love" with their distinctive qualities. Neither do they fit well in the contemporary understanding of how the language functions. That said, *agape* and *eros* have been found by various thinkers to be helpful in expressing certain concepts even in the case of disagreeing with Nygrenian distinctions. As Paul S. Fiddes suggests, "Eros . . . is always mixed with agape."[59] The same may be also said the other way around.[60] God's love, the greatest love of all, seems to contain clear parallels to people's erotic longings, and at the same time, the most common Hebrew usage of "love" entails a strong sense of loyalty. The intertwining of these loves can also be observed in the theology and practice of friendship which would display many of the aspects typical of the third type of Greek understanding of love, *philia*, yet would also contain elements of faithful care as well as particularity and passion.

What other interpretative tools then may be helpful in approaching the theme of love in the context of Christian marriage and singleness? Here I choose to look at several formative stories which seem to shape the understanding of love, at least in the Western context.[61] I first came across them in the thought of James Wm. McClendon, who suggests two of such: the Freudian myth of libidinal drive and the myth of romantic love, especially as explicated by Dennis de Rougemont.[62]

---

59. Fiddes, "Creation Out of Love," 172.

60. Cf. the argument of Allen, *Love*, 3–4 and passim; Williams, *Spirit and the Forms of Love*, 2–3.

61. On the nature of "myth" and its power "[to win] over us, usually without our knowing," see de Rougemont, *Love in the Western World*, 19.

62. McClendon, *Ethics*, 139–60. Another author who looks at the myths of romantic and libidinal love is Diogenes Allen. He makes a distinction between four types of love—Christian, Platonic, Romantic, and Freudian, but concentrates largely on the interplay between the Romantic and Christian understandings of love. See Allen, *Love*, 62–90 and 136–38.

The Reign of the Libido

This myth came to the fore during the twentieth century and remains prominent in many ways. Its influence and power is perhaps best observed in the transformation of Eastern Europe, especially the former states of the Soviet Union, where a few decades ago "there was no sex"[63] and today, *sex-appeal*, a term rapidly gaining a place in the dictionaries of various Eastern European languages, seems to be all-pervasive, from the requirements of TV presenters to advertisements for mobile phones. These images and sounds attacking the eyes and ears, the pictures of the interplay of sexual desire and its satiation, are parts of but only one of the stories "explaining" love that have shaped Western societies. The unending fascination with sex is captured by the theory of the most outspoken of its exponents, Sigmund Freud: alongside the instinct of agression, libido is *the* drive underlying all our behaviour.[64] Besides Freud's narrative about the permeation of this drive in all our acts and desires, a "softer" version of the myth would ask that we do not complicate matters by trying to look for the deep meaning of our sexual urges but simply accept the constant presence of sex in people's lives. Sex has become accepted as "an all-purpose healing instrument, a kind of glorified patent medicine for everything that might ail us";[65] an instrument working on an assumption that "sexual satisfaction constitutes the good life."[66]

In another variant, sexual drive is appropriated as "god" in the sense of the divine, or the best bliss of heaven we might hope for; at times associated with marriage[67] (and thus a sort of merger with the romantic love), it now seems to increasingly be less so. In the antipodal version of the myth, it may be seen to represent the most dangerous of the demonic powers, the opposite of all that is good, the "bad god," the force playing a central role in the lives of the people trying to preserve themselves from its destruction (or, alternatively, to be subdued by its power in the pornographic acts of sex as technique).

---

63. I am referring here to the answer of a Soviet woman on one of the US-Soviet "TV Bridges"—telecasts that were broadcast in the time of *perestroika* toward the end of the Soviet empire. Somebody on the American side asked, "What are your attitudes towards sex?" The Soviet woman replied, "Why, there is no sex in the Soviet Union."

64. Freud, *Civilization and Its Discontents*.

65. Marin, "A Revolution's Broken Promises," 169.

66. Williams, *Spirit and the Forms of Love*, 232.

67. May, "Four Mischievous Theories of Sex," 189–90.

The story claiming that everything ultimately boils down to libido is not a story typically accepted by the disciples of Jesus. Yet it creeps in, especially the aforementioned version of the demonic, when human nature is taken with so much suspiciousness and scepticism that relationships, especially between the opposite sexes, are seen to need stringent regulations, to the extent of a Christian college dormitory having separate staircases for men and women, as they cannot be trusted to pass each other without inappropriate thoughts.[68] What happens, however, when these students graduate and suddenly have to use the same staircase with other people? Freud should be delighted to see such places as they confirm his point. He would also be happy about the numbers of married Christians gathering to attend seminars or buying books on "Christianity and sex," yearning for a "legal achievement" of the bliss of intercourse that seems to be so fascinating and beautiful in books and on TV screens. Again, polls might show more than the churches might want to know about the deep, if muted, fascination with the subject in Christian circles.[69] Hence some theological voices have been calling for a reconsideration of sexuality as a key motif of human existence—indeed, sex understood as a means of communication[70]—without lapsing into a worship of sex: "We can recognize the omnipresence of sex without asserting its omnipotence."[71] These are certainly worthwhile questions to explore in the context of not only marriage and family life, but also within the whole faith community—a theme I will return in chapter 7.

---

68. So, for instance, the policies of the Pensacola Christian College, as described in its Student Handbook 2001–2002, or in a copy of a memo to chaperones (!) reminding them of their duty to be especially vigilant during the spring season, in "The Student Voice," Pensacola Christian College. My thanks to Vanessa Lake for providing some background information on such practices in a US fundamentalist setting. There are variations of such "suspicion culture" in Europe, too, partly due to American influence, but certainly also as an "indigenous" mistrust toward people's abilities to stay chaste in the presence of sexual temptation. It ought to be noted that the form of such temptation tends to be a woman in trousers or without head covering, or even worse, a short skirt, as reflected in the fact that the dress codes of decency first and foremost apply to women. For a first-person account from a Russian-speaking context, see Disterchett, "Kogda traditsiya gubit nas i nashikh detey."

69. For a firsthand story, see Schaeffer's reflection on the conservative Evangelicals' fascination with sex in *Sex, Mom, and God*.

70. Williams, *Spirit and the Forms of Love*, 221–24.

71. Ibid., 220.

However, it is the other myth which has much firmer roots in the life of the church, and it is to that myth that I turn now.

"A Fatal Love":[72] Consuming Passion of Romance

> The moderns, men and women of passion, expect irresistible love to produce some revelation either regarding themselves or about life at large.[73]

It was Denis de Rougemont, a Swiss Reformed thinker, who presented one of the most forceful arguments on powerful myth of the romantic love. This myth, argued de Rougemont, had its roots in a Gnostic heresy, then, through the Cathars, was reinforced in the practice of courtly love, and since then has played a major role in shaping the European psyche.[74] As far as de Rougemont was concerned, the roots of this myth were platonic and dualist, and the consummation of such love was found in the death of the lovers, through which fulfillment and deliverance are achieved. Medieval literature indeed provides us with such stories—consider Tristan and Isold, Aucassin and Nicolette, Romeo and Juliet, etc.[75] The myth "has been agitating us for eight hundred years as spell, terror, or ideal"[76] and "operates wherever passion is dreamed of as an ideal instead of being feared like a malignant fever; wherever its fatal character is welcomed, invoked, or imagined as a magnificent and desirable disaster instead of as simply a disaster."[77]

Different variations and echoes of the myth can be recognized in today's Western cultures.[78] As Diogenes Allen puts it,

72. De Rougemont, *Love in the Western World*, 15.

73. Ibid., 282.

74. Ibid. An interesting case of the critique of the influence of the troubadours comes from Christine de Pizan (ca. 1365–ca. 1430), the earliest European female professional writer, who saw the courtly love motif as representing great danger for women. Nowacka, "Reflections on Christine de Pizan's 'Feminism,'" 88; Krueger, "Questions of Gender in Old French Romance," 145.

75. De Rougemont also suggests the example of the first known European story of such passionate love—that of Abelard and Heloise (*Love in the Western World*, 74). For Abelard and Heloise's story, see, e.g., Radice, *Letters of Abelard and Heloise*.

76. De Rougemont, *Love in the Western World*, 23.

77. Ibid., 24.

78. De Rougemont highlights the typically asexual expression of romantic love and fuelling an unfulfilled desire. However, such a version does not seem to represent the narrative of the present culture which certainly does not seem willing to give up sex

> Not only did tragic love become a favourite theme in literature, music, and art, so also a falling in love with love itself increasingly became a preoccupation. There was an urgent longing for, and belief in, the powerful passion that would sweep people off their feet and restore vitality. The individual love object, male or female, hardly mattered.[79]

This is where the myth reveals itself at its cruellest: the love object is merely an object; it is about being in love with love, or more precisely, the idea of love.[80] Or consider the following summary of the romantic story:

> The natural expectation of every boy and girl is that each will fall in love, once, in the bloom of youth, suddenly, intensely, and at first unhappily, desiring infinitely more than sexual fulfilment but desiring that as well; that each will fall in love with a person of the opposite sex, also young and beautiful, who is unattached and falls just as much in love in return; that they will marry and experience a bliss which cannot even be talked about.[81]

This story has several similarities to de Rougemont's mythical love. For one thing, such a take on love frequently has a character of exclusive particularity—there is no lover for Heloise after Abelard; nor does Romeo contemplate trying his luck with someone else, friendlier to the Monagues. "They were meant for each other," and that is that. In this sense, the myth of romantic love goes way beyond the Cathars and medieval Europe. The idea that human beings cannot help but be looking

---

for a heavenly vision and in many ways does not see a problem in blending Freud's insistence on the fundamentality of sexual acts as part of the bliss of finding "that one." A similar argument is being developed by Stone, "Passionate Attachments," 180.

Some have reacted to de Rougemont's proposal pointing out the distinction between romantic love and courtly love, the latter being a narrative of an unfulfilable love based on the unattainability of the pursued woman. Cf., for instance, Allen, *Love*, 2. Yet another argument has been put forward by Anthony Giddens who argues for a distinction between passionate love—a phenomenon common across cultures and times—and romantic love, a creation of Western modernity as the motif for organising individual life and the journey to self-discovery (*Transformation of Intimacy*, 37–48). These few examples, pointing to the range of differing interpretations of romance and passion in love, also hint to the range of possibilities for their incorporation into the Christian story—a possibility explored in the next section of this chapter.

79. Allen, *Love*, 63. Allen links the myth to the growth of the industrialisation of the nineteenth century and its consequences.

80. De Rougemont, *Love in the Western World*, 41.

81. Gould, *Platonic Love*, 11–12, quoted in Allen, *Love*, 64.

for "their other half" is at least as old as Plato's *Symposium*. Such search, Aristophanes argued, is the longing for the bliss of fulfillment: "I believe that if our loves were perfectly accomplished, and each one returning to his primeval nature had his original true love, then our race would be happy."[82] The idea is also easily found in today's churches, not only in the half-joking reference to the spouse as "the other half," but also in the implicit notion that one marries "the one (and only) given by God"—or otherwise stays single.

One can also discern in the myth strong overtones of salvation.[83] Yet, paradoxically, another element of the myth of romantic love, as de Rougemont has discerned it, has often been its necessary termination by a tragedy; or at least, "unless the course of love is being hindered there is no 'romance.'"[84] At its roots, such love is therefore unsustainable; it loses its attractiveness when consummated. Following the myth of Tristan and Iseult, de Rougemont insists that even when it remains implicit, the course of romantic love in its pure form is directed toward death or self-annihilation; this is what explains the unsustainability of such romantic love. As far as European literature is concerned, claims de Rougemont, "happy love has no history."[85] Even in the case of a happy end of the fairytales, the "happily ever after" suffers from content-lessness: "Romantic love cannot even provide us with a description of 'ever after.'"[86]

As de Rougemont would argue, this myth of love comes into conflict with the notion of married life. "There are cases of passion in Christian marriage, and in passion cases of the married status,"[87] but generally the myth of romantic love stands in diametrical opposition to Christian marriage which is perceived as the shackles of commitment and duty in which romance and passion die.[88] Certainly, there have been attempts

82. Plato, *Symposium*.

83. See, e.g., a discussion on one of the love songs by Nick Cave and his band The Bad Seeds by Kelton Cobb who comments how the lyrics "are thick with the theme of advent, of the irresistible approach of someone unknown but long awaited, one who has long been an anticipated source of comfort and consolation." Cobb, *Blackwell Guide to Theology and Popular Culture*, 239.

84. De Rougemont, *Love in the Western World*, 52.

85. Ibid., 52.

86. Clapp, "From Family Values to Family Virtues," 198.

87. De Rougemont, *Love in the Western World*, 299n1.

88. One of the examples de Rougemont provides is a document issued by the Countess of Champagne in 1174: "We declare and affirm . . . that love cannot extend its

to marry the myth of romantic love and marriage, and it is such attempts that de Rougemont tackles.[89] He argues that such romantic interpretation of love is "a religion in the full sense of the word."[90] For him, that also means that "underlying the modern breakdown of marriage is nothing less than a struggle between two religious traditions"[91]—that is, between the theology of what de Rougemont understands to be Christian marriage, and the heresy of romance.

The religious function of this myth can be seen in the perceived power that such romantic love is supposed to have: love is something that *happens* to human beings, inescapably and uncontrollably. However, if, following de Rougemont's critique, emotions would be understood to constitute a part of the convictional set—which I explore later—things would look rather different. Emotions, such as love, certainly may not be easy to control, especially when we are led to believe that we are victims of emotions "stronger than ourselves." Here I am following Robert C. Solomon's exploration of why and how we are formed and encouraged to feel a certain emotion—in fact, to "do" this or that emotion.[92] Emotions[93] reflect our dispositions, fears, and hopes, and are shaped by guiding myths, such as those reviewed here.[94] Their rationality and

---

rights over two married persons. For indeed lovers grant one another all things mutually and freely, without being impelled by any motive of necessity, whereas husband and wife are held by their duty to submit their wills to each other and to refuse each other nothing. May this judgement, which we have delivered with extreme caution, and after consulting with a great number of other ladies, be for you a constant and unassailable truth, Delivered in this year 1174, on the third day before the Kalends of May, Proclamation VII." Quoted in de Rougemont, *Love in the Western World*, 34.

A similar stance is echoed in the nineteenth-century wit of Oscar Wilde: "I really don't see anything romantic in proposing. It is very romantic to be in love. But there is nothing romantic about a definite proposal. Why, one may be accepted. One usually is, I believe. Then the excitement is all over. The very essence of romance is uncertainty. If ever I get married, I'll certainly try to forget the fact." Algernon in Oscar Wilde, *The Importance of Being Earnest*, 3.

89. In a later postscript de Rougemont makes a point that he was never arguing that "marriage and passion . . . [are] mutually exclusive, as had been decided by the courts of love" (*Love in the Western World*, 368). What he seems to be focusing on, however, is exclusively *passionate* love as unsustainable in the long run of marriage.

90. De Rougemont, *Love in the Western World*, 137.

91. Ibid.

92. Solomon, *Not Passion's Slave*.

93. By this I do not mean to say that love is *only* an emotion. However, emotion is certainly a key aspect of the type of love reviewed in this chapter.

94. See Solomon, *Not Passion's Slave*, 20; McClendon, *Ethics*, 159.

intentionality may not be visible on the surface, but it is there. On this point de Rougemont and others are indeed right: the myth of helplessly "falling" in love, the treatment of love as something that happens "to us" is powerfully and continuously rekindled by many narratives floating in the cultural air.

Attending to the uncontrollable passion of romance as an alternative religion has obvious implications for both the single and married. Although probably not many would attempt to seriously argue for the exorcism of romance from the birth of a marriage, it is worthwhile remembering that romance is *but* a part of the story. Dethroned from the divine throne, the myth and the type of love behind the myth lose its demonic power too, as de Rougemont argues, and "finds [a] proper place in the provisional economy of Creation and of what is human."[95] By ceasing to inhabit the very center of one's life, it ceases to function as a severe limitation on many aspects of the everyday. When "spontaneous emotion and exotic adventures [are not] definitive for the grammar of love," the patterns of predictable relationship between the spouses do not need to be perceived as lifeless and boring.[96] This is especially important to bear in mind given the lurking danger for married life which starts in the typical Western fashion, that is, the height of passion and romance.[97]

Refuting the myth offers a way to escape the deadly end of a fizzled-out romance. Such an outlook comes to terms with the limitations of marriage and ceases to demand from it what it cannot possibly give. "Ask too much—ask for everything—and then even that which human beings *can* give is lost," noted Allen.[98] When the myth of romantic love

---

95. De Rougemont, *Love in the Western World*, 312.

96. McCarthy, *Sex and Love in the Home*, 161.

97. The juxtaposition of the opposite starting points for marriage in high-context and low-context cultures reminds us that there is no advantage to the "fireworks" of love in a typical "Western way" compared to the quality and satisfaction within the arranged marriages as traditionally practiced in the East. The idylle of the arranged marriage is at times presented too idealistically, but it is a point worth making.

One also ought to consider the biochemical aspect of erotic passion, such as the soaring levels of phenylethylamine, an amine responsible for "the giddiness, euphoria, optimism, and energy lovers experience in early stages of infatuation" (Jankowiak and Fisher, "Cross-Cultural Perspective on Romantic Love"). The roles of oxytocin ("the hormone of love") and vasopressin in long-term pair bonding should also be noted (e.g., Wagner, *Brain Imaging: The Chemistry of Mental Activity*, 189).

98. Allen, *Love*, 83.

is dethroned, the egotism of romanticism[99] is shattered; there begins a journey of experiencing love in the variety of its colors: passionate and calm, practical and emotional, warm and demanding, ebbing and flowing, and, above all, supported by the larger network of community which both benefits from the contribution of a particular family and also gives it focus by requiring commitment and service.

The consequences of dethroning de Rougemont's god of romantic love have even more straightforward implications in the framework of the single life. As chapters 2 and 3 demonstrated, one of the elements of struggling with singleness is the notion that, by not experiencing intimate, romantic human love, one misses out on the most important part of life—if not salvation, then at least something that can be called happiness. The strength of the myth has to be acknowledged: one is immediately confronted by it upon turning on the radio, watching television or movies, or browsing the offers in a standard bookshop. If, however, the myth ceases to function as the leading interpretative motif, so many new vistas of meaning-making are suddenly wide open. The god of romance indeed deserves to be taken off that pedestal of ultimate loyalty and given a proper place.

However, I wonder whether de Rougemont, in his reaction to the demonic grimaces of romance, might have underestimated its role in the "provisional economy of Creation." His insistence on this being a European creation can be challenged by the presence of romance described in terms similar to de Rougemont's yet arising from other, non-Western, cultures, as well as pre-medieval examples,[100] not to mention the Song of Songs of the Bible, with its obvious story line of sexual passion of a man and a woman. Indeed, there is a growing scepticism regarding the social constructivist approach relegating romance to the doing of the troubadours à la de Rougemont.[101] The examples he has chosen to dem-

---

99. McCarthy notes: "Married life does not allow us to gaze long into each other's eyes—thankfully, because the 'two in one' may readily become an attenuated egoism of two." *Sex and Love in the Home*, 147.

100. Gottschall and Nordlund, "Romantic Love," 432–52. For an overview of several studies on the universality of the notion of romantic love, see Pillsworth and Haselton, "Evolution of Coupling," 99–100.

101. See, e.g., a sociological argument for the cross-cultural prevalence of the notion of romantic love of Jankowiak and Fisher, "Cross-Cultural Perspective on Romantic Love," 149–56. On the literary side, see Gottschall and Nordlund, "Romantic Love," 432–52.

onstrate the myth may be argued to represent the extremes rather than the standard pattern of the notion of romance.[102] Romance continues to be debated among cultural anthropologists, literary scholars, neuroscientists, evolutionary psychologists, and others interested in the subject, partly because of its complexity and a quality of mystery even in the light of biochemical explanations about what is happening when a human being experiences an attraction to another human being. Culture plays a crucial role in providing ways of expression for such enchantment, but the nature of the interplay between culture and neurological-physiological reactions of the human body is open to various suggestions (in other words, "did poetry invent love, or love poetry?")[103]

These considerations suggest that the presence of romance is somewhat more widespread than the Cathar-affected Western world, even if it may not have the same connection with marriage as in the Western tradition[104] and may be viewed not with enthusiasm, but with distrust or opposition.[105] Yet if it is impossible to reject the myth as a whole—indeed, if it is also impossible to reject the role of the libidinal drive in the lives of most human beings—what should be done with these myths?

"Immanuel lives indeed in this city of mortal love"[106]

> The truth in the Gospel which cuts into all our loves is that every love must be offered up to the creative transformation which God is bringing about in the whole creation.[107]

De Rougemont provides one of the clues himself by noting that "passion and the passion myth are active in many other ways than in which our private lives are affected. Orthodox mysticism in Europe has been another passion, and its metaphorical language is at times curiously akin to that of courtly love."[108] For de Rougemont, however, there is no question of the superiority of this "orthodox mysticism"; directed by the desire of

102. Williams, *Spirit and the Forms of Love*, 230.

103. Stone, "Passionate Attachments in the West," 177.

104. Jankowiak and Fisher, "Cross-Cultural Perspective on Romantic Love."

105. Jankowiak, "Introduction," 17n2, quoted in Gottschall and Nordlund, "Romantic Love," 441.

106. Williams, *Outlines of Romantic Theology*, 50.

107. Williams, *Spirit and the Forms of Love*, 209.

108. De Rougemont, *Love in the Western World*, 137.

union with God, it differs from the intoxication of passionate love.[109] Yet the relationship between romantic love and Christian mysticism could be looked at from a different perspective: "If the Church ever considers the problem of marriage seriously Romantic and Mystical Theology will find themselves closely akin."[110] The quote comes from Charles Williams, who, in his study of medieval literature, and especially taking the case of Dante's love for Beatrice, maintains that romantic, passionate love has a direct relationship to knowing God: what it can result in is "Romantic Theology."[111] The experience of the depth and passion of love of one human being for another is seen by Williams as a legitimate means of revelation—an insight so far much more explored and appreciated by people of art rather than theologians.

So, perhaps love which can be called "romantic" can be at least a glimpse into God's glory and goodness—God who in the Scriptures presents himself as a lover. Not that it would be the only—or sufficient—way of knowing or perceiving God; one of the greatest mistakes would be to assume self-sufficiency of such love, or indeed expect it to be endless.[112] However, passionate love for another human being, the experience of "falling" and "being" in love,[113] is capable of revealing something about God and God's love, and about ourselves.[114]

---

109. One may also note the expressions of desire for union with God present in evangelical circles, especially the worship songs in which mysticism, romance and eroticism intermingle to a degree that is worthy of further exploration. I will return to this theme in chap. 7.

110. Williams, *Outlines of Romantic Theology*, 67.

111. See ibid., and especially the last article, "Religion and Love in Dante," 89–111, a reprint representing his thoughts on the subject toward the end of his life; and *The Figure of Beatrice*. As an interesting side note, Thomas C. Owen observes that the views of Williams and de Rougemont must have been at least partly formed in their ecclesial traditions—high-church Anglican and Reformed, respectively.

112. Williams, *He Came Down from Heaven*, 78–81.

113. "Falling/being in love" seems to have different usages. Neuroscientists, for example, are clear about the limited and comparatively short period of this euphoric state, whereas the arts can easily depict a character toiling long years away from the object of love (or, in Dante's case, long years after his beloved's death) with the same passion. This already seems to be an important distinction. Can it be, however, that even the fleeting nature of the euphoric state can be seen not as a failure, but as "a part of the mystery of love"? Cf. Williams, *Outlines of Romantic Theology*, 19.

114. As Day Williams observes, such erotic love also grounds the experience of ourselves: "Selflessness with no *eros*, no vital impulse, no love of life, is not real selfhood." *Spirit and the Forms of Love*, 203; emphasis original.

For Williams, there is no contradiction between love and marriage, although they are not necessarily synonymous. Many marriages might fall short of their full potential, but they signify a possibility which is ours through God who himself is Love. "Nothing is easier than to overrate this experience of love [i.e., marriage]; it is, for most of us, weak and paltry enough. But it is the most illuminating—not necessarily the strongest—we have probably ever had, and it is renewed."[115] Such an approach would also allow a new look at the scriptural references to love, wedding feast, and marriage with a possibility of fresh insights and new embodiment in a particular marital experience.[116]

Romantic theology has implications far beyond the realm of marriage. Laura Smit has linked Williams' thought to the experience of unrequited love, an experience seldomly deemed worthy of a theological reflection and yet a profound reality for many human beings. Unrequited love can be especially significant for a single person for whom it is not merely an episode before marrying and settling down. It can be—as Williams aimed to illustrate by the story of Dante—an experience providing a strong color for the whole of life. Here again passion's connection, rather than the break, with the love of God is evident. As Daniel Day Williams notes, alluding to the same story of Dante and Beatrice, "To love is to enter relationship in which the growth of love transforms the initial motivation."[117] Dante's love for Beatrice becomes a starting point for his growing awareness of the love of God. This is why growth and development of the initial love is a must; "preoccupation with origins is fatal to love."[118] The object of love may serve in ways hardly predictable, as one is reminded of in the sight of a lover suddenly aware of the goodness of the world she was blind to previously. Surely some may deem such a state to be an illusory one—but it could be argued that such a love-filled vision was precisely the moment of truly seeing.[119] The way

---

115. Williams, *Outlines of Romantic Theology*, 28.

116. In yet another observation of Day Williams, "Between sentimental kinds of romanticism at one pole, and the cynical despair . . . at the other, sexuality is seen only in a half-light of distortion, violence, prettiness and ugliness. It is not easy to grasp its potential for wholeness and creativity amid this distortion, but we must try." Williams, *Spirit and the Forms of Love*, 227.

117. Ibid., 119.

118. Ibid.

119. As beautifully put by Williams: "Love for another person opens the way to a kind of knowledge which can never be given without it . . . The familiar saying, 'love is

a lover sees the beloved may not be an illusion or delusion—at least not entirely—but how God sees us constantly, and how we can be when the *shalom* of God's reign is at hand. As for illusions, they may also have a (limited) role: "Perhaps love must begin with illusions, for without them we might never break through the preoccupations with self that so fiercely grip us all. But love can grow only when we pass through or beyond the illusion to the reality it had presented in disguise."[120]

The way such romance changes the outlook to the whole world suggests that it may not even require a particular human as an object of one's love, not even in terms of unrequited love. As Charles Williams himself puts it,

> The complex art of this knowledge [of a Way towards God] is certainly not confined to romantic love of the male-female kind. Wherever the "stupor" is, there is the beginning of the art. Wherever any love is—and some kind of love in every man and woman there must be—there is either affirmation or rejection of the image, in one or other form. If there is rejection—of that Way there are many records. Of the affirmation, for all its greater commonness, there are fewer records. "Riguarda qual son io"—we have hardly yet begun to be looked at or to look.[121]

A different understanding of love—romantic, erotic love—thus emerges: love which can be expressed also in the delight for life itself. While still taking seriously de Rougemont's warning regarding the idolatrous divine claims of romantic love, it is possible to see human romance incorporated into the biblical story of God's romance—costly romance!—thus responding to de Rougemont's worry about romance's "proper place."[122] However, "costly" is an important word here. If the Cathars are to be blamed for the myth of romantic love, then they would be right at least in their insistence on the suffering aspect of love, although not on its deadly nature. Love is costly in many ways—a theme to be explored in chapter 9.[123] Yet those different experiences of love, lived

---

blind,' is a half-truth stressing one side of love's knowledge. But it really means, or ought to mean, that love sees *more* clearly. Love is light, insight, and understanding. It reaches the other's being and yields an awareness otherwise impossible." Williams, *Spirit and the Forms of Love*, 291.

120. McClendon, *Ethics*, 159.

121. Williams, *Figure of Beatrice*, 232.

122. See McClendon, *Ethics*, 155–60.

123. For a profound reflection on the connections between love and suffering, see Williams, *Spirit and the Forms of Love*, passim.

and suffered, can become threads in the tapestry of life which can be truly called "happy."

> For love is strong as death,
>   passion fierce as the grave.
> Its flashes are flashes of fire,
>   a raging flame.
> Many waters cannot quench love,
>   neither can floods drown it.
>
> (Song of Songs 8:6b–7a)

I have sought to address the nature of the difficulties which have beset the so-called traditional, coupledom-based nuclear family, both within and without the church context. I first looked at the indications of the so-called "crisis in families," which is often seen as inseparably linked to the diminishing social role of the church in contemporary European societies. I reviewed some of the factors which have brought about the current shape of the nuclear family. After comparing it to the general outline of family shapes and functions found in the Bible, I considered several theological insights arising from the New Testament's insistence that the church is the primary family in relation to which all other structures should be aligned. The current practice of marriage and family may well undergo a significant change, yet the change itself presents an opportunity to rethink family in terms of faithfulness to the Christian story, and the reflection on, and practice of, love.

"We live largely by our loves," wrote Day Williams,[124] but the intimate, sexual loves which are the topic of this chapter have been powerfully shaped by their cultural interpretations. Thus the last section of the chapter looked at two important myths of the nature of love: libidinal drive and romantic love. I focused on the latter and its powerful grip today's appropriation of love, with a reminder about the dangers of making such love the object of one's ultimate loyalty.

However, the experience of human love also points to its gift in enabling human beings to see life's challenges and possibilities in a different light. Such energy and passion can mark not only the specific ex-

---

124. Ibid., vii.

periences of being in love with another person, but also "being in love" as a way of life, or perhaps even "being in love with life." An exploration of love and sexuality will continue into the subsequent chapters.

5

Convictions behind the Surface

Defining a Theological Perspective

Where is the front line for each of us: in our hearts; in the society; in the church itself?[1]

THE PREVIOUS CHAPTER SET out to understand the development of the modern notions of love, marriage, and family, and hinted at some helpful theological themes in responding to the challenge of singleness. In order to explain the line of thought I hope to develop in the remainder of this book, here an explication is due of the methodology guiding my work.

One of the features of the method is evident in the very point where such explication is taking place, pointing to a belief that theological inquiry starts, as Rowan Williams would put it, "in the middle of things."[2] Such an understanding assumes two levels of theological discourse. The first-order, or primary theology, concerns theological practice within the believing communities in their primary expressions: songs, prayers, testimonies, verbal and non-verbal expressions of reactions to particular events or circumstances, and to some degree, sermons and other occasions of teaching and admonishing. The second-order theology is concerned with making sense, analysis, and appraisal of the first-order material and the convictions expressed therein. Both types of discourses

---

1. Zorn, "Slovo redaktora. Novosti s fronta," n.p.
2. Williams, *On Christian Theology*, xii.

have been present with the churches, both are needed, and neither has a clear priority over the other.

Starting "in the middle of things" requires a way of making sense of what is discovered along the way, and this is where the heart of the method lies. One of the terms used for it is convictional theology: a stance that is committed to a careful examination of deeply-held beliefs of people and communities about what is really important in life; and on the basis of that examination and in relation to professed theology, to steer the discussion further, hopefully to some sufficiently realistic transformation. McClendon, my guiding voice in such convictional theology, described it as a threefold task of theology: describing, analysing and evaluating "the convictions of a convictional community, including the discovery and critical revision of their relation to one another and to whatever else there is."[3] In the context of this work, the challenge posed by the growing numbers of single people represent one such case of "whatever else there is."

The roots of the focus on convictions lie in the thought of several thinkers who suggested that such an approach could be a more helpful way to discuss the human beliefs which often remain at the theoretical level, and often seem to clash with the actual lives lived by those making such theoretical claims. The term "convictions" enabled a response to the conflicting reality of Christians in general, and theologians in particular, agreeing on things which may have sounded good in theory, yet which seemed to have little influence over the Christian life as experienced by particular communities of faith. Thus Willem Zuurdeeg pointed out the value of "conviction talk" or, as he put it, "convictional language."[4] Convictions stand for those persuasion that shape and direct

---

3. McClendon, *Ethics*, 23. McClendon's understanding of the theological task would fall into a larger field of a renewed interest in models of theological reflection which seek to heal the rift between "practical"/applied theology and what has been often implicitly understood as "proper" (systematic, biblical, philosophical, etc.) theology. McClendon's theological method provides the lead for my exploration of singleness and the response of the church. The key work exploring convictions is McClendon and Smith, *Convictions* and McClendon's three-volume systematic theology: *Ethics*, *Doctrine*, and *Witness*. I also engage with the work of several other convictional theologians, such as Stassen, "Critical Variables in Christian Social Ethics," and my own teacher and now colleague, Parush R. Parushev, "Convictions and the Shape of Moral Reasoning," 27–45; "Baptistic Theological Hermeneutics," 172–90.

4. Zuurdeeg, *Analytical Philosophy of Religion*, 9. There are different ways of describing realities which here are termed "convictional." Examples can be encountered

human lives, most of the time implicitly. Zuurdeeg describes convictions as "all persuasions concerning the meaning of life," followed by persuasions about good and evil, political ideas, and so on.[5] Importantly, various elements of convictions, such as the meaning of life, need not be explicitly religious: "We find convictional language . . . also in political and philosophical statements,"[6] as well as in any of the other spheres of human activity and experience. Such an understanding was already employed in the way I approached the theology of culture, whereas the question of the meaning of life, which, as Zuurdeg argued, forms the core of any convictional set, will be explored in the last section of this chapter.

Thus, convictions, in contrast to opinions or preferences, are understood as the drives behind our motivations which make us who we are and therefore cannot be easily changed. "We cannot stop being ourselves, that is, being our convictions";[7] at least, not if we are to retain some sort of integrity. If we undergo a radical change of convictions, we become a significantly different person, and if holders of significantly different convictions arrive at a mutual understanding of the issue in question, they both—or both groups—will have been considerably changed in the process. It is in this context that a profound change of convictions can be called "conversion," although it is not likely to be an appreciated concept when used outside the religious context.[8] As Darrell L. Guder has helpfully noted, there is a need for a *continuing* corporate conversion of the church.[9] My hope is that with a transformation of convictions in regard to the church's witness to human love and its theology of singleness a small conversion might take place.[10]

---

in different fields of inquiry. See, for instance, Ron Ritchart's usage of terms such as "dispositions," "inclinations," "mental models" or "fixed and developed beliefs" from an educationalist perspective, in Ritchhart, *Intellectual Character*, or Taylor's "basic" (or "fundamental") "orientation" (*Sources of the Self*, e.g., 29–30).

5. Taylor, *Sources of the Self*, 26.
6. Ibid., 35.
7. Zuurdeeg, *Analytical Philosophy*, 49.
8. McClendon and Smith, *Convictions*, 7–8.
9. Guder, *Continuing Conversion of the Church*.
10. I am also aware that an insistence that the church must be examined in the light of such conflicting, yet stable convictions which it holds, extends to the one or ones doing such an examination.

A particular convictional set[11] may carry different, and even rationally conflicting, convictions. These may come from different groups which the person (or community) pays loyalty to—different "convictors," to use Zuurdeeg's terminology.[12] An example of this would be a tension between certain Christian and patriotic convictions.[13] What I attempted to demonstrate in the preceding chapters was an illustration of similar tensions between convictions arising from the Christian story and those impressed by the ideology of coupledom. Convictions are not necessarily logically ordered, and some convictions will be much more central than others.[14] Convictions which are more at the center of the convictional web, and therefore related to a greater number of other convictions, would signify an especially monumental change when altered. Another way to speak of such central convictions is to use Tillich's "ultimate concerns"[15] or Stassen and Gushee's term of "ultimate loyalty."[16] Stassen and Gushee discuss such loyalty in relation to God, but, although this is the context in which such loyalty is expected to be professed in the communities of Christian faith, such ultimate loyalty may *de facto* lie in other matters; to use McClendon's apt observation, such loyalties—and the convictions they form—may well be about "guns, girls, and gold."[17] Culture at large, in its hermeneutics of love and happiness, no doubt is a

---

11. On convictional set, see McClendon and Smith, *Convictions*, 91–101.

12. E.g, Zuurdeeg, *Analytical Philosophy*, 40–44.

13. Much of Christianity seems to be unaware of such a tension or conflict. Such unawareness does "not so much reveal an admirable naïveté as a misleading glossing over of a factual situation: man is a complicated and ambiguous being, not all of a piece, but full of contradictions and conflicting loyalties. The suspicion widely felt, that being a Christian requires a considerable amount of hypocrisy, is connected with the awareness that so many 'Christians' share in the 'naïve' denial of man's [sic] ambiguity." Zuurdeeg, *Analytical Philosophy*, 41. Such a hypocrisy is "a laudable attempt to construct a respectable façade behind which he can live his real life in peace" (ibid., 41–42). A fanatic, in Zuurdeeg's understanding, is a person who does not see this complexity in herself or himself. "The fanatic denies part of his own convictions: that is to say, he ignores, hates, and rejects part of his own being." Ibid., 41.

14. As McClendon and Smith would put it, "Conviction sets . . . are seldom deductive systems or theoretical constructs. If they possess a unity, it is rather first of all the unity of their coinherence in the organic unity of a community of persons." McClendon and Smith, *Convictions*, 99.

15. Tillich, *Dynamics of Faith*, 1–4.

16. Stassen and Gushee, *Kingdom Ethics*, 63–64.

17. McClendon, *Ethics*, 23.

far more significant convictor in shaping the theology of churches than they might be ready to admit.

At some point, the tension between conflicting convictions begins to tear the web apart, and convictional change of some sort becomes unavoidable. Yet the process of such change will be a complex one. A reordering of the convictional set is not a result of a single decision, or an adjusted teaching on singleness. Whenever a genuine change takes place, it will be connected to a change in practices that shape the virtues reflecting and upholding a new conviction.[18] The communal aspect, therefore, will be very important: "It is in the context of relationships, ways of life and institutions—in the corporate traditions we inhabit and help to form, reflexively, as they are shaping us—that the virtues are forged and demonstrated."[19] I will return to the question of communities and their role in the formation of convictions in chapter 7.

The three parts of the book approximately represent the three theological tasks, although they overlap in a number of ways. Thus in Part I, I concentrated on describing the situation as I saw it, both inside and outside the believing community and its single women. In Part Two, I am focusing on interpreting the situation. The third part will then consider more concretely the implications of a different look at singleness.

Happiness Revisited

How [to be] free from the idea that a happy life belongs to the married and others are either waiting or already hopeless?[20]

I return now to the question of the perception of happiness as a prime case of a convictional clash which has tremendous implications regarding the attitude toward singleness in baptistic communities. Although Christians may feel obliged to emphasize God's will and the meaning of life as the ultimate questions to be asked in regard to one's life, what is often assumed by these, or substituted for as a synonym, is the notion of happiness. Our communication, verbal and otherwise, of conditions necessary for happiness—or alternatively for the signs of being in God's

---

18. Here I broadly follow the thought of Alasdair MacIntyre. His ideas on practices, virtues, and tradition will be explored in depth in chap. 7.

19. Graham, "Virtuous Circle," 230.

20. Vershina, "Gift I Would Like to Return," 32.

will—is one of the mirrors of the convictions we hold. "As I reflect on what I mean when I say my life is or is not happy, I see that I have judgments in mind about myself, the world, what is satisfying now and over the long term, what is worth pursuing and avoiding, and so forth."[21]

It is helpful to recognize that the Christian understanding of happiness and good, meaningful life does not emerge exclusively out of the Christian narrative; it will always be related to the particular context shaping that understanding. Indeed,

> people draw their concept of the good life from a variety of sources, Christians being no exception; the point of contention is what aspects of such influences—Scripture, the corporate narrative of tradition, secular reason, experience—should prove ultimately binding. Understandings of happiness are lived out and formed in a variety of settings—and the complexity of modern life is such that any mature adult will inevitably encounter a plethora of such messages in the course of a single day, just by watching a television soap opera, passing advertising billboards, reading a bedtime story to their children, listening to politicians, let alone reading the sacred texts of their tradition (which are not in themselves monolithic in their visions).[22]

Where the problem lies is in the assumption that the theology of happiness centered around marriage and family is Christian through and through and, by implication, a good one. Churches which cannot see the cultural influences which shape their life are not able to see where change is needed, and even less to bring about this change. They may fiercely cling to what they consider to be Christian language and Christian practices, but these will be either neutralized by their much greater loyalty to culture's gods, or subverted to serve the purposes of this religion and reflect its narrative.

As was noted earlier, one of the ways to deal with this convictional clash is to insist even stronger on separating the notions of happiness and the will of God. It is certainly true that some of the hedonistic shades of the term would stand in direct opposition to the classical Christian notion of the will of God. However, what would not stand is an insistence that it is either helpful or possible to ignore the notion of happiness altogether; that Christians are not, or should not, be interested in happiness.

---

21. Griswold, "Happiness, Tranquillity, and Philosophy," 15.
22. Graham, "Virtuous Circle," 232.

At least for the children of the Western culture, happiness, with all its multiple interpretations, is something which "is consistently described as the object of human desire, as being what we aim for, as what gives meaning and order to human life."[23] Therefore the discussion will now turn to the secular explorations of happiness in order to see how they can speak into the Christian discourse on the same subject.[24]

Gleanings from the Secular World

Happiness is not an easy concept to work with. "Are you happy now?" may be a question asked after someone gets an ice cream they have been demanding for a while on a hot afternoon. "Only in God (or children, or serving the motherland) can we find happiness" is a claim of a different calibre, and the talk of "happy utterances" in the philosophy of language is yet another one. In resorting to additional qualifications to the word, Jussi Suikkanen proposes "happiness$_p$" to refer to a happy sensation (such as could be applied to the person licking the ice cream on a hot afternoon), "happiness$_g$" to denote "global" happiness, that is, one extended throughout a substantial period of one's life, and "happiness$_w$" as a more objective description signifying a life characterized by well-being.[25]

Then, in another set of issues, there are questions such as how happiness is related to the chemical balance in the person's body. Furthermore, is it a state, or a process? Is it mostly known only by its aspect of "longing" rather than that of fulfillment? Perhaps, even, such perpetual yearning—so intense, and so elusive at the same time—is the sole point of it?[26] Or, as others would suggest, is happiness really possible, but only as a by-product, rather than the goal to be chased?[27]

---

23. Ahmed, "Happiness Turn," 7.

24. The following reflections do not aim at comprehensiveness; that would be a different project altogether. My purpose here is to engage in dialogue with some of the threads in political and moral philosophy and psychology that can inform the current Christian understanding of happiness.

25. Suikkanen, "Improved Whole Life Satisfaction Theory of Happiness," 149–66. Some researchers have been employing the terms "hedonia" and "eudaimonia," referring to psychological, subjective well-being and meaningful, satisfying life respectively. See, e.g., Deci and Ryan, "Hedonia, Eudaimonia, and Well-Being," 1–11.

26. E.g., Farley, *Wounding and Healing of Desire*, 6–7.

27. Mihaly Csikszentmihalyi, among others, has worked to demonstrate how happiness—in Csikszentmihalyi's positive psychological terms, "the flow"—can only

The broad diapason of meanings which Alasdair MacIntyre referred to as "the polymorphous character" of happiness[28] may be part of the reason why, in spite of the prominence of the word in popular culture or sociology, the modern times have seen happiness receiving comparatively little attention until recently.[29] Whereas much of sociological research has been based on comparing various measures of happiness, there has also been a suspicion as to the accuracy of such measurements: can happiness be really quantified? Do people really mean the same thing when answering the question as to how happy they generally are? Are they honest when answering, or could they be presenting a picture of happiness (or unhappiness) that for some reason they feel they ought to present? How much meaning can one expect from a respondent reporting in a questionnaire that they are "overall happy" or "mostly satisfied"?[30]

The answer to these questions is both "yes" and "no." The vagueness with which the term is used can be exasperating.[31] This is one of the reasons why other terms had at times been preferred, yet the introduction of these terms and the inconsistent variety of ways they are employed by psychologists and philosophers alike simply illustrates the difficulty rather than eliminates it. On the other hand, happiness preceded by such words as "lasting" or "deep" does seem to suggest a comprehensible notion of a life which can be called "good" in a sufficiently profound way, referring to something without which life is lacking something at best or is unbearable at the worst. Such conceptions of deep, "true" happiness stand in contrast to a temporary emotional state that is strongly dependent on circumstances or mood.[32] This may be expressed by considering

happen when the subjects completely immerse themselves in an enjoyable activity. Csikszentmihalyi, *Flow: The Classic Work on How to Achieve Happiness*, 2.

28. MacIntyre, *After Virtue*, 64.

29. Griswold, "Happiness, Tranquillity, and Philosophy," 13–14.

30. See, e.g., Haybron, "Life Satisfaction, Ethical Reflection, and the Science of Happiness." On the difficulties of comparing the results of seemingly similar polls on life satisfacion, see Bjørnskov, "How Comparable Are the Gallup World Poll Life Satisfaction Data," 41–60.

31. See, e.g., an overview of different conceptions of happiness and the stories of their founders by Götz, *Conceptions of Happiness*.

32. Thus, for instance, Haybron distinguishes these two senses of happiness in *The Pursuit of Unhappiness*, 29–31, and so does Martin Seligman, one of the originators of the Positive Psychology approach: "The sum total of our momentary feelings turns out to be a very flawed measure of how good or how bad we judge an episode—a movie,

a difference between a person who is referred to as "happy" (happy, for example, because they ate a cake a minute ago, or are known to be of optimistic disposition) and a conversation about a "happy life" which has much more to do with a complexity of well-being—including, but not limited to, feelings and circumstances—and a concern for life which can be called good and meaningful. It is to this latter understanding of happiness that a whole cluster of related terms is attached and often used interchangeably (even as arguments about the precise meaning of each term and its relation to others continue): "deep happiness," "authentic happiness," "contentment," "harmony," "well-being," "human flourishing," "fulfilling one's potential," leading a "good life," or "a coherent, realistic, and durable style of life that reflects our deepest concerns."[33]

The latter words are those of philosopher John Kekes, whose stance reflects the disappointment of many with the resources for a good or "happy" life offered by religion or a political structure, and provides a good illustration of the contemporary thrust of the multiplicity of possible route to a happy life. These routes require an appropriate set of virtues (or personal excellences, as Kekes puts it)—be they integrity, reflectiveness, self-direction, decency, honor, and so on. Such a stance is representative of a popular emphasis on the complexity of factors contributing to a fulfilled life, the multiplicity of ways for increasing the levels of happiness, and the focus on traits, virtues, or skills as an integral part of generating happiness.[34] Thus, for instance, positive psychologist Martin Seligman sees good life in terms of "using your signature strengths . . . every day to produce authentic happiness and abundant gratification."[35]

---

a vacation, a marriage, or an entire life—to be" (Seligman, *Authentic Happiness*, location 192).

33. Kekes, *Enjoyment*, 270.

34. The focus on traits goes back to Aristotle and his *Nicomachean Ethics*. Aristotle noticed that while some associate happiness with simple pleasures and avoidance of suffering, and others with the honour and status they are able to get for the activities performed, both of these are highly dependable on the circumstances. Thus, although for some this may seem to be happiness, true and long-lasting happiness, Aristotle suggested, is an activity arising out of something which is not easily taken away from the person, and is best exemplified by those who "contemplatively" (i.e., philosophically) are seeking to achieve their goal by developing such traits of character which are required for the realisation of the person's full potential. Aristotle, *Nicomachean Ethics*, books 1 and 10.

35. Seligman, *Authentic Happiness*, location 317.

The word "authentic" preceding "happiness" here returns the discussion to an observation made back in chapter 3. An offer of a broad spread of possibilities for journeys to happiness has been popularized both by the successful industry of self-help books as well as by the media. Happy lives involve different "arts-of-living."[36] Kekes sums it up thus:

> In normal circumstances, we all want to enjoy life, but, in wanting that, we do not want the same thing. Differences in our characters and circumstances assure that we find different things enjoyable and that we find the same things more or less enjoyable. The contrary also holds: different lives can be miserable in countless different ways and for countless different reasons. Human nature and world limit what could make the lives of beings like us enjoyable or miserable, but within these limits there is a very wide range of possibilities. This is one reason why there are many forms of good and bad life and why there can be no universal and impersonal prescription of how to live a good life.[37]

How is it, then, that such insights still seem to be largely unable to change the way people (and women in particular) go about their own happiness? One of the answers could be that even among this broad spectrum of possibilities, marriage is still considered one of the key factors—or, alternatively, an *indicator* of happiness.[38] When emphasising the link between high levels of happiness and marriage (or romantic love more generally), researchers continue to debate whether it is the marriage which makes people happy, or happy people are more likely to get married.[39] One may recall an earlier mentioned claim regarding the bias of the researchers themselves in the assumption of the strong link between romantic relationships and a happy life when it may not necessarily be so strong.[40] Yet even if that is the case and the bias in research results in romantic love receiving a much more prominent role, that still does not quite explain the strength of the happiness-through-romantic-

---

36. Veenhoven, "Arts-of-Living," 373–84.

37. Kekes, *Enjoyment*, 250.

38. On the critique of the links made between marriage and happiness by much of the "new science of happiness," see, e.g., Love, "Compulsory Happiness and Queer Existence," 52–64.

39. Seligman, *Authentic Happiness*, 1136. For an overview of the discussion, see Lucas and Clark, "Do People Really Adapt to Marriage?" 405–26.

40. See n34 in chap. 3.

love motif in popular culture given the emphasis which is placed on various other paths to well-being.

Alternatively, it could be argued that the enormous pressure by industries such as advertisement is much to blame. The advertisement industry is heavily dependent on sex-appealing images to promote a variety of products, and images of couples play an important role as the marketeers seek for the most convincing ways to advertize.

> When couples are used as part of the visual information in sexualized advertising, they may be seen as proof that using products makes people more sexually attractive or more likely to engage in sexual behavior . . . In other words, the image of a couple is not simply to attract attention, but is an essential part of the ad's message.[41]

Thus, it could be argued, if only there was more money and effort invested into subverting the current ideology of advertising, things would change.

Perhaps they would, to some degree; the power of advertising certainly should not be taken lightly.[42] However, there seems to be another problem in the perceptions of happiness. Interested as it is to see human beings flourishing in a variety of ways, much of both academic and popular literature on happiness shies away from suggestions of which particular goals and routes to flourishing are appropriate.[43] It is left to the individuals themselves to figure out. "Nothing can make you better off that goes against your all-things-considered (informed, etc.) preferences, desires, or judgment."[44] Individuals themselves must make deci-

---

41. Reichert and Lambiase, "How to Get 'Kissably Close,'" 129.

42. As Dorothee Soelle observed a few decades ago, "We may understand the advertising experts as high priests of a new religion." Soelle, *To Work and to Love*, 121.

43. On the variety of happiness advice, see *Journal of Happiness Studies* 9.3 (2008), and especially the editorial article by Bergsma, "Advice of the Wise," 331–40. Seligman offers a list of six ubiquitous virtues of good character: wisdom and knowledge; courage; love and humanity; justice; temperance, and spirituality and transcendence (Seligman, *Authentic Happiness*, location 2611). For another example of an exploration of character traits and happiness, see a special issue of *Journal of Happiness Studies* 7.3 (2006). However, such lists presuppose an understanding that the same virtues mean the same thing across different contexts.

44. Haybron, *Pursuit of Unhappiness*, 178. This is not the stance Haybron promotes but his summation of the subjectivist take on figuring out the routes to happiness.

sions "to create their future lives by selecting and combining personal excellences, projects, prevailing rules, and aspects of themselves."[45]

Such a stance also assumes that people actually know what will make them happy. But do they? Can they? The happiness stereotypes which still govern the day would suggest they do not.

> Indeed, sometimes our best source of information about how happy we are is other people, or observing ourselves from a third-person perspective. Those who have spent much time gaining the perspective of living outside mainstream civilization are liable to find it a truism that many of us may not have a clue how happy, or unhappy, we really are.[46]

Thus, more is left wanting in the discussion on happiness. Although the above explorations of the exciting variety of avenues toward a good life have their value and are marked by some deep insights into the way humans function, they suffer from insufficient attention to the necessity of a larger framework—the visionary and the corporate.[47] They struggle to speak satisfactorily into complex situations involving suffering (and even more, death), the inevitable struggle with rivalling theologies of culture, or the multifaceted and at times painful relationships with other people. The motifs of happiness most widespread in and practiced by popular culture end up serving the function of the corporate and the visionary. "The successful pursuit of happiness may be less an individual affair, and more a matter of living in the right social and physical context, than the modern tradition has normally assumed," notes Haybron.[48] The same is true for those who profess to be the followers of Christ, as they also are easily caught in these popular motifs despite an intention to keep the Christian message at the center.

---

45. Kekes, *Art of Life*, 6.

46. Haybron, *Pursuit of Unhappiness*, 150.

47. This is not to claim, however, that the awareness of the need for a community and some sort of spiritual focus is entirely nonexistent in such explorations. On the sociological side, for example, there have been proposals to expand the Personal Well-Being Index (PWI) to include the category of spirituality and religiosity as the eighth domain to be considered in research. Wills, "Spirituality and Subjective Well-Being," 49–69.

48. Haybron, *Pursuit of Unhappiness*, 255.

Christian Happiness: Two Perspectives

Can the explicitly Christian reflection on happiness shed more light? I will briefly explore the proposals of two rather different authors, one working strongly at a second-order theology level and another employing much more of a church-language. The first of them, Pierre Teilhard de Chardin, represents a larger Christian tradition.[49] A scientist, philosopher, theologian, and a Jesuit priest, Teilhard points to some of the interconnections between theology, philosophy, and science which are of interest to this book: the themes of believers not as individuals but one body, of suffering, of centrality of love and the redeeming power of suffering-love. However, here I focus on a little book entitled *On Happiness*. Teilhard acknowledges "an essential craving for happiness" that is present in all human beings.[50] He outlines three approaches to happiness[51] and concludes that it is the third one—striving "to attain a fuller measure of being"—which deserves to be truly called "happiness."[52] His threefold proposal can be summarized thus: "If man is to be fully himself and fully living, he must, (1) be centred upon himself; (2) be 'de-centred' upon 'the other'; (3) be super-centred upon a being greater than himself."[53]

The first step, "centration," or "organic development," for Teilhard involves continuous personal development in physical, moral, aesthetic, and intellectual terms:[54] "being is in the first place making and finding one's own self."[55] This is then followed by "decentration"—that is, connectiveness to others. Teilhard is deeply aware of the interconnectedness of human beings. Union with others is central for Teilhard's interpretation of organic development:

---

49. Most of Teilhard's thought on theology has been published only posthumously, as he was prevented from publishing by the church authorities during his lifetime.

50. Teilhard, *On Happiness*, 6.

51. Teilhard starts with the "pessimists" for whom the "best of all would be not to be at all," and then proceeds with the "hedonists," for whom life is about enjoying the "static pleasure" of the present moment, finally pointing to the "enthusiasts" who search for "happiness of growth," "for whom living is an ascent and a discovery." Ibid., 15–22.

52. Ibid., 19.

53. Ibid., 33.

54. Ibid.

55. Ibid., 34.

> Broadly speaking, we cannot reach our own ultimate without emerging from ourselves by uniting ourselves with others, in such a way as to develop through this union an added measure of consciousness—a process which conforms to the great law of complexity. Hence the insistence, the deep surge, of love, which in all its forms, drives us to associate our individual centre with other chosen and specially favoured centres: love, whose essential function and charm are that it completes us.[56]

Such a union most obviously means romantic and organic connection, especially when these words are followed by three "toasts" on occasions of the weddings of Teilhard's friends which have been added to the back of the booklet. Teilhard refers to "a union . . . between bodies and souls that are made to complete one another and come together as one."[57] However, it must also be remembered that Teilhard speaks of such "centers of affection" as a Jesuit priest who evidently felt he was partaking of such decentration himself.

These centers of affection continue drawing to themselves others. Such "super-centration" is about consciously becoming part of the one big Whole and is expressed in "subordination of our own life to a life which is greater than ours."[58] Such time will come "when men will understand what it is, animated by one single heart, to be united together in wanting, hoping for, and loving the same things at the same time."[59] Teilhard is rather hopeful that such emergence will take place in the near future.[60] As with much of current happiness discussions, it is accompanied by an insistence that each a person will have to discover the unique way of super-centration.[61] It is in discovering such a way that "the explosive hoy of a life . . . at last [finds] a *boundless* area in which to expand."[62] Or "in other words: first, be. Secondly, love. Finally, worship."[63]

---

56. Ibid., 36–37.

57. Ibid., 43. Teilhard does have a very high view of marriage as one of the manifestations of divine love and purpose. "Who was the fairy who, without ever breaking her thread, worked alone to weave today into one perfect whole the double web of your two lives?" (71).

58. Ibid., 50.

59. Ibid., 40.

60. The lecture which formed the basis for this booklet was given in 1943 in Peking.

61. Teilhard, *On Happiness*, 51–52.

62. Ibid., 47; emphasis original.

63. Ibid., 42.

Such "triple beatitude" of happiness[64] represents three strands of human life which will be argued for in the next section: organic, corporate, and visionary.

Nevertheless, the way this vision of the triple beatitude is presented is rather foreign to the character of the churches which are the focus of this book. This would be especially true in regard to the visionary element which, for Teilhard, is boundless indeed: "an ideal or a cause, the secret of collaboration and self-identification . . . with the universe as it advances."[65] Something more would be helpful to ground this vision.

I now turn to an author of a very different caliber who also was attracted to beatitudes. Very few others among baptistic figures have attained a standing as high as Billy Graham. One of his works which has been translated into many languages and has enjoyed great popularity among Evangelicals, including clandestine publishing and circulation in countries under Communist regimes, was a book called *The Secret of Happiness*.[66] In contrast to Teilhard, it focuses on a particular biblical passage from an evangelistic, rather than scholarly or spiritual perspective. By focusing on a biblical text, Graham has been especially appealing to baptistic communities for whom "biblicism" represents one of their identity features.[67]

The Secret of Happiness starts with a similar insistence which was expressed earlier in this chapter and was also present in Teilhard: that happiness is only worth discussing if what is meant by it is something deep, secure, permanent—and for Graham, that certainly meant

64. Ibid.

65. Teilhard, *On Happiness*, 48. It ought to be noted that Teilhard proceeds by pointing out the Christian message about the loving nature of this universe in "God who not only creates but animates and gives totality to a universe which he gathers to himself" (60).

66. Graham, *Secret of Happiness*. As a young child, I was witnessing its publication by *samizdat* into Lithuanian.

67. The intention with which Graham approaches Scripture reflects what McClendon termed "the baptist vision": an intention to show how the "secrets" disclosed a long time ago in a very different context, can be readers' today (McClendon, *Ethics*, 31–35). In other words, the present time and circumstance can be identified with that which Jesus addressed in his Sermon on the Mount, and the implications of living out the Sermon lead to the future of the realm of God in its fullness. Even those in academia, sceptical as they were of writings of such order, could admit that Graham's sermonic practice was able to make Christ visible "in such a way that [the hearers/listeners] are not listening to ancient history but are entering into personal spiritual encounter with the Word made flesh" (Osborn, review of *Secret of Happiness*, 202).

rooted in God and God's goodness.[68] He also laments the state of the Christianity of his day which "has become well versed in Christian terminology, but is remiss in the actual practice of Christ's principles and teachings."[69] His response is an invitation to "retrace our steps to the source" and return to a life of christlikeness.[70]

The chapters follow the individual Beatitudes found in Matthew 5:3–10, with the rendition of the recurring Greek word, *makarios*, as "happy," "contended," "joyful," "blessed." Graham explores happiness through poverty in spirit; happiness while mourning; happiness through meekness; happiness through hunger; happiness through showing mercy; happiness in purity; happiness through peacemaking; and happiness in persecution. He concludes with a chapter illustrative of the primary audience for which Graham was writing, with "steps to happiness."

Although simplistic in his argumentation, Graham goes a step further in disclosing the concrete virtues befitting the vision, not only a vision itself. He is also right in his basic intuition that the Beatitudes must be the core text for those who claim to follow the One who uttered these words. This is important, as in spite of its clearly central role for Christian theology, the Sermon on the Mount has been overlooked both in the teaching and the practice of the churches for much of Christian history.[71] Granted, Graham takes up only the introductory part of the Sermon, the Beatitudes, but this is a start nevertheless.

Yet a question similar to the one asked above in regard to secular culture needs to be asked again, now in the context of the believing communities. How is it that these same communities who were so familiar with Graham's *Secret of Happiness* and, it must be assumed, the Sermon itself, have been so quick to adopt a stance toward happiness which goes against the Sermon on the Mount? I wish to argue that Graham's secrets of happiness still suffer from a lack of grounding in a fuller story of salvation. They largely miss the "*they*," the third person *plural* which later switches to second person plural, "*you*," of the Beatitudes them-

---

68. Graham, *Secret of Happiness*, 14–19.
69. Ibid., 9.
70. Ibid., 10.
71. As Stassen and Gushee note, such "evasion . . . has seriously malformed Christian moral practices, moral beliefs and moral witness . . . When Jesus' way of discipleship is thinned down, marginalized or avoided, then churches and Christians lose their antibodies against infection by secular ideologies." *Kingdom Ethics*, xi.

selves. Graham offers his insights from the Beatitudes as "a formula for personal happiness."[72] Surely, living out the Beatitudes can "transform the world in which we live," but such application is secondary to their personal significance.[73] What is omitted is the thrust of the Sermon on the Mount being lived out in a community—a "school of virtue"[74]—where such humility, such poverty, such hunger and thirst for righteousness—are worked out together. No wonder, then, that the remainder of the Sermon on the Mount (Matt 5:11—7:27) is ignored. Without such community, the practice of what Stassen and Gushee call "transforming initiatives" of the Sermon on the Mount can easily become a project of a madman.[75] Thus, if the Beatitudes are indeed to be the manual for happiness, the Sermon's larger context in the story of Christ must be kept in mind. Only then can the virtues which Jesus calls for in the Sermon on the Mount be embodied and developed in appropriate Christian practices and embedded in the Christian narrative. What can be retained from the present discussion is an appreciation that, following Teilhard and Graham, a Christian theology of happiness does contain the visionary element. However, taken as an abstraction, it allows too easily for morphing into the world's order of things—where the "will of God" becomes surprisingly similar to my own wants which in their turn mirror the common views of happiness.

Where God's Will Might Lead: Meaning(s) of Life

Our joys and sorrows
Have been so strangely intertwined
Our lives so colorful with tears and gladness . . .
So we sing hope, Lord
Seeing an image in the dusk

72. Graham, *Secret of Happiness*, 9.
73. Ibid.
74. I take the phrase from Graham, "Virtuous Circle," 229.
75. Stassen and Gushee's interpretation of the Sermon on the Mount follows the Anabaptist tradition over against the persistent attempts to moderate its radical call which have marked most of other Christian sub-traditions. In contrast to the antithetical reading of the Sermon, Stassen and Gushee argue for a triadic structure of the commands, where the first component represents the teaching of the tradition, the second describes the vicious cycle which characterises the reality in which human beings often find themselves, and the third element represents the teaching of Jesus which delivers people and communities from the vicious cycle (*Kingdom Ethics*, 123–45).

> As in a mirror, in our daily journey
> Trusting and knowing
> A time will come when all the parts
> By your love will be made complete and perfect.[76]

What might that "less abstract" look like? For the further exploration of the visionary element in the theology of happiness, I will now return to that more comfortable synonym for happiness in the Christian language: that of the "meaning of life."[77] As argued earlier, I will use it synonymously to happiness, i.e., assuming that making sense of the meaning of life is linked to happiness, over against those who hold happiness to be a trivial matter in the larger scheme of things. The term is considerably less polymorphous compared to the term "happiness" and has enjoyed much more respect in Christian talk; however, there is a danger that the phrase may remain abstract, with no applicatory meaning. Here again it is helpful to recall the convictional framework of the present discussion. The question of the meaning of life is central for any convictional set, although it can be seen most explicitly in those worldviews which are openly religious.[78] It does not necessarily follow that the definition of the meaning of life must be narrowly singular, even if it may look so on the surface.[79] The role of the church includes the task of concretising such a meaning for a particular time or place; a task which demands much more attention within church life—songs, sermons, occasional remarks,

---

76. Andronovienė, "I Sing Life."

77. While earlier sections dealt with some of the philosophical distinctions and intricacies in regard to the usage of this phrase, here I focus on the implications of such a meaning to one's way of life—what John Hick has termed "practical meaning." See Hick, "Religious Meaning of Life," 268.

78. The verbalisation of the meaning of life, as well as its non-verbalised living-out on an everyday basis, forms a part of any convictional set (even the one which argues there is *little* or *no* meaning in human life). Michael Steger has remarked that exploring the meaning of life "is about understanding where we've been, where we are, and where we're going" (Steger, "Meaning in Life"). As such, it is the staple of any convictional discourse.

79. Cf. the observations of Viktor Frankl, out of his experience of the Nazi concentration camps, that finding a meaning of life in the midst of horrific suffering was the single most important factor in survival, and that particular meanings differ "from man to man, from day to day and from hour to hour. What matters . . . is not the meaning of life in general but rather the specific meaning of a person's life at a given moment." Frankl, *Man's Search for Meaning*, 130–31.

non-verbal cues—so that meaning-making can become a deeply integrated practice. The meaning of life surely must be about following Jesus and doing God's will. This is how far the account goes much of the time. Yet the question often remains as to how it is to be embodied, not in a high moment of singing praise on a Sunday morning, or upon hearing a moving sermon, but in a day-to-day working out of one's life.

Of course, certain instructions are likely to be given: one is to have one's daily devotional time of reading the Scriptures and praying, to listen to God's voice in order to understand the specific will of God, and so on. Yet these elements of the practice of discipleship seem to be insufficient in providing a framework for life which would be strong enough to resist dominant cultural understandings of requirements for happiness, and to sustain one when life gets hard-going or different from one's expectations. Thus, further exploration is required: smaller, yet concrete meanings that would sustain Christian life in a variety of situations. The ease with which the plural of the phrase—"meanings of life"—can be employed is another reason why it is a helpful term; "happinesses" does not quite work, and the ever-singular "happiness" fails to convey the plurality of its expression.

David Schmidtz provides a metaphor to illustrate such plurality:

> Life is a house. Meaning is what you do to make it a home. Giving life meaning is like interior decorating. It is possible to overdo it, so that the walls become too "busy." But if our walls are bare, the solution is not to stare at bare walls, or philosophize about their meaning, but to put up a few photographs, making the walls reflect what we do, or care about, or making them reflect our judgment about what is beautiful or worth remembering. Activity can be meaningful, and philosophical reflection can be meaningful activity if done in the right way and if kept in its place—if we take it seriously without taking it too seriously or taking it seriously the wrong way. We need not be afraid of bare walls or deceive ourselves about their bareness. Neither is there any reason to dwell on the "fundamental underlying" bareness of walls we have filled with pictures. If we do that, we are not being deep. We are pig-headedly ignoring the fact that the walls are *not bare*. We are failing to take our pictures seriously, which is metaphorically to say we are failing to take seriously what we do with our lives. We are saying, what would be the meaning of this life (the wall) if the

activities that make it up (the pictures) were not real? But they *are* real.[80]

Just like with interior decorating, so with meanings: they involve intentions and choices of some sort. "Persons can choose to see their lives (or other lives) as meaningful. The less inspiring corollary is, persons also can choose to see their experiences, and by extension their lives, and other lives, as meaningless."[81] This is where single people's consciousness about such intentions and choices is likely to be sharper. Living in singledom, one is often more aware of one's own demons challenging the meaningfulness of one's life. Coupledom can provide elements that are conducive to bringing a (commonly accepted) meaning, but it also carries with it a danger of assuming that *this* way of decorating is the *only* way; otherwise it's not a proper house. No wonder that singleness is met with fear or suspicion: alongside other reasons, it reveals and challenges the insecurities of married lives. A sudden loss of marriage equals a sudden loss of Schmidtz's metaphorical house and its standard decorations.

One of the ways to look at the task of meaning-making is to recognize a special calling of singles as witnesses to its dynamic and creative nature. The restlessness which can visit many human beings, but which is known to many singles especially, can help them—and others, through them—to improve in their decoration practice. As Diogenes Allen put it, "Our need for God is sensed in our restlessness, but the goodness of other things keeps us hoping that we shall find fullness of life in the world."[82] Surely, there are other ways beside marriage to keep oneself busy for the sake of avoiding the imagined or real monsters of meaninglessness, but the dynamic and creative nature of meaning-making has to do with the positive angle of the aforementioned restlessness. "To be happy with things as they are is to risk detaching oneself from God's project . . . A theological understanding of human happiness will need to embrace some notion of continual struggle rather than being posited on the completion of a discrete process of change."[83] "Static bliss" is an illusion. Such an awareness also helps to stop the obsession with "happy

---

80. Schmidtz, "Meanings of Life," 184; emphasis original.
81. Ibid., 181.
82. Allen, *Love*, 122.
83. Brown, "Happiness Isn't Working," 76.

endings" and instead turns our attention, as Malcolm Brown puts it, to "happy middles."[84]

The choice involved in meaning-making also entails accepting the limitations of the circumstances: one cannot have all the desired pictures. All the states of life involve limitations of some sort, and so it entails working with what is there, rather than with what is not.[85] And yet yearning for something one does not have is a human characteristic, and this needs to be recognized. As chapter 3 has sought to show, single life can involve yearning for marriage even while celebrating singleness. The same, of course, can apply to the married state, and it can arguably be a more challenging problem to wish not to be married than the other way around. Meaning-making is less difficult when one is aware of such tendencies, and when yearnings for whatever it is we do not have are approached constructively. "If this life is to mean what we want it to mean, it will happen as a result of attending to the path life actually takes, not dwelling on what might have been, or even on what might yet be."[86]

The meanings of life become an especially important synonym of happiness when viewed from the perspective of life's ending. Some thinkers, reflecting on suffering and death, have spoken of "letting go." "Abandon the struggle against death. Just gather in life, freely given, like manna," wrote Rubem Alves.[87] The theme of struggling and letting go will be explored in greater detail in chapter 9, but here it must be at least noted that a deep sense of happiness must include making peace with the prospect of death.[88] One of the ways to approach it is to declare all the concerns for happiness to be "vanity, sheer vanity," following Ecclesiastes and Teilhard's "pessimists."[89] Yet that does not do justice to the other motifs of the Christian story which celebrate life and hold it to be God's gift. Rather than playing down the importance of this life, the reminder of death gains its full meaning in the light of the message of the resurrection and of life which awaits its fulfillment at the dawn of a new age. That "not yet" aspect of the realm of God is also true of happiness. It is also, in

---

84. Ibid., 84.

85. Rodney Clapp helpfully observes that both marriage and singleness very clearly represent limitations of a sort. Clapp, *Families at the Crossroads*, 112.

86. Schmidtz, "Meanings of Life," 185.

87. Alves, *I Believe in the Resurrection of the Body*, 62.

88. I thank Lydie Kucová for her comments on this issue.

89. See n51 in chap. 5.

all its varied expressions, both common to all human beings and unique to the Christian experience, a foretaste of what is yet to come.[90]

How life-meanings come vary, but they will certainly have one element: they will be relational. Though some argue for the meaning of life based on a principle or an idea, ideas and principles come to us through language which has been passed down by others. An objection to the relationality of meaning would lie in the suspicion of the fleeting nature of situations and of relationships. Indeed, one of the gifts of singleness for the life of the faith community is an embodied message against the illusory panacea in which relationships often invest—until, that is, they crumble, reminding those involved, yet again, that human bonds are a fragile reality.[91] However, this is where the baptistic theology of community formation has a strong contribution to make: what is at stake is not just any relationship, for, although they do give meaning, they are indeed subject to change and therefore to creating havoc in a person's life. Instead, these are relationships aligned (to a greater or lesser degree) to the above-mentioned visionary thread of life based in a community of the followers of Jesus Christ, sharing the same convictional set.[92] When one such member moves away and joins another faith community elsewhere, the change is likely to be painful and involve aligning to a different group of particular people, but the common vision provides sufficient stability.

Such communal framework should not only enable one to keep one's meanings, but also serve by giving meanings when a particular member loses hold of them. "Meaning can be our gift to each other," notes Schmidtz.[93] Such meaning, received as a gift, can be especially poignant in times of crisis.

> We give ourselves away to others in words, enabling them to be themselves by words of encouragement, building them up by words which efface ourselves and thereby, in the mystery of love, finding ourselves as persons also. God, supremely, has given himself away to us in his word of self-expression. Above all, the cross of Jesus is the word in which he gives himself away most deeply. It is a self-communication in the non-verbal medium of

---

90. Graham, "Virtuous Circle," 233.
91. Nouwen, *Clowning in Rome*, 38–40.
92. Alignment to a particular convictional set in the context of the church will be explored in more detail in chap. 8.
93. Schmidtz, "Meanings of Life," 181.

suffering, which communicates where literal words cannot, so that we are persuaded through the very situation and the feelings of God. At the same time it *is* the point of origin of a story, which has power to give us the courage to be and to accept. As this story of suffering is retold in the preaching and worship of the church it gives new words to those whose meaningless suffering has struck them dumb.[94]

This is where family-oriented churches have often failed those members who differ from the "coupled standard."[95] When singleness is experienced as suffering, whether sudden or prolonged, the calling of the faith community is to be a source of inspiration for meanings which celebrate the person's unique contribution to the body of Christ. How disappointing it is when even those meanings which the single person comes up with are looked down upon.

The suffering and the hope of resurrection make another important link. Jürgen Moltmann describes how the hope of the resurrection ought to change our bodily life:

> The person who loves life in the light of the resurrection hope becomes capable of happiness. All the senses come awake, the understanding and the heart become open for the beauty of this life. But with this love for life we also become capable of suffering, and feel the pains, the disappointments and the trouble of this mortal life . . . We experience what life and death really are when we love, for in love we go out of ourselves, become capable of happiness and at the same time can be hurt."[96]

How the bodily and the communal can be aligned with the visionary aspect of happiness and meaning-making will be explored in the subsequent chapters. What I attempted to demonstrate here is the presence of these three threads—organic, social and visionary. I borrow the metaphor of the three strands from McClendon, who suggested it as a way of

---

94. Fiddes, *Creative Suffering of God*, 173; emphasis original.

95. Kristin Aune suggests that marriage and children represent God's created order, whereas a single woman is a picture of the new creation, of the age to come. It might be perceived in dichotomic terms—juxtaposing God's creation as something which "will pass" with that which is to come, as often is the case with the absence of theology of creation care in many a church—but Aune certainly has a point that "the gospel's witness will continue to be harmed unless far more people than at present take up the challenge to be willingly single in order to symbolise the coming new creation." Aune, *Single Women*, 129.

96. Moltmann, *Sun of Righteousness, Arise*, 64.

reflecting on Christian ethics.[97] Thus, the bodily strand, or personal life; the strand of community, or the corporate personality; and the strand of the anastatic, or resurrection ethics, which colors and aligns the other two strands with the vision of the newness of life through Christ. These three constituents are interwoven in a variety of ways, so it must be kept in mind that their dissection, although helpful at times, is never completely accurate.[98] Yet whether together or separated for the sake of better understanding, they all have a role to play in the experience of happiness, bringing meanings into life. Only in such context does the Christian talk of life in abundance (following John 10:10) can actually be meaningful.

The beginning of this chapter sought to delineate the theological perspective guiding this book, arguing that a careful examination of deeply held beliefs of persons and communities in relation to their professed, or wished-for, theology allows for considering possibilities for their better alignment. I then turned to the question of the perception of happiness as a prime case of a convictional clash, with tremendous implications for the way in which singleness is viewed. A serious clash appears between what the church feels it ought to be saying (and may believe it is saying) on the subject of happiness, and what it actually conveys about the purpose and goodness of the (Christian) life. I looked at some attempts both outside and inside the field of theology and Christian practice to find a larger framework for happiness, and suggested that although these findings are enlightening, the communal dimension was strongly lacking both in the secular and the Christian discourse on happiness. The wide-open vistas of authentic happiness were not able to overcome the constraints of the stereotypical, but clear and confirmed motifs of happiness.

---

97. McClendon, *Ethics*, passim. McClendon discusses organic, social, and "anastatic" ("resurrection") ethics as a way of organising a reflection on Christian life with its challenges and opportunities. For a concise description, see McClendon, *Doctrine*, 109. For the third strand, I am also employing Parush R. Parushev's term "visionary" to describe the realm of human life which has to do with the vision "of construing the world according to . . . [the] best aspirations" of its holders. Parushev, "Convications and the Shape of Moral Reasoning," 37.

98. McClendon, *Ethics*, 78.

The last section sought to understand how strong visionary proposals could become a reality. I switched the vocabulary to employ another synonym to happiness—that of "meaning-making"—and began an exploration of the interconnectedness of the visionary element with the organic and social spheres of human life. In what follows, I proceed to explore how this interconnectedness can be worked out.

6

The Fight of the Tamars

Feminist Interpretations

IN THE LAST CHAPTER of this part, I turn for assistance to feminist theologians. This book began with the story of Tamar from Genesis 38 and an observation that feminist theologians were among the few to explore it seriously, and in the story's androcentric setting unearth insights suggesting a gynocentric dimension.[1] That they should have insights into singleness, then, is hardly surprising, even if such insights do not explicitly arise out of or are related to singleness as such.[2] I start with an overview of feminist theologies in the light of the baptistic context. The rest of the chapter looks at two motifs of meaning-making arising out of the intersection points between feminist voices and the issue of singleness. The middle of the chapter reflects on patterns of reweaving personal identity in relation to the dynamics of the community of be-

---

1. See, e.g., Bos, "Out of the Shadows," 48. Such a gynocentric perspective can be sensed in the story, as well, especially in the irony and the "tone" in which the men are described. For a number of feminist theologians, such as Bos, the story represents a clear interest in the oppressed. "Tamar does not change the patriarchal structures of her world, but her story challenges at least the notion . . . that the promises of God are advanced through male initiative alone" (49). See also Jackson, "Lot's Daughters and Tamar as Tricksters," 29–46.

2. As Reynolds notes, "Singleness is an important topic for feminism: however, it is a topic that has also remained at the margins of feminist theorizing. While feminism has drawn attention to the possibilities for women to live independently of men and actively shape their own lives, much of the debate has focused on the imbalance of power in relationships between men and women." Reynolds, *Single Woman*, 12–13.

On the Fringes of the Familial Circle

I am a woman
and the blood
of my sacrifices
cries out to the sky
which you call heaven.
I am sick of you priests
who have never bled
and yet say:
This is my body
given up for you
and my blood
shed for you
drink it.
Whose blood
has been shed
for life
since eternity?[3]

Impressions of Feminism(s)

Discussing the relationship between feminism and the church can be a rather challenging task. For many churches, especially in the East of Europe, feminism is a curse word which can be conveniently applied to others and is assigned the same value as liberalism, homosexualism, or Communism.[4] It is one of the words one uses to call somebody names.

---

3. Excerpt from Dietrich, "Blood of a Woman," 34. Used with the permission of the author.

4. It should also be noted that post-communist Europe is largely marked by a very reserved stance toward feminism. The reasons are complex, but the experience of the Communist regime has resulted in suspicion toward ideologies of emancipation: feminist mottos can be a reminder of too much of the old Communist propaganda (and some of those mottos were actually included in Communist propaganda). Meanwhile, on the ground, governmental systems of childcare and strong encouragement for mothers to be fully employed has meant that most women have been juggling a career and family responsibilities for several generations, and tend to see themselves as strong women and often concerned about the loss of their own femininity. These factors

The issue is also sure to raise eyebrows in more "Western" contexts, even if feminism is more established there, or when one needs to take care to remain "politically correct."[5]

"Feminism" and "feminist theology" are loaded and elastic terms, and thus easily misused. Technically speaking, one should speak of "feminisms" and "feminist theologies" rather than employing the singular form. The kinds of feminism range from a reformist approach which argues for changes within existing societal structures, to ecofeminism which elaborates on the nature of relationships between women, men and the non-human world, to radical feminism which contends that the symbolic world our societies inhabit must be overturned completely. The major, Euro-American, streams of feminism have also been critiqued in their turn by the non-white and majority-world feminists, as represented by womanism (African-American), feminista/mujerista (Latin American), Asian feminists, and so on. Then there is an area of discussion on distinguishing and evaluating the waves of feminism, while some others are naming the current era as already "post-feminist" or hoping that with the corrections brought by feminist insights, it has achieved its purpose and "can be absorbed into a new, broader, more inclusive theology."[6]

Such a rich variety does make matters more complicated, as there are always exceptions and variations to which one may point. In the broad strokes, however, feminism will be treated here as an ideological critique of patriarchy, arguing for equal treatment of women and men in all aspects of life.[7] An important part of the background for the development of feminism, from its early expressions in the fight for suffrage rights to the (still incomplete) struggle for equal wages for the same quality of work, are the experiences wrought with pain for being treated

---

help to explain why even in the glaring cases of gender inequality feminist discourse can be met with opposition by the very women it addresses. For an insider overview, see Rovna, "Women in New Member States"; Mudure, "Zeugmatic Spaces," 137–56.

5. Such an observation is a personal one, arising from numerous conversations with women in leadership in supposedly women-affirming contexts. Many of them note more subtle, implicit ways of discrimination and disregard—ways that are more difficult to tackle than direct confrontation.

6. Slee, *Faith and Feminism*, 106.

7. A minority of (separatist) feminists would explicitly argue for feminine superiority and thus a kind of model of power relations which mirrors patriarchal order, the most renowned of these being Mary Daly (referred to below in this chapter).

as not-fully-human, the manifold instances of abuse and the patterns of being silenced, ignored, despised, or blamed. These stories and their analyses are, not surprisingly, frequently born out of pain and anger.

When it comes to Christian feminisms, the state of affairs in the church is a consistent focus of concern and critique. "The more one becomes a feminist the more difficult it becomes to go to church," as Rosemary Radford Ruether would put it.[8] In some expressions of feminism, such as that of Mary Daly's, religion *per se* is seen to be the tool of patriarchal oppression of women, where the only alternative for such a church can be "sisterhood" or "antichurch."[9] On a more sympathetic side, one of the notable developments in feminist ecclesiology is related to the women-church cluster of base communities inspired by Elisabeth Schussler Fiorenza's powerful idea that "women are church" (as contrasted to "women in church" or "women and church" or the like).[10] Such networks, started chiefly among Roman-Catholic women in the United States, but also operative in Europe and the Majority World and in non-catholic or ecumenical backgrounds, seek to challenge the traditional church to seriously consider the feminist vision of justice and peace, refusing to give up the claim of belonging to the believing community, yet also refusing to accept the injustice in a church so patriarchal and unwilling to change. Such groups see themselves as a challenge to the institutional church and are developing their "gendered ecclesiology" separately from, and sometimes in fierce criticism of, the existing tradition(s) of the church. A number of people, women and some men, belong to such communities at the same time remaining a part of the institutional church.[11] Their practices reflect the expected concerns of feminist theology: an encouragement for women to develop their voice and a need for retelling the story of women as followers of Christ, both in the past and in the present:

> We come to telling Christ's story as the people we are, but who we are is in turn shaped by being part of this story, which is Christ's story and that of women. Sexual identity, being male or female,

8. Ruether, *Sexism and God-Talk*, 193–94.

9. Daly, *Beyond God the Father*.

10. For a sketch of the movement's vision in its early years, see Ruether, *Women-Church*.

11. Slee, *Faith and Feminism*, 89. For a description of one such community, see Graham, *Words Made Flesh*, 53–59.

as it is shaped by the particular context in which we live, is an important aspect of understanding what it means to be human, being an actor in the performance of Christ's story.[12]

Feminist ecclesiology, thus seen, has the purpose of "the recovery of the ambiguity of history and tradition of the church as not only the history of women's oppression to be remembered and transformed, but also as the history of women's transformative presence to be made available to the church as a whole."[13] The church can hold a variety of meanings and be expressed in a variety of forms, understood as

> Christian community as *prophetically marginal, as the place for creative boundary-living*... [It includes] a spectrum of meanings, from Exodus from institutional Church (Mary Daly), exodus specifically from alienating forms of Church (Rosemary Ruether), to base-communities of justice-seeking friends (Mary Hunt), and to the idea of a space, open yet bounded, where diverse communities of women and justice-seeking men are in dialogue with each other and with other faith communities (Schüssler Fiorenza and others).[14]

Such new expressions of church, often cross-denominational, marked by vigorous creativity in their worship practices, have already affected the liturgical life of the churches, especially those with high social awareness, though not identifying themselves with feminism *per se*.[15]

However, much of feminism, and even much of feminist theologies, does not hold a strong link with the life of the church in any particular form. This feature highlights not only the problem with the church, but also the problem with those feminist perspectives which take the insistence on the equality of women to men as *the* guiding perspective. In a New Testament scholar Stephen C Barton's words, such reading of reality represents certain "tribal interests" to which Scripture (or, in this case, theology in general) is made captive.[16] Or, as noted by McClendon, such ideological methodologies

---

12. Watson, "Reconsidering Ecclesiology," 73. Watson takes the lead from Loughlin, *Telling God's Story*.

13. Ibid., 76.

14. Grey, *Beyond the Dark Night*, 21–22; emphasis original.

15. Slee, *Faith and Feminism*, 90.

16. Barton, *Life Together*, 62, as an example. Guarding the Bible against "tribal in-

place some political, economic, or social proposal prior to the gospel. Typically, they propose singular cures for what they think ails the world . . . Preoccupied with context, these risk overlooking the content of Christian teaching, failing to see that an authentic practice of Christian doctrine grows from the gospel, not from ideological assumptions however insightful.[17]

A number of those interested in feminist thought have acknowledged the inherent problem of such ideological assumptions and have called for the reformulation and refocusing on the task of confronting and redeeming injustice and oppression in its broader framework and scope. If the battle against patriarchy is the lens through which all phenomena are seen, the movement is largely precluded from becoming constructive. The main thing it does is deconstruction: a task needed yet insufficient. While rightfully pointing out the areas of male abuse/hegemony, feminists are often unaware of the same danger in their own movement. In the words of Angela West, "If the old hierarchies of value are declared false, it is certain that new ones will immediately appear. To condemn all hierarchies as such is [thus] about as useful as cursing the weather."[18] By struggling with the maleness of Jesus, for example, some feminisms fail to see how it is exactly his position of "power" out of which he challenged the accepted status of women that is a striking illustration of the new order into which he called his followers.[19] If another

---

terests" is one of Barton's key concerns throughout his work. Feminism represents one such particular group; the same can be said, Barton contends, of conservative fundamentalism or liberal biblical criticism.

17. McClendon, *Doctrine*, 53. The ideological (i.e., religious) nature, especially of radical feminism, is markedly highlighted by examples such as Mary Daly's central image of "antichurch" (e.g., *Beyond God the Father*, chap. 5). In her own words, "The affirmation of being by women is a religious affirmation, confronting the archaic heritage of projections that deny our humanity. However, since the conflict is more on the level of creation than of struggle for equal ground in sexist space, the term Antichurch must be understood in a positive way. It is the bringing forth into the world of New Being, which by its very coming annihilates the credibility of myths contrived to support the structures of alienation" (Daly, *Beyond God the Father*, 139).

18. West, *Deadly Innocence*, 154, quoted in Spalding, "'Right Relation' Revisited," 58.

19. Interestingly, this seems to be more readily grasped by theologies done by women in the majority world—those that could be considered to be the most oppressed. Althaus-Reid and Lisherwood, *Controversies in Feminist Theology*, 82ff. It is the same conviction which is underlying this project, arguing that it should not have to be the single women themselves who have to fight for their well-being in the church, but that those who are currently in a position of power and convenience within faith communi-

ideology becomes the weapon for opposing the ideology of patriarchy, it is akin to chasing a dream that is not only unrealistic but potentially abusive and unjust.[20] The old dragon, when killed, can be succeeded by a new dragon; only a "girl dragon" this time. In other words, feminism as an ideology can, and does, bring a needed unsettling prophetic challenge to the structures of life, yet the framework of sex/gender binaries or other similar kinds of cultural critique cannot transcend itself and bring about the envisioned embodiment of the fullness of Christ.

These reservations in regard to feminism as ideology in no way mean that feminism can be ignored. Even the churches that treat feminism as their greatest enemy in fact live in the shadow of the effects of the first and second waves of feminism. It is arrogant to think that feminism did not affect the lives of women in a variety of ways, and it is arrogant not forget that feminism picked up very serious abuses within the structures of society and of the churches. It is arrogant not to recognize that feminists are at least trying to tackle the issue of involuntary singleness and loneliness in churches, whereas many churches have often opted for silence in the face of the problem. Feminists keep reminding us—perhaps in a way which the "mainstream" ("malestream"?[21]) church finds too loud, uncomfortable, or irritating—of the pain and injustices which have not been amended. As feminists have often insisted, perhaps the church might learn to listen better to those who are on the fringes.

Thus, taking a lead from some intersections between feminist voices and the challenge of involuntary singleness, the remainder of this chapter explores reimagined and reworked ways to address the challenge.[22] While wisely escaping the trap of resorting to marriage as the

---

ties should seriously engage in changing personal and churchly ways in order to make a difference.

20. So, for example, Anne Spalding assesses Mary Daly's (aggressive) critique of church as lacking the "practice of right relation": "[Daly] unfortunately gives the impression that the elect are only those of like mind while everyone else is collaborating with evil to the detriment of women, society and the planet. Her be-friending is not a welcoming climate for others (such as men, heterosexuals or non-white women)." Spalding, "'Right Relation' Revisited," 60.

21. Chopp, "Eve's Knowing," 116–23.

22. Once again, I return to the multiplicity of feminist perspectives and note that the intention here is not to work through the texts extensively (volumes have been, and still are being, written on the subject), but, though risking the critique of those who consider a particular feminist stance not sufficiently highlighted, wade through the insights which I have found helpful for working out the major concerns of the present work.

solution, can feminist insights contribute to a change for single women and the whole of the faith community? If so, in what ways?

Reweaving the Patterns: Personal Identity and "Community of Connections"

> A new language must be created to express women's experience and insight, new metaphors discovered, new themes considered . . .[23]

The Business of Finding One's Single Self

At the start of her autobiographical novel, a Lithuanian author Ieva Simonaitytė describes little Ėvikė, the main character, coming to a realization of her personhood: "She felt herself to be. That felt so strange, as if it was hurting. But it didn't hurt, no, only . . . there was no way to put it differently."[24] This epiphany takes place in the middle of the night, as Ėvikė realizes that from now on, she would not be saying anymore "Ėvikė wants"; "no, she will now always say clearly: 'I want.' Come to think of it, why hasn't she yet ever said 'I'?"[25] The night continues with Ėvikė exercising the usage of "I"—as could only be expected, to the irritation of everybody in the room trying to sleep. She has a difficult life ahead of her, as the rest of the novel will reveal, but the awareness that descended upon Ėvikė that night makes it clear that in the morning, "she will already wake up as a person."[26]

An author sympathetic to feminist concerns, Simonaitytė illustrates one of the sustained interests of feminist theologians. How is the view of the self formed and sustained? Do aspects of personhood look different from a woman's perspective, and if so, how? What sort of view of the self makes life meaningful and worth living? Keeping such questions in mind when approaching materials of first-order theology of baptistic communities can bring rather perturbing conclusions. How, when, where do I matter—how can my self be affirmed and celebrated—

---

23. Ruether, *Women-Church*, 168.
24. Simonaitytė, *O buvo taip*, 7.
25. Ibid., 10.
26. Ibid., 13.

if my life does not seem to follow the standard stream of marriage and motherhood?[27]

Matters are complicated by biblical materials such as Jesus' words about the value, indeed the necessity, of "denying," "disowning oneself"—which seems to discourage attempts to give much thought to the issue of the self. Yet, as it has been noted by many, in order to obey this commandment, one must know what this self is that one needs to deny and disown. Not surprisingly, feminist theologians have commonly pointed out that women end up sacrificing much more of the self than men. Grey observes, among others, that because women have been encouraged to forego themselves and have been rather good in doing that, "the lack of sense of self, or self-abnegation" is nothing less than "the female sin,"[28] and therefore redemption for women is directly connected to self-affirmation.[29] She maintains, "Unless we develop our own personal strengths and face our 'aloneness' in the world at quite a deep level . . . our *interpersonal* relating will continue to make unrealistic demands."[30] Developing such personal strength requires that a woman abandons her passivity and begins to struggle, often through suffering and anguish, to see how her own experiences, thoughts and aspirations, perhaps seemingly unshaped and fragmented, may be worthy of nurture and attention. Such experience of dark lonesomeness and struggle with one's timid self can emerge into a fresh sensing of the reality of God's presence in this journey of discovery: "It is to free darkness of its overtones of evil and sin and see it as potential richness, fertility, hidden growth and contemplation, as nature broods and contemplates in winter, seemingly inactive, yet preparing for the birthing of spring."[31]

Yet here one immediately runs into one of the constant points of divergence for feminist studies. Is a woman's selfhood rooted in the difference of gender and its construct? Must it be? Some feminists would agree, elaborating, in a variety of ways, on features that make women

---

27. On the other hand, however, "not fitting the woman-mould" in the first place may become a spur to challenge the patriarchal arrangement and initiate change. The history of the church provides numerous examples of women who, because they were single, were able to launch in directions which would have been unimaginable in the case of a married woman.

28. E.g., Grey, *Redeeming the Dream*, 70.

29. Ibid., chap. 4.

30. Ibid., 39; emphasis original.

31. Ibid., 80.

essentially different from men. Others have found the notion of essentialism to be the main supporting pole of patriarchal hegemony.[32] Here, I acknowledge the complex interplay between the biological and cultural variables shaping women's perception of their selves, both individually and collectively. Although there may be no universal "female nature" as such, there are differences insofar as women happen to be shaped by certain factors which are significantly different from those typically encountered by men. As Grey puts it, "Men and women see both the world and themselves differently not primarily because of inbuilt physiological and psychological differences but because they actually have vastly different experiences (including the view of others in regard to their identity) and these lead to disparate understandings of their own identities."[33] The "vastness" of the different experiences of women and men would need to be continuously qualified, especially given how fast life continues to change for women in the West today.[34] Furthermore, gender-based differences represent only one type of distinction; other categories, such as upbringing and social context, may be just as significant for the formation of personal identity.[35]

The feminist questioning of the (modern) notion of personhood has often been accompanied by a critique of its links to the hegemony of the male experience and the patterns of thinking arising from such experience. The question of knowledge and power are seen to be related, and the knowledge system which has dominated the modern Western discourse is recognized as integrally connected with the perception of personal identity. Hence one of the foci of feminist studies has been the exploration of the significance and the role of other ways of perceiving, arising from experience in all its variety (physical, social, practical,

---

32. For a critical overview of the faces of essentialism, see Grey, *Redeeming the Dream*, 20–24.

33. Ibid., 24.

34. That said, for many women and men belonging to the communities I have been describing, one place where their experiences are likely to be "vastly" different, sadly, is often the church.

35. In this respect, biological variables such as intersexuality, transsexuality, etc., which challenge the binary of male and female, are a helpful reminder. It is notable, for example, that the intersex condition is gaining more publicity, such as in the recent introduction of the "indeterminate" option for gender identification in Germany, New Zealand, and Australia. "Australian Passports to Have Third Gender Option," *Guardian.com*; Evans, "Germany Allows 'Indeterminate' Gender."

numinous, cerebral, aesthetic, etc.),[36] and especially the "intuitive" or "imaginative" or "deep" knowledge—a way of conceiving, sometimes understood in contrast to "logical" rationality,[37] or increasingly as a necessary counterpart of the latter for a more thorough wisdom about the nature of things.[38] Marginalized and despised, "the chaotic, the imaginary, the obscure have been seen as enemies and indeed requiring of a cure that can be achieved largely by reason."[39] The feminist call, together with those educationalists who have recognized the inadequacy of an information-imparting, head-only, top-down type of education, has been that of reintegration into a wholeness which merges these various ways of knowing in a process akin to birthing.[40]

For Christian feminists, the importance of such knowledge is often confirmed by the reaffirmation and embrace of Christ as Sophia, and frequently runs alongside the rituals, the purpose of which is to help the women to understand, express, and affirm their way of being and especially various passages of life with the acknowledgment of the wisdom gained and needed for the next stage of life.[41] Explorations of these other ways of knowing have at times been described as an autonomous journey into oneself. "The inward path [to wisdom] promises healing for the crisis of knowing and deep-seated self-doubt."[42] Separation (from other relationships, commitments, emotions) has been at times accentuated as an essential aspect of developing one's own personality and therefore as a way of liberation for women from oppression—including the oppression of family ties:

> I revel in my singleness. I treasure it. Every morning I awake aware that, this day, I need only please myself. This may sound

---

36. Copeland, "Difference as a Category," 144.

37. On the dominance of patriarchy in the tradition of scientific inquiry and a feminist critique of it, see Graham, chap. 9, "Feminist Epistemologies and Philosophies of Science," in *Making the Difference*, 192–213.

38. For a concise overview of "many ways of knowing" and feminist strategies in interpreting and challenging "malestream" [i.e., modern] epistemology, see Chopp, "Eve's Knowing," 116–23.

39. Boyce-Tillman, "Unconventional Wisdom," 319.

40. Grey, "Feminist Images of Redemption in Education," 221–23. Grey is referring here to Belenky et al., *Women's Ways of Knowing*.

41. On the overview of human practice as the locus of knowledge, see, e.g., Graham, *Making the Difference*, 209–13.

42. Barger, *Chasing Sophia*, 162.

selfish, but it isn't. The fact that it pleases me to serve womankind . . . is irrelevant, because I *choose* to do so and there's no one on which I must wait . . . I find it imprisoning even to contemplate another close relationship in which I would, because of gender, be forced again into a subservient role.[43]

At this point it is worthwhile to review the storied understanding of one's identity and the narrative construction of one's self. From the convictional perspective employed in this work, on its own, the task of finding oneself only in terms of oneself fosters an isolationist and illusionary non-vulnerability. While it is important to recognize the efforts of "finding" oneself, and the need for women to develop their authentic languages or "voices," for the understanding and communicating of such knowledge, the task is impossible to complete when taken in isolation:

> We can never gain the necessary distance from our own experience and point to ourselves by saying, "Here, that's me." We know the self indirectly. How we understand the pursuit of self-knowledge through an inward journey will determine how successful we will be at obtaining both self-knowledge and wisdom.[44]

Having reflected on the limits of the isolated search for the self, some feminists have thus turned to "an emergent world-view based on connectedness."[45] Grey, for instance, contends that the whole of Western culture suffers from being permeated by a fractured and detached worldview of "separative individualism"; thus "invitations to connect, re-connect, or build relationships around the notion of mutuality will make no difference until the all-pervasiveness of the notion of separation—even within theology itself—is recognized, together with the difficulties of moving away from this to re-structure on the basis of connection."[46] In the perspective based on connectedness, the perception of selfhood will be necessarily pluralist.[47] As Boyce-Tillman puts it, "The self emerges within a web of complex relationships rather than a heroic journey."[48]

---

43. Way-Clark, "My Second Life: Single Again," 68; emphasis original.

44. Barger, *Chasing Sophia*, 171.

45. Grey, *Wisdom of Fools*, 74.

46. Ibid., 67.

47. Ibid., 68.

48. Boyce-Tillman, "Unconventional Wisdom," 326. Such a narrative understanding of the person as "bestowed selfhood" has far-reaching implications. Think of the children raised by some animal or other before they are discovered by horrified

Wendy Farley observes that perception of the self will also be related to the experience of suffering and the distortion of desire.[49] The way of making us whole in our perception of ourselves, she maintains, lies in the realization that

> personhood is organized by awareness located in a particular ego. The vividness of this awareness produces the illusion that we exist alone, trapped with our ceaselessly nagging fears and hopes, sufferings and desires . . . Our emotional and spiritual life degenerates into a struggle with passions that bind us ever more tightly to our sorry attempts to ease our pain.[50]

But if egocentrism—and illusion itself—begins to fade, those same "passions become powers of the soul. Terror is transposed into freedom. Rage becomes the divine energy of compassionate wrath. Addiction becomes eros: loving delight that others exist."[51]

Bearing these insights in mind, the invitation of Jesus to deny oneself may be responded to in a way that brings growth to one's self-perception, so that the promise of the self being found anew in the very losing of it may indeed be true. Yet to see how that can happen requires further exploration of the themes of connections and loving delight, to which I turn next.

A Community of Connections

This, in my reading, is one of the most significant motifs of the feminist thought: "to discover 'the connected self' in a connected world."[52] The relationality of women has been one of the predominant topics of interest among scholars concerned with the psychology of women, as, for example, expressed among those working with the "new paradigm" emphasising the need and capability of affiliation.[53] The theory of *self-*

---

members of human society attempting to integrate them: what sort of story can these children live? I owe this insight to Linas Andronovas.

49. Farley, *Wounding and Healing of Desire*, 34.
50. Ibid.
51. Ibid.
52. Grey, *Wisdom of Fools*, 67.
53. Such a paradigm was initiated by Jean Baker Miller in her influential work, *Toward a New Psychology of Women*. She was followed by those like Carol Gilligan who have pointed to a "different voice" arising from experiences of women which are often significantly different to those of men. See Gilligan, *In a Different Voice*.

in-relation, or *connection,* focuses on exploring what was believed to be the most distinct quality of a woman's present psychological makeup: that of relationality, affiliation, or empathy.[54] Another way to express this reality of connections is relational theology, as in Grey's "connected self," where one's identity is developed by it "being made and re-made through the very epiphanies of connection which are the stuff of community experience."[55] Pointing out the importance of relationality, mutuality, and connectedness has far-reaching implications highlighting the need for interconnections and a framework of just relationships that can constructively shape identity.[56]

However, such just, or "right," relations presuppose a social setting. Where is the community where these relations can be practiced? A number of feminist thinkers have proposed support groups centered around the idea of sisterhood and the friendship which can be practiced within it.[57] Such sisterhood was seen as especially meaningful in terms of its support for the experience of singleness: "a new understanding of the solidarity of sisterhood as a basic support for the single woman."[58] In feminist thinking, such sisterhood may or may not involve the sexual element. However, relationships not based on marriage are helpful in developing "new paradigms of sexuality which evoke celebratory, creative, mutually-empowering and sensuous relationships, and [accuse] the Church of being out of touch with those who are discovering these forms, and thus of the vision of God which is being made incarnate in this struggle for justice."[59]

The idea of a community of sisterhood remains a challenge to the church. Throughout the many centuries of its existence, the church often left no option for the women but to organize themselves into female-only intentional communities. One only needs to think of the legacy of some of the convents, but especially communities such as the Ursulines or the

---

54. The scholarship elaborating this theory, especially connected with the Wellesley College Stone Center, have been influential in calling for a paradigm shift in the male-biased psychological models and their implications on various fields such as ethics or philosophy of education.

55. Grey, *Prophecy and Mysticism*, 56.

56. For an overview, cf. Spalding, "Being Part of 'Right Relation,'" 43–66.

57. Spalding, "'Right Relation' Revisited," 57ff.

58. Fulton, foreword to *Single Women*, xii.

59. Grey, *Redeeming the Dream*, 159. Grey here is summarizing the thought of Beverley Harrison, "Human Sexuality and Mutuality."

Beguines, and their remarkable impact on the society of their times.[60] The life of most of these communities was cut short by the ecclesiastical authorities and the secular powers "terrified of these mobile, active and, in their own words, apostolic women."[61] Not necessarily wanting to limit their communities to women only (but often forced to), they made the most of their circumstances.

Out of these experiences of exclusion and suppression arise calls such as the now classical proposal of Mary Daly who, in speaking of the sisterhood of liberation, sees such sisterhood as necessary to create a new world, free of oppression.[62] Men, even those displaying signs of understanding, empathy and commitment, cannot be a part of this group, for "women and men inhabit different worlds."[63] Nevertheless, since such a covenant of the antichurch "is an agreement that is found rather than formed, men who are 'graceful' enough to have fallen into the new space and find themselves in agreement are in fact part of the covenant."[64] The necessity of such a community of sisters is described by Daly in no uncertain terms:

> We have been locked in this Eden [of God the Father] far too long. If we stay much longer, life *will* depart from this planet. . . . The freedom-becoming-survival of our species will require a continual, communal striving in be-ing. This means forging the great chain of be-ing in sisterhood that can surround nonbeing, forcing it to shrink back to itself. The cost of failure is Nothing.[65]

---

60. As the Franciscan Friar Gilbert of Tournai struggled to describe the Beguines in 1274, "There are among us women whom we have no idea what to call, ordinary women or nuns, because they live neither in the world nor out of it" (quoted in Stoner, "Sisters Between"). Without belonging to a religious order as such, engaging either in manual work in the textile industry or teaching, the Beguines followed a certain faith-based pattern of living, out of their own choice and only for as long as they wanted. The tradition was later continued in other forms, such as the *beatas* or *filles seculières* of southern Europe. See Lynch, *Individuals, Families, and Communities in Europe*, 161–63.

61. This specific observation is a comment to the reaction stirred by the French Ursulines by Malone, *Women and Christianity*, 98. All three volumes of Malone provide a fascinating overview of numerous and sometimes outstandingly original initiatives of women in the strangest and most difficult of times.

62. Daly, *Beyond God the Father*, 59.

63. Ibid., 171.

64. Ibid., 172.

65. Ibid., 198; emphasis original.

Yet so far, such sisterhood failed to emerge in any significant way, and the whole talk of sister solidarity has become much less vocal. "Among feminists," observes Anne Spalding, "sisterhood seems to be taken for granted without there being a single concept and praxis for it."[66] Moving away from the essentialist notion of sisterhood, terms such as "difference," in regard to diversity between genders as well as within them, are increasingly employed in working out constructive proposals for imagining and celebrating a better world.[67]

A number of feminists have been interested in exploring the role and the nature of community as a vehicle of right relationships and right life, including the distinction between community and "pseudocommunity."[68] Some have been particularly doubtful of the idea that a "true" community can be made exclusively by women. Grey points out that the isolationism of sisterhood testifies most strongly to the impossibility of any redemption from power-based relationships if one closes one's eyes to women's potential for evil and therefore "[prolongs] the scapegoating process from which women themselves have continually suffered."[69] The temptation of power remains real for women who can easily mirror the same wrongs that the males have been accused of.[70] Grey speaks powerfully of the feminist stance of suffering for and with the church:

> [Staying] in this place of pain for the sake of the Church, for community, for new patterns of relating, out of fidelity to the Spirit, who is the very energy of relation, connection and the vitality of all living things. Not out of a sense of self-inflicted injury, or a futile wallowing in despair, but, first, out of a sense of compassion with the vulnerable God, a ministry to "bear up God in the world" (the root meaning of compassion), and because of the conviction that there is a new way of being Church (or an old one, reclaimed) and this is the only way it will be born. So, "I said

---

66. Spalding, "Being Part of 'Right Relation,'" 52.

67. Copeland, "Difference as a Category," 142.

68. Spalding, "Being Part of 'Right Relation,'" 49. For an example of a feminist vision of the church as a community of welcome, see Russell, "Hot-House Ecclesiology," 48–56.

69. Grey, *Redeeming the Dream*, 163.

70. Grey notes: "There is evidence which we cannot ignore that women in power behave in exactly the same over-assertive, over-ambitious manner as men, even towards other women." Grey, *Redeeming the Dream*, 19.

to my soul, be still" is not the stillness of opting out, of despair, but a free, communally-chosen act of hoping.[71]

The context of such community requires the prophetic gifts of some of its members, a role which has been carried out by a number of feminist theologians, inside faith communities, on their margins, and also outside the organized church. However, as Grey points out, community itself should strive to become a prophet, subverting, in yet another way, the transgression of individualism. "By all means let us give honour to women and men of courage, but let us also take the responsibility of becoming the kinds of communities which challenge society and live by a transforming ethic, communities which 'shine like stars' because they are 'offering the word of life' (1 Peter)."[72]

Such a transformational ethic requires a careful look at another aspect of existence: the organic sphere of human life.

Self as Organic Relationality: Loving Delight

> [A] feminist critique of ecclesiology would take its starting point from the assumption that it is our bodies, women's bodies into which the story of Christ is inscribed and which perform it, without which the story of Christ can in fact not be performed.[73]

"For salvation, you need to have a personal relationship with Jesus." This standard evangelical insistence on the reality and the necessity of a personal relationship with Jesus, so much part of the grammar of baptistic churches, reveals a key to the spirituality of such communities. It could be rightly objected that the terms—"personal relationship with Jesus"—are not even biblical. Yet the phrase itself does speak of a reality as a piece and parcel of Christian life with God which is at the center of the evangelical vision and experience.[74] Connectedness is experienced not only with other human beings, but also with God. Yet although part of virtually every testimony, this "personal relationship" is not much

---

71. Grey, *Prophecy and Mysticism*, 52.
72. Ibid., 62.
73. Watson, "Reconsidering Ecclesiology," 74.
74. See, e.g., Ian Randall's claim that personal relationship with Jesus forms the core of evangelical spirituality in *What a Friend We Have in Jesus*, 23.

explained or elaborated on. Does the organic existence of the Christian play any role in it? Some feminist theologians would suggest it does.

However, bodiliness remains a very problematic area, especially in the realm of theology. The world which the churches inhabit is marked by polymorphous suspicion and ambiguity toward the body.[75] For the West, this has been a long story, tightly connected to the dualist body/soul tendencies in Christianity or the Enlightenment's version of the body/mind split. "Few other human societies have achieved such an effective split between these elements,"[76] and in some ways we cannot help but live in these categories, however consciously attempting to oppose them.[77] In this context, connection between the "body" and the "human being" tends to go via "woman," bodiliness being one of the features of the feminine[78] alongside other qualities such as non-rationality, subjectivity, and nature—a reflection of the parcel of a patriarchal portrayal of women "as misbegotten . . . males."[79] It is not surprising, therefore, that some feminist thinkers have chosen to focus on the psychosocial reality of personhood which transcends bodily limitations, as in this way one can dismiss the way the body seemed to "imprison" women. The relegation of women to the realm of the bodily, and their exclusion from the matters of the mind, encouraged the resistance to such division by focusing on the latter and "[transcending] . . . bodiliness."[80] As Graham puts it, "Many feminists have shown themselves nervous about women's embodiment because it is associated with all manner of patriarchal theories of female inferiority, whether that be hormones, maternal instinct, penis envy or brain deficiency."[81]

The split between the body and the mind has also been encouraged by some developments in contemporary society. Boyce-Tillman points

---

75. Barger, *Chasing Sophia*, 105; see also Sarah Coakley's edited *Religion and the Body* for an extended discussion on the role of the body in different religions with special attention to some practices which shed light on the way "body" and bodily functions in their societal milieu are understood.

76. Boyce-Tillman, "Unconventional Wisdom," 334.

77. Farley, *Just Love*, 115.

78. Bynum, *Fragmentation and Redemption*, 200.

79. Graham, *Words Made Flesh*, 81.

80. Ibid. Another way to critique focus on the body was to equate it with biological essentialism, holding therefore that such an approach submits to the dualist patriarchal framework. (See ibid.)

81. Ibid.

to the examples of the body-mind split such as computer work which "requires most people to use a mind with minimal movements of the body which now has to be exercised separately almost with no mind. Work for the mind and leisure for the body, religion for the spirit if your cosmology includes one."[82] Therefore "the biggest hurdle to overcome is that of dualistic thinking, the notion that we are somehow not really our bodies. We have to put to one side the idea that lurking deep within is the 'real' me and the body is a mere unruly covering for this reality."[83]

Thus, interest in embodiment in feminism has been one way to explore and "redeem" that which had been seen as less valuable than the non-material realm of mind or spirit. Such reflections have highlighted how any "disembodied" talk, that is, a perspective which does not acknowledge its location in the particular context *and* a particular body or bodies, is a serious (self-) deception. However suppressed, our bodies never cease to shape our life, often in unaccounted and therefore even less controllable ways, as with all things unacknowledged or denied, yet ever surfacing. It has been observed that "it is only by understanding the cultural presentation of women's bodies in social space that we can ultimately begin to understand the problem of sexuality and spirituality in human societies."[84]

Some feminists have chosen to see the female body as the locus of identity, such as in the francophone psychoanalytic feminists' notion of "writing the body."[85] The area of the organic is explored in order "to find ways of speaking which cast bodies as the primary source and medium of our relationship to the world, as a kind of 'vantage-point' for experience, while lending diversity and provisionality to such accounts."[86] Yet such a "vantage-point" may be a challenging one given how extensively women have been suffering from the body and soul/spirit/mind split. Often they have seen their bodies as repulsive or problematic, a stance at times quite explicitly affirmed by theologies around them. One's view toward one's body is further complicated when there is no affirmation of its value and beauty by a specific beloved. It is no wonder, therefore, that some women reflect such disregard toward their body by giving it

82. Boyce-Tillman, "Unconventional Wisdom," 334.
83. Isherwood and Stuart, *Introducing Body Theology*, 39.
84. Turner, "Body in Western Society," 25.
85. Jones, "Writing the Body," 247–63.
86. Graham, *Words Made Flesh*, 76.

minimal attention, while others have felt compelled to hide behind fakeness made available by the beauty industry.

Yet the delight in the existence of the embodied self and engagement with the reality beside one's self is a deep force, a source of the joy of living: or as some others term it, the erotic.[87] Thus Sally McFague reflects on the role of "bodily intimations" as one of the ways in which we make sense of life—"looking through the filter of physicality in seeking for God, they highlight the sensuous, bodily, physical, basic aspects of life."[88] This kind of erotic appropriation of life is illustrated by Grey's description of her vision of what is included in redemption:

> What I seek is a concept which includes a dynamic flow of passionate energy, capable of being nourished between persons, through sexual relationships or friendships of which sexuality is a dimension . . . , but also in other ways because it is the *fundamental creative and healing energy of existence*.[89]

A similar theme is echoed by Audre Lorde, who speaks of the erotic as a deep feeling of involvement into whatever one is doing, and therefore a deep sense of "satisfaction and completion."[90] For her, the erotic is "an assertion of the lifeforce of women; of that creative energy empowered, the knowledge and use of which we are now reclaiming in our language, our history, our dancing, our loving, our work, our lives."[91] Lorde also speaks of how the spiritual has been divorced from the erotic, making spirituality "a world of the ascetic who aspires to feel nothing."[92] Lorde is adamant that such delight in life does *not* require marriage, a help of a divine figure, or a consolation of life beyond death: it can come here and now, in spite of whatever patriarchal, "anti-erotic" society might tell.[93]

---

87. For some feminists, this meant working in the area of pointing out the sacredness of female sexuality. This would be the direction of queer/lesbian feminist theology, such as in the liberal feminist work of Isabel Carter Heyward, *The Redemption of God*. Heyward's provocative musings on Christology in erotic terms represent an interesting, if uneasy, subversion of the standard (patriarchal) perception of the relationship between power and eros.

88. McFague, *New Climate for Theology*, 106.

89. Grey, *Redeeming the Dream*, 87; emphasis original.

90. Lorde, *Uses of the Erotic*, n.p.

91. Ibid., n.p.

92. Ibid., n.p.

93. Ibid., n.p.

This is a theme well familiar for the mystics of medieval times, though often avoided by other experts of Christian tradition. By and large, "'knowing God'—despite the passionate and erotic language of the Song of Songs and the mystics—has been much more an affair of mind than of heart or body."[94] Yet, regardless of the widespread discomfort about human bodies, the testimony of the Song of Songs compellingly reminds us that these bodily intimations can be true and real, both in their primary sense of sensuous connection of two human beings, and also in the allegorical interpretation of the relationship between God and God's people. Here one finds mystery as piece and parcel of the "journey into God."[95] Such mystery entails fascination as well as pain, fear, and anxiety for the unknown or unknowable. Yet "in God's light of truth . . . humanity's relationship to all other created things is clarified. In this intimacy with God, there is no attempt to escape our sensual and social experiences; rather they are placed in the light of God and seen in new ways."[96]

Just like reflections on the Song of Songs beyond the metaphor of Christ and the Church, such mystical-erotic language would be largely strange in an evangelical setting. However, the erotic aspect surfaces even when it is not much spoken about. One of the most ready examples may be the presence of the erotic vocabulary and imagery in contemporary worship songs.[97] Whether such public outlet is good could be disputed, but the point here is that eroticism surfaces even in contexts deeply affected by ambivalence toward bodily expressions of devotion. Here a convictional perspective can again be of help in clarifying what is going on. Erotic language in its explicit and implied variants is a way of trying to express, and to cope with, the drives and passions deeply set within our convictions, longing for wholesomeness and healing, the need of which arises from our experiences of injustice, pain, incompletion. In these wounded convictional webs, passions play a very central role. Wendy Farley calls them "deeply rooted dispositions that shape the way we orient ourselves in the world."[98] Like other convictional ele-

---

94. Grey, *Wisdom of Fools*, 12.

95. Grey, *Prophecy and Mysticism*, 57.

96. Barger, *Chasing Sophia*, 181.

97. On the eroticism of charismatic worship, and especially the songs, see Percy, "Sweet Rapture," 71–106.

98. Farley, *Wounding and Healing of Desire*, 45.

ments, they have a habitual nature.[99] Their centrality, especially when they are unaccounted for, makes them dangerous. These "erotic powers" can disintegrate into separate bits and disconnected urges, losing the wholesomeness of the creature made in the image of God, "[leaving] us open to the relentless wiles of the demons."[100] The healing of these wounded convictional webs and their disintegration requires a framework larger than ourselves and a setting where bodily narratives can be learned to be told. If such stories of the bodies, such "disclosures of Divine reality and activity"[101] are to be told, they will have to be learned in the community of faith, interweaving with other sub-narratives in the great fabric of God's and God's people's story. This theme will require further exploration; here, however, several points are offered in the light of the insights gathered so far.

If genital sexual activity, important as it is, is not the center of gravity of life, and if erotic capacity is to be understood as loving delight in God and God's gift of life, then various bodily activities have to be attended to in order to understand the stories our bodies tell. Any theology offered for the life of the church will need to seriously reflect the proposal that "we thus begin with bodily experience, in the narratives of our bodies; but we end, too, with bodily practices and sacraments as the incarnations of the Divine in our midst."[102]

Another important avenue is reflecting on the bodily from the perspective of eco-theology. The connection between women and nature has received considerable thought among feminists both from the negative and positive sides: for one thing, it seemed to some to reinforce the subjugation of women in the same way nature was being subjugated, yet on the other hand, eco-awareness was pointing out the requirement of repairing wrongs done to both nature and women, as well as serving as a constant reminder of the embodied nature of life.[103] Many voices in Christian theology insist on the urgent need of a theology of creation.[104] As Grey points out, it is not about the romantic development of the world

---

99. Ibid., 45–48.

100. Ibid., 77.

101. Graham, *Words Made Flesh*, 86. Graham points to Nancy Eisland's reflections on the sacramental message of disability as one example of the power of such narratives.

102. Ibid., 88.

103. Maeckelberghe, "Across the Generations in Feminist Theology," 67–68.

104. Mary Grey, who I have used extensively in this chapter, is one of the examples.

or the enrichment of human experience; the living out of such embodied theology brings with it ethical demands to rectify the distorted connections, as well as to acknowledge those connections which have gone in a harmful way, to bring about their transformation, participating in their redemption.[105] The way to bring such connections about are various, from giving attention to the language of the architecture of the church's gathering places to holding services (not to speak of baptisms) outside buildings and into various natural settings.

Such a search for wholeness has brought about concrete proposals as to how the organic sphere can be aligned with other aspects of our human existence. "Our desire," notes Margaret A. Farley, "is for an integration that destroys no desire but transforms it, that ignores no love but makes it just, that harms no one, not even ourselves." Yet to what extent can such appropriations be found in actual, flesh-and-blood communities of disciples of Christ? Can the good news about life in abundance emerge "from the blood, sweat and tears and delight of encountering God involved in all creation's travail"[106] (a theme of chapter 9)? Some feminists believe it can, and not only in the communities of sisterhood. Grey offers examples of communities bound in "solidarity, mutuality, interdependence and commitment to the ongoing process of liberation."[107] Beside examples arising directly from women's movements, she discusses groups which I have referred to as baptistic—"House-Church movements, Adventist Groups, and charismatic and pentecostal groups across the denominations."[108] Herself a Catholic, Grey contends that these communities, often characterized by narrow theology (certainly in feminist eyes), can hold a vision sufficient to offer an opposing, prophetic stance which offers hope for the body as well:

> I think we should not underestimate the positive points of such a grouping. In times when the traditional family structure has clearly changed, if not broken down together with even basic traditional morality, I see this group as providing a structure and discipline that gives people of all age ranges a quality experience of community belonging, beyond what they could have imagined. The sheer affection and commitment to community

---

105. Grey, *Wisdom of Fools*, 61–62.
106. Ibid., 129.
107. Ibid.
108. Grey, *Prophecy and Mysticism*, 62–63.

members, the quality of support systems set up, the enthusiasm of the liturgies—this is not lightly to be underestimated. I know many young people set on fire for Christianity, many older people whose marriages were rocky, whose faith was lukewarm or tired, whose lives have been completely regenerated. In the larger scheme of things, these groups have a valued place.[109]

Confirmations such as these strengthen the thread running throughout this book: there seems to be sufficient potential within the baptistic tradition to address issues such as involuntary singleness. However, it will require listening to other voices, including those explored in this chapter; voices which remind that God is on the side of the powerless and the ignored.

When I first set out to explore the subject of singleness in Christian community, I was surprised by the scarcity of theological reflections dealing with (female) singleness on its own terms, both in the life of the church and in second-order theology. Moreover, whereas the church occasionally brings out a popularly-written book or a booklet about strategies for finding that God-given spouse or learning to enjoy life as a single person, theologians are mostly silent: except for feminist theologies. Hence this chapter.

As my task here was not to provide a comprehensive overview of the many manifestations of feminism, many things had to be left unsaid. What this chapter sought to achieve was to discuss some routes to wholeness offered by feminist thought. First, there was a recognition of alternative accounts/perceptions/notions of human personhood arising from women's studies. Notably, they also shape the perceptions of what counts as a life well lived.[110] I also looked at the feminist emphasis on the "community of connections" and the dynamics of those connections. Lastly, I asked whether and how, given the strong baptistic emphasis on the visionary dimension of faith and the necessity of a relationship with God through Jesus, these can be expressed organically.

---

109. Ibid., 64.
110. Meyers, "Feminist Perspectives on the Self."

PART THREE

Costly Companionship
The Shape of the Journey

7

Community and Its Practices

Previous chapters have explored the problems in how both singleness and marriage are understood and practiced throughout the majority of baptistic communities in the Western world. I have argued that singleness and marriage are intrinsically connected, the theology of one inevitably reflected in the theology of the other. However, this connectedness often goes unrecognized. The result is a clash between the two, arising from the supposed concern for the well-being of the one (that is, the institution of marriage) at the expense of the other (singleness).

Are there different, and better, ways of practicing both family and singleness? Perhaps the most straightforward conclusion, in the light of the unequal numbers of men and women in the church, would be a reintroduction of polygyny, as in the case for some early Anabaptists and still some communities today.[1] This would no doubt result in a fascinating piece of research. Indeed, there may not be anything inherently wrong with the practice of polygamy as such; it has been a cultural norm for much of thes period of the writing of Hebrew and Christian Scriptures.[2] Yet it is precisely here that one of the practical obstacles to

---

1. For the practice of polygyny in the Anabaptist Münster, see Haude, *In the Shadow of Savage Wolves*. It is notable that women outnumbered men by three times in Münster at the time when polygyny was introduced (Jelsma, *Frontiers of the Reformation*, 68). Other examples include the current practice of polygyny among Christians such as in an African context (Zeitzen, *Polygamy*, 38ff.) or among Mormons (Altman and Ginat, *Polygamous Families in Contemporary Society*).

2. A careful look confirms that there is no explicit condemnation of polygamy as such in the Bible. For a helpful summary, see Gitari, "Church and Polygamy," 6–7. One important aspect of polygamy is its frequent intention to take care of "unattached"

such a solution lies: being so removed from our cultural norms of today, "it just will not happen," at least not in any foreseeable future and not in a constructive way. Of course, Christianity should not shy away from breaking down cultural norms. Yet cultural norms are not toys easily replaced; altering them is an extremely long and difficult process. One had better have strong reasons to engage in such an uphill battle, and it is here that the attractiveness of a polygynous solution begins to fade. Arguments for the effectiveness of such a model of the structuring of society, although not condemned in the Bible, are not terribly strong either, not to speak of the fact that polygyny is completely out of the picture in the New Testament. That by itself does not disqualify it, but hardly makes a strong case.

Returning back to the connection between our theologies of singleness and marriage, I argue that unless the church learns to foster the practice of singleness, it will continue to fail in its practice of marriage. Both are in need of transformation. Yet what may be those possible avenues of transformation? I have been keeping an eye on three intrinsically interwoven areas of human life: the bodily; communal realities; and visionary concerns of human existence. In this part, I turn specifically to the communal framework. The chapters below demonstrate further that in no way can this "thread" of life be fully separated from the other two, the organic and the visionary.[3] However, there has to be some entry point. The "spot light" on the communal as the way to highlight the holistic picture seems to be the most helpful for the purposes of my argument. As a point of intersection of the experiences of the presence of God and organic joys and troubles, community life is a ready tool for those ecclesial groupings which are the main concern here.

The importance of a larger framework, of a community in which the practices of marriage and singleness are shaped, sounds like a very acceptable idea. Moreover, baptistic ecclesial types tend to be especially marked by strong communal ties and a common vision. However, communal dynamics are a very complex business. As described in the previous chapters, even churches which assume communitarian language can end up ignoring important deficiency points in their actual communitarian expressions and may remain blind to the conflicting claims

---

people by the ties available through the extended family. The same intention is reappropriated in this work, although not through the vehicle of polygamous structures.

3. McClendon, *Ethics*, 75–78.

they seem to be holding. In his discussion of singleness and the great failure of the church in addressing and upholding it, Wilson calls, once again, for a different community—a "radically distinctive Christian community where structures exist to empower members to befriend one another in relationships of Christian love and support, irrespective of one's marital status or blood ties."[4] The problem which precludes the formation of such community, in Wilson's view, is that many churches function "in a very hierarchical and rationalistic way," like a political party, consisting of "The Electorate" (those who are rather disinterested in the church, although loosely belonging to it), "The Party Faithful" (those who are supportive of the structure), "Voluntary Workers" (self-explanatory), "The Legislature" (e.g., the elders), and "The Executive" (often salaried).[5] Such a system is encouraged, even in relatively small Christian communities, by the "growing professionalism of pastoral care." Friendship becomes impossible, as it would involve "crossing professional boundaries." Boundaries, though mostly unspoken, are clear and rigid. "The most a professional can really do is to be *friendly* which is certainly better than nothing, but quite different from actually being a person's *friend*."[6] Similarly to other communitarians, Wilson proposes removing the individual from the center and focusing on the Christian community, empowered by the Spirit, for the sake of together forming the sign of the gospel.

Yet how does such theologically accurate statement become a communal reality? The language of the Spirit, quite familiar to the communities which are my focus here, suffers from the dominance of individualistic grammar. In contrast to much of biblical material,[7] the individual remains the primary level of discourse and interpretation of reality even if the importance of community is theoretically acknowledged. In turn, the role of community is incessantly underestimated. Take the aforementioned "empowerment by the Spirit": any look at the theological material, both popular and academic, will demonstrate how habitually it is understood in strictly individual terms.[8] Ever-obscure if

---

4. Wilson, *Being Single*, 183.

5. Ibid., 183–86. For an Eastern European, this is a curious reminder of Communist party structures.

6. All quotations from ibid., 186; emphasis original.

7. Kallenberg, "All Suffer," 2–6.

8. Ibid., 2–9.

not outright Gnostic, the concept of the reality of the power of the Spirit continues to hold theoretical significance with very little implementation in the life of the believing community and its members:

> We are only fooling ourselves (not to mention attempting to fool outsiders) when we maintain in the absence of concrete practical differences between our community and others' that, nevertheless, talk about the Spirit's presence must mean "something." No. If our theology is to resonate with the NT and second-century apologists, we must ground our pneumatological statements in concrete descriptions of community life.[9]

It is because of these concerns that I turn to another perspective and a different conceptual language. The idea of community and its practices is closely related to a larger understanding of the way the universe works, from its smallest particles to macro-phenomena. It may seem to be far from my theme, but as with all philosophy, churches are influenced by it even if they are not aware of how one or other explanation of the workings of the world shapes, among other things, their retelling of the Christian story and their approach to various ethical issues. Thus, I turn next to the notion of metaphysical holism, suggesting that such conceptual language provides a helpful corrective to the understanding of the function and significance of community and its individuals.[10]

Community as an Emergent Structure

> There is a longing in my heart not just for personal wholeness and oneness with a husband but also for being woven into a community of people whose whole is greater than the sum of the parts, whose purpose is bigger than itself.[11]

---

9. Ibid., 8.

10 What I mean by "metaphysical holism" is a cluster of related conceptual developments involving rejection of metaphysical atomisms of various sorts, the recognition of the emergence of new entities and causal processes, and downward causation of these higher-level processes. I was first introduced to the concept and the theory of metaphysical holism by Nancey Murphy, and am grateful for her help in finding my way through the tangle of this very complex discussion.

11. Gilliam, *Revelations of a Single Woman*, 189.

Although ideas about how there is a certain potential in things to evolve and new, radically different things to emerge[12] have been present here and there in the field of science and philosophy since ancient times, they were more-or-less completely discarded in the face of fascinatingly rapid progress in early modern physics. Certain optimism was in the air that the key to the understanding of the universe was at hand. All the complex questions about the make-up of the universe could be answered by proper scientific investigation—which, it was assumed, was about reducing all that is to basic physical particles and forces. Such an approach came to be known as reductionism.[13]

What such reduction assumes went much further than methodology in the sciences. It presumes that it is the smallest building blocks of the universe that determine the behaviour of the "stuff"[14] on the higher levels of complexity. In other words, all that happens in the world is caused bottom-up—that is, it is wholly determined by the properties of the constituents on the lower level of complexity, eventually boiling down to physics. The whole, then, is the sum of its parts, something which could be derived from, reduced to, and accounted for using the vocabulary and the concepts of, the level of its composite parts.[15] Christian community would be one such example: from the reductionist point of view, the properties of this entity could be entirely explained by properties possessed by the individuals constituting it (and, if one did not stop here, individuals, in their turn, could be explained by their own composite parts all the way down to the most basic physical properties).

It would certainly be difficult to argue that this is not true—*in part*. The whole cannot be explained without taking into account its constituent parts. However, with further developments in the philosophy of sci-

12. The terms can be confusing indeed. "Emergence," for example, has been used in several distinct ways and, for clarity's sake, I will use it as a synonym for "anti-reductionism."

13. On different expressions of reductionism, see Murphy and Brown, *Did My Neurons Make Me Do It?* 47–48; Stoeger and Murphy, *Evolution and Emergence*, esp. Murphy's chapter "Reductionism: How Did We Fall into It," 19–39.

14. "Stuff" is the word used quite frequently by emergentist scholars, thereby reflecting the difficulty of finding an adequate term to describe the reality which has to refer both to objects such as electrons and, for example, consciousness. Cf. Clayton, "Conceptual Foundations of Emergence Theory," 3–4; see also the hierarchy of structure presented by Ellis, "On the Nature of Emergent Reality," 80; and an especially helpful discussion by Peacocke, "Emergence, Mind, and Divine Action," 258–61.

15. Ellis, "On the Nature of Emergent Reality," 86.

ence, including its relation to theology, complex relationships between entities studied by different disciplines prompted some to suggest that the properties on the more complex levels could not be described or explained simply by referring to those on the lower level of complexity. This is an understanding especially held by a number of researchers working on the connection between the mind and the physical world. These more complex levels were characterized by new—emergent—properties and behaviours which did not seem to be reducible to the lower level when it came to explaining them. Thus, if atomism was insufficient to explain these mereological dynamics, then the life of each of those levels of complexity needed to be imagined and described differently: more holistically, acknowledging the way the parts were affected by each other and by the whole. For one thing, it meant that each level could be described as having a distinct and equally "real" life of its own:

> There is no sense in which, for example, subatomic particles—with their properties—are to be regarded as "more real" than, say, a bacterial cell, a living organism, or a human person. New and distinctive kinds of realities at the higher levels of complexity may properly be said to have *emerged*. This can occur with respect either to moving synchronically up the ladder of complexity or diachronically through cosmic and biological evolutionary history.[16]

The same would apply to social realities; thus it can be argued that various social constructs are no less real than any biological or physical entities.

The way these different levels of complexity relate is often described as involving downward causation. The concept conveys an understanding that not only more basic levels account for the developments higher in the system, but that the whole also has causality in relation to part, and that properties which emerge on a higher level can in their turn affect the life of the next lower level. A ready example of such causality would be observed by neuroscientists in the way mental processes seem to be able to affect the physical conditions of the brain, suggesting that although genetic and neural processes play an essential role in shaping the behaviour of human beings, morality of humans could not be explained as a sum total of genetic factors. In fact, neuroscience explores how habits can in their turn affect the brain itself in the long term;

---

16. Peacocke, "Emergence, Mind, and Divine Action," 259; emphasis original.

this is exactly what a "top-down" or downward causation represents.[17] Similarly, community, far from being an aggregate of individuals and somehow less real than individuals, represents an "irreducible social reality"[18] and has a critical role in determining the identity and functioning of the individuals that belong to it. Communal dynamics then can be shown to possess properties which cannot be derived from its elements, i.e., persons comprising a particular community: "the Body of Christ emerges from the system of individuals that embodies a particular form of life."[19]

What such reconceptualisation achieves is that it points to the way emergent communal properties influence, in a top-down fashion, the life of individual believers—positively as well as negatively.[20] Some of those negative influences have been observed in the preceding chapters: as any social reality, the church is capable of ignoring and discouraging certain members and applying partial treatment of others. However, the inevitability of such top-down influence and the possibility of the positive points to the way the presence of the Spirit in the life of the church can create emergent phenomena in ways which then can transform individual lives: "there is a patternedness and reality to the whole that must itself display Christlikeness if we are to intelligibly say that the Spirit is present among us."[21] One way to describe it would be to suggest the "catalytic effect of a kenotic community,"[22] a concept to be explored more fully in chapter 9: "given the intactness of the normal neural substrates (as yet not fully spelled out), kenotic capacities may be enlarged and enhanced by participation in a kenotic community, i.e., a top-down effect."[23]

---

17. Jeeves, "Nature of Persons," 87.

18. Kallenberg, "All Suffer," 20.

19. Ibid., 19. Another way to speak about emergent properties is employing systems-theory approaches, currently explored by authors coming from a variety of disciplines. Murphy and Brown, *Did My Neurons Make Me Do It?* esp. 67–104. For one interpretation of systems theory for missiological purposes, see Hiebert, *Gospel in Human Contexts*, chap. 6, "Systems Approach," 127–59.

20. Kallenberg, "All Suffer," 19. A similar concept is the notion of peer pressure, with its capacity to bring about both positive and negative effects.

21. Ibid., 20.

22. Jeeves, "Nature of Persons," 88.

23. Ibid., 74.

Viewed thus, transformation becomes a two-way process: not only are there certain influences which an individual believer, or a smaller group in a large church, can apply in order to make some difference, but community as a whole exerts its downward causal powers which affect individual believers: "*Multiple top-down action* as well as bottom-up action *enables the self-organisation of complex systems*, in so far as it enables higher levels to coordinate action at lower levels which otherwise would not have occurred."[24] The potential of applying these ideas to community life lies precisely in the insistence that the reality of a more complex level is something which could not have been derived from the properties of the components of the lower level—that is, individuals, who themselves are to be understood as dynamic systems.

Such relationship between the individuals and the community they form is something that Terrence W. Deacon calls "pull of yet unrealized possibility";[25] something that can bring transformational developments of an unexpected nature.[26] Yet how does this pull actually become realized? It is here that another concept employed in the field of metaphysical holism can shed light. Alongside the notion of emergence, philosophers refer to the concept of supervenience. In a very basic definition, it can be said that for A to supervene on B means for A to be dependent on B, but not reducible to it.[27] As Murphy puts it,

> Holism recognises that in many systems there are dynamic interactions between parts and wholes,—that is, there are both bottom-up and top-down causal influences. In fact, the very nature of parts often has to be reconceived in relational and functional terms. For example, an animal is composed of functional systems such as the circulatory and digestive systems, that can only be what they are *as* components of the organisms. In systems of this sort (in contrast to mere aggregates such as a pile of sand and mechanisms such as clocks) the system manifests "emergent"

24. Ellis, "On the Nature of Emergent Reality," 89; emphasis original.

25. Deacon, "Emergence: The Hole at the Wheel's Hub," 144.

26. For an example of Baptist thinking on these lines in the United States, see Gunderson, "Emergent Wholeness," 360–67.

27. Kallenberg, "All Suffer," 26. For the purposes of this work, I am employing a simple definition of supervenience which emphasises dependence (i.e., of the higher-level properties on the lower-level properties) without reduction; however, it has to be noted that the notion of supervenience, although used widely, does not have a single agreed definition. For a summary of the development of the term, see, e.g., Murphy and Brown, *Did My Neurons Make Me Do It?* 205–9.

properties and causal capacities that cannot be reduced to the properties or causal capacities of their components. The description of these higher-level systems calls for new concepts (e.g., social concepts) that can be said to "supervene" on concepts from the lower-level (e.g., personal characteristics and actions). So, for example, a community can be tight-knit, which an individual cannot. But there must be a variety of behaviours and traits of the individuals that warrant the community being described as tight-knit.[28]

What it means for the witness of the Christian community is that for Christian discourse to be intelligible, the form of life embodied by a Christian community *must* exist in order for the claims about God's presence, God's deliverance, happiness provided by God, church as a true family to be true: "descriptions of God's presence supervene upon descriptions of the believing community's form of life."[29]

There are different ways to evaluate the reality and the degree of such embodiment. What I chose to do here is to look at tradition-laden practices which constitute a particular form of life called the church. As practices are linked to certain virtues (or vices![30]), they are a condition necessary for the church's claims about itself and the reality of God to be truthful. Therefore next I explore the concept of practices and examine their potential for reconsidering and realigning the church's understanding of singleness and the support it should provide to those who are not directly participating in the practice of marriage.

The Practice of Witnessing to the Realm of God: Vision and Virtues

> When we are comforted by the presence in our lives of others who are committed to giving us affectionate and caring guidance, we will be less likely to go off on unhealthy tangents, including painful love relationships. This is not about licking wounds; this is about being grounded in some-

---

28. Nancey Murphy, personal communication, 26 January 2011.
29. Kallenberg, "All Suffer," 26; emphasis removed. In a helpful example of Murphy, a killing of a sheep in a similar fashion could be described on several different levels, which could include a biological explanation of what is taking place as well as a religious one, where the man sacrificing the sheep turns out to be doing it to appease a god. In this case, the religious explanation would supervene upon the biological. Personal communication, 25 January 2011.
30. I owe this insight to Parush R. Parushev.

thing genuine and real at the root of our lives, something that models right and wholesome love. Intentional community is where we can find it.[31]

First of all, what exactly is meant here by "practice"? The word itself can be employed to refer to activities as varied as singing in a choir, being a dentist, or regular attendance at church services. I will, however, use the concept as described by Alasdair MacIntyre, for who a practice is

> any coherent and complex form of socially established cooperative human activity through which goods internal to that form of activity are realized in the course of trying to achieve those standards of excellence [that is, virtues] which are appropriate to, and partially definitive of, that form of activity, with the result that human powers to achieve excellence, and human conceptions of the ends and goods involved, are systematically extended.[32]

One of the parameters of practices is their historical and contextual grounding, making them therefore necessarily intricate activities aimed at certain goals and requiring a considerable degree of expertise gleaned from other participants, past and present, for achieving those goals. Growing in such expertise is what makes one a genuine participant of a particular practice. Practices are not merely habits, such as brushing one's teeth twice a day, reading before sleep, or even greeting one another with the holy kiss in the church. These do not presuppose progress and growth in the particular action, and thus do not qualify here as "practices." However, similarlto habits, practices are an inseparable part of an individual life. They are the "stuff" without which any talk of individual personality is essentially meaningless. Indeed, "in a strict sense there is no such thing as 'individual practice' at all; the phrase is an abstraction from a tissue of relational conduct."[33]

That said, the way people engage in various practices reflects varying distances from other people and communal life as such. The loners and the mavericks are just as much a part of this communal framework as those at the core of the community's activities. At times, people prefer-

31. Sheridan, *Unwilling Celibates*, 36.

32. MacIntyre, *After Virtue*, 187. There are numerous works exploring the meaning and the implications of this complex definition. On the benefit of MacIntyre's argument for the further development of the Christian tradition, see esp. Murphy, Kallenberg, and Nation, *Virtues and Practices in the Christian Tradition*, and McClendon, *Ethics*, 167–91.

33. Connell, *Gender and Power*, 222.

ring the margins have a prophetic role to play; the critique they provide may be extremely valuable. Yet for them, as much as for other members, community of some sort is an indispensable web[34] in which particular skills, or virtues, can be cultivated in their narrative connectedness.[35]

The contextual grounding also presupposes that practices always belong to a certain tradition—in MacIntyre's words, a certain "historically extended, socially embodied argument."[36] What the "argument" is about is the "goods" which constitute the tradition; in other words, the goals which the tradition deems worth pursuing. These goals may be adjusted over time; they "themselves are transmuted by the history of the activity."[37] However, for a practice to be a practice, there will always be goals, for it is the visionary dimension of a practice which sustains it and gives it shape. From a non-reductionist point of view,

> that particular actions derive their character as parts of larger wholes is a point of view alien to our dominant ways of thinking and yet one which it is necessary at least to consider if we are to begin to understand how a life may be more than a sequence of individual actions and episodes.[38]

The social embodiment of this argument presupposes a strong narrative dimension. Practitioners internalize, in various ways, the developing story of why certain goals are central, and how they can be reached. The "why" has to do with the overall (narrative-shaped) understanding of the goal of human life, and is accordingly reflected in the set of practices developed in a form of life. The "how" is reflected in the virtues which become associated with particular practices; in other words, certain skills, or personal and communal qualities, which are recognized as needed for the successful participation in a practice. These virtues are intrinsically linked to the context in which a practice takes place and

---

34. This web will have an institutional expression of one sort or another: see MacIntyre, *After Virtue*, 194–95.

35. It is precisely this web and its narrative connectedness that preserves the virtues from the danger, out of very good intentions and with much effort, of concentrating on a context-less virtue, thereby potentially turning it into something harmful. I owe this insight to Farley, in *Wounding and Healing of Desire*, 77.

36. MacIntyre, *After Virtue*, 222.

37. Ibid., 194. The "argument," therefore, entails conflicting interpretations of the goods or the goals as a necessary constitutionary element of a tradition.

38. Ibid., 204.

the narrative which provides it with the meaning and links it with other practices.[39]

In order to be counted as a virtue, it has to be characterized by a sufficient degree of stability. A certain virtue has to be a consistent feature of one's character (and indeed the character of a particular community) if it is to be called a virtue. An accidental show of kindness, hospitality, courage, or any other quality held to be a virtue by Christian tradition, may provide a spur to rethink things and occasionally even lead to significant life changes, but it is only when it becomes a permanent feature in one's life that it becomes a virtue. Alongside the virtues, there are also vices—those qualities of a stable nature which are detrimental to the practice's achievement of its goals. Moreover, virtues can also be feigned.[40] What seemed like kindness may turn out to be an attempt to ensure self-directed gain; patience may turn out to be passivity, disinterest or fear. Yet, as is usual with forgeries, falsifications will be eventually recognized and disclosed as qualities which are detrimental to the progress of the practice.

The quality of those virtues constitutes the test of a tradition, its feasibility, superiority, and sustainability. Thus one key virtue needed for a successful participation in the practices, claims MacIntyre, is "the virtue of having an adequate sense of the traditions to which one belongs or which confront one."[41] The absence of this virtue is exactly the problem identified in this book: singleness presents a problem because of the confusion of the allegiances to the Christian tradition and the fragmented remains of a worldview of Enlightenment, with strong hedonistic undertones.

The way practices are aligned is therefore crucial for their progress. There is more than one way to align them, and indeed a change in context may require a reconfiguration of the practices in terms of their achievement of the goals set by the tradition; but coherence must be a feature of the set of practices belonging to a particular life form. MacIntyre's claim is that

---

39. Thus care needs to be taken to recognise the context. The virtue of courage for a Greek philosopher is something completely different, indeed, opposite, to the courage of Jesus Christ in his death on a cross (cf. Macintyre, *Short History of Ethics*, 66–67).

40. MacIntyre, *After Virtue*, 241.

41. Ibid., 223.

unless there is a *telos* which transcends the limited goods of practices by constituting the good of a whole human life, the good of human life conceived as a unity, it will *both* be the case that a certain subversive arbitrariness will invade the moral life *and* that we shall be unable to specify the context of certain virtues adequately. These two considerations are reinforced by a third: that there is at least one virtue recognised by the tradition which cannot be specified at all except with reference to the wholeness of a human life—the virtue of integrity or constancy . . . This notion of singleness of purpose in a whole life can have no application unless that of a whole life does.[42]

The Complex Practice of Witnessing to God's Realm

The concept of practices thus understood entails a certain structure of how they are aligned in the case of the baptistic perspective on the church. The central, or complex, practice would be the one that holds the disciples together, and holds them not for their own sake, but in expectation and the challenge of transformation into the newness brought by the resurrection of Christ.[43] The purpose of this overarching practice can be formulated as being the sign—or, following John Howard Yoder, a foretaste—of the realm of God, thereby inviting others to join in the life of that realm.[44] It can be named, following McClendon, the practice of community formation,[45] or as I have chosen here, the practice of witnessing to God's realm. Such witness, in biblical understanding, is essentially communal.[46] If witnessing to God's realm is seen as the core practice, then all other and various churchly practices—such as worship, social outreach, or preaching—constitute the simpler practices, or what Murphy names subpractices,[47] of the Christian tradition.

This is where the practice of marriage and family belongs too, as do some forms of single living.[48] It could be argued that the practice of

---

42. Ibid.; emphasis original.

43. MClendon, *Doctrine*, 103ff.

44. See Yoder, *For the Nations*, 228. Cf. also Murphy, "Using MacIntyre's Method in Christian Ethics," 32.

45. McClendon, *Ethics*, 221.

46. For one description of the features of this complex practice, see Yoder, *Body Politics*.

47. Murphy, "Using MacIntyre's Method in Christian Ethics," 39.

48. Consecrated celibacy would be the clearest and the most common example

marriage is not essential to the life of the church. Whereas it is impossible to imagine a church without a practice of worship, one can easily imagine—and history provides examples of—Christian communities not engaged in marriage, such as the religious, or where married people constitute an insignificant minority and the encounter with the practice of marriage for that community is therefore peripheral. Community may be impoverished by the absence of different generations, but then the latter can be present in more creative structures by fostering orphans, engaging with young people, caring for the elderly, all possibly done without family ties. Indeed, the practice of marriage can be seriously doubted as to its beneficial nature, especially given how it has usurped a role more central than it would be legitimate, sometimes claiming, in very real terms, to be what is meant here by the central practice of the church. The virtues that it was supposed to nurture have at times turned into vices. Some more radical voices have therefore found it to be entirely beyond redemption.

However, the way forward seems hardly to be in rejecting the practice of marriage and family as such. If it is discovered to be seriously deficient, the primary Christian response is that of engaging in redeeming it.[49] A thorough attempt to propose possible routes of redemption is a separate project undertaken by others.[50] Here I simply point, by way of illustration, to some markers which would be especially tightly linked with the challenge of singleness, all in the context of the overarching practice of witnessing to God's realm.

Re-Christianising marriage would surely require attending to the challenge of the narrative which sustains the life of this practice.[51] Practices always cohere around a certain ultimate loyalty which can be called God or which fulfills the function of a divinity. I have attempted to show how powerful the gods of culture seem to be in shaping the narrative, both of the Western culture, and the church. Finding a proper place for the practice of Christian marriage, therefore, requires evaluating it from the perspective of the central practice of the witness to God's realm and therefore being subsumed by the overarching framework of

---

of singleness as a practice. Much of involuntary singleness, in contrast, would not be constituting a practice but more accurately could be described as a state or a situation.

49. McClendon, *Ethics*, 181–82.

50. E.g., Clapp, *Families at the Crossroads*; McCarthy, *Sex and Love in the Home*.

51. McClendon, *Ethics*, 176–77.

the community—or family—of the disciples of Jesus, as was the case with the early Christian practice of marriage.

The modern version of the practice of marriage has frequently bred the vice of selfishness. In this context, hospitality can be seen as a key virtue of the *Christian* practice of marriage, arising out of the narrative understanding of the purpose of family:

> The church is not interested in community simply for family's sake. We practice hospitality and build community because the story of Israel and Jesus calls for it. The necessity of hospitality converts our homes from insulated havens into adventurous mission bases. Hospitality gives families a purpose beyond themselves. They exist to serve God and the world through the church.[52]

Among the ways the skills of hospitality can be nurtured, two seem to be particularly important for the purposes of my theme. One of them is the most basic expression of hospitality: that of sharing a meal. Theological implications of taking the common meal seriously are profound and possess an enormous potential, although, sadly, ignored too often.[53] Enjoyment of a meal together is one of the most common activities among friends, and this is not by accident: "the pleasure of good food and conversation with people one enjoys and trusts is symbolic of fulfilment at a very deep level . . . Sharing of food, like friendship itself, is potentially a more inclusive phenomenon than sex."[54] The longing for such an inclusion and deep connection is expressed in these words of a single woman: "My dream is that if I am elderly and single . . . people will drop by my house a lot, and I will be often at my friends' families' homes—without needing appointments for either . . . that there will be a feeling of safety, comfort, and familiarity."[55]

Such expression of hospitality will depend on how the believing community as a whole responds to the call of embodying the hospitality

---

52. Clapp, *Families at the Crossroads*, 162. Although some Bible translations urge to "practice hospitality" in Rom 12:13 (NIV, e.g.), hospitality would be better understood as a virtue, as reflected in some other translations which urge, in the same verse, to "extend" (NRSV), "be given to" (KJV and ASV), "seek to show" (ESV) hospitality or "pursuing" it (New Advent Bible).

53. On the interconnections between Anabaptist theology and the practice of the Lord's Table, see Kreider, *Communion Shapes Character*.

54. McFague, *Models of God*, 167.

55. Gilliam, *Revelations of a Single Woman*, 191–92.

of God.[56] The celebration of the Eucharist—also called Communion or the Lord's Supper[57]—ought to be its definitive expression, although so often it has become a highly formal activity without so much as a hint of anything resembling a real intake and enjoyment of food and the intimacy with other people with which common meals would be associated.

Another aspect where hospitality is deeply needed is in the role of the church in bringing up the next generation. Those baptistic churches which have been emphasising their conviction regarding the baptism of (adult) believers have also to face a gaping hole in terms of the theology of children. However, the baptistic view of the church as community implies that, in a very real sense, the children belong not only to parents, but to the whole community. Hospitality is to be extended toward children, loving them as such—as God's precious gifts—over against the consumer approach of society which tends to treat children as commodities. Parents would do well to recognize that they need the help of others—including childless people—in raising their children, echoing the witness of the monastic tradition at its best, giving witness that *all* believers are called to be fathers and mothers in many ways, and this calling has to transcend familial bonds. Such hospitality can be expressed in creative ways and could be measured (in positive terms as well as negative), at least in some small way, by the way activities such as Mother's Day or "Mothering Sunday" services are employed (or not).[58]

Thus,

> the Christian life represents an entirely different kind of homelessness, where we accept hospitality as a gift and settle into a place. Christian singleness and marriage alike form an alternative. In each, we are called to resist self-serving habits, to give ourselves over to the needs of others, and to be critical of our own desires. [. . .] We should accept that it is a mark against our faithfulness when we lack the kind of communities that can sustain the single life as one that is rich in friendship, intimacy, purpose, and love.[59]

---

56. Rossi, "Sojourners, Guests, and Strangers," 121–31.

57. For the usage of the three terms to describe this practice and a helpful reflection on the implications of a deeper Eucharistic theology for the life of the church and, see Jones, *Shared Meal and a Common Table*.

58. Such events are frequently an uncomfortable, if not disturbing, experience, to childless or single people. See, e.g., "Single-Minded: Single People in the Church," 13.

59. McCarthy, *The Good Life*, 61.

Much needs to be rethought and transformed in the practice of marriage and family within the context of the church. Much remains unsaid here, given that it is not marriage but singleness—not as a practice, but as a state—which is the focus, though the two are interrelated. The above, hopefully, pointed to the importance of the way the church engages in practices such as marriage. The implications of the discussion held in this chapter on the concepts of practice and virtues will be explored further. Before that, however, I will revisit the theme of the body in the context of the insights gained so far. In what ways can a single life find meaning in its bodily expressions? In what ways can it be called truly happy, truly good?

Goodness of Life and the Theology of Bodiliness

> That God loves human creatures in their fullness and that human beings are called to love God fully is hardly a topic of debate in theology ... What is more difficult to see is the place of embodied sexual desire and erotic yearning in this relationship. It is surely a part of it—but how?[60]

> "I believe in the resurrection of the body" (from the Apostles' Creed).

Now comes the right moment to address the most controversial and frustrating issue related to singlehood: the bodily matter of human existence, including its sexual expression. One can almost put an equality sign between these two, "the bodily" and "sex": so little of essence is said in regard to the body which would *not* be about its sexuality. It is intentional, however, that I address it explicitly only at this stage.

Why Only Now?

The subject of sexuality is often seen as the ultimate "can of worms" for many a church community, but this is not the primary reason for the issue to be addressed only at this point. True, the topic of sexuality is one of the most explosive materials to be released in the church; thus the common reaction of the church has often been to limit the whole discussion to sex being reserved for marriage (in more conservative circles) or to point to the respect for freedom of choice and the privacy of the

---

60. Jones, afterword to *Embrace of Eros*, 302.

individual (in more liberal communities).[61] Such restriction of the topic is often an indication of fear and a lack of concern for persons struggling with their—and others'—sexuality. Moreover, for much of its history the church could not be said to have nurtured a positive message in relation to the human body:[62] for those with legitimate sexual relations, the body could be a pragmatic tool for producing progeny, but otherwise a site of *sarx*, all things opposite to salvation. No wonder that, in the words of one single woman, "I began to feel more comfortable in my own body [only] after leaving the church."[63]

However, there are serious reasons why sex should not be a central question for the church when discussing singleness. For one thing, keeping sexual issues away from the forefront of the church's agenda echoes the minor role sex plays in the Christian Scriptures, the New Testament particularly.[64] At the time of a "sexually *disoriented*"[65] culture, this is one of the ways the church can present a powerful witness by providing a space where sex does not rule the agenda—to the relief not only of the unwillingly single people, but also the asexuals and many a married couple feeling the pressure to "perform to the standard."[66] In this sense, the church can help paint a more accurate picture of the nodes connecting the network of a human life. When the church refuses to concentrate on sexual matters for *this* reason, it is responding to its prophetic task, which in this case consists of pointing out the illusion that sexual intercourse is a self-evident necessity for a fulfilled life at all times and places. In contrast to what one may conclude from being bombarded by the subtle-and-not-so subtle suggestions of sex as *the* driving force, many human beings spend considerable periods of their lives without

---

61. Some churches will insist on celibacy as a non-negotiable requirement for single believers, whereas others will want to talk about responsibility and various degrees of commitment. However, even those that will allow for responsible sexual relationships in a non-marital context will see some of their single members struggling with various aspects of such relationships, such as, obviously, the shortage of available partners, irregularity, or indefiniteness of such arrangements.

62. For a critical look, see, e.g., Lawrence, *Sexual Liberation*.

63. A former Baptist, age 28, quoted in Sharma, "When Young Women Say 'Yes,'" 81.

64. Cahill, "Sexuality, Christian Theology," 350.

65. Grenz, *Sexual Ethics*, 1; emphasis original.

66. As pointed out by researchers, couples indeed can suffer from the guilt for not having an exciting enough sexual life. Cossman, *Sexual Citizens*, 80–83; Brunner, "Low-Sex Marriages."

engaging in sexual acts. Moreover, sexuality cannot be fully understood without the larger framework of communities shaping one's so-called private life. It is, as Hauerwas has noted, a public matter.[67]

Postponing the discussion does not entail, however, that sexuality is minor in terms of significance—an error committed only too often by the church historical and contemporary. For many human beings, sexuality is of tremendous importance, even though they may prefer not to admit it. It is not only naïve to think that saying "don't do it" will suffice; it is also extremely insensitive.

> It's a bit like being taken to a huge sweet counter where all these amazing goodies are on display, under glass of course, and you're told by the person who's taken you there, who incidentally is quite at liberty to stuff his face full, that you can have a good look at them all, you're just not allowed to eat any![68]

That it does not hold is also demonstrated practically, as can be seen from the numbers of instances of sex before marriage or extramarital activities taking place in the context of the church.[69] The starting point should be admitting that herein lies an immense challenge which cannot be taken lightly. If the church shuns discussions of sexuality, or limits them to the Bible study group for wives and husbands, its members (especially those without husbands or wives) will learn of it in other ways: from other people, through books, through TV, and perhaps especially through the information available on the internet. Convictions will be formed not reflectively, but in much more accidental ways which will make this part of one's convictional set much less coherent and, at times, downright destructive.

---

67. Hauerwas, *Community of Character*, 189. See also the whole chapter, "Sex in Public: Toward a Christian Ethic of Sex," 175–95.

68. Keay, *Letters from a Solo Survivor*, 141. Reproduced by permission of Hodder & Stoughton.

69. Given the sensitivity of the issue, the data is, unsurprisingly, scarce. However, closer acquaintance with the life of particular churches would often reveal vigorous dynamics of a sexual nature hiding under the surface of silence. For the resources indicating or documenting the extent of sexual issues in the context of the church, see Grams and Parushev, "Comparative Mapping," 51, 56–60, on Eastern European Baptist communities and the concern for problems related to sexuality; Charles, "(Almost) Everyone's Doing It," 65–69, on the extent of sexual activity among unmarried professing Christians which hardly differs from that of non-Christians; Miller, "What Pastors Are Saying," for a Northern American account.

Thus the need to address bodily matters is certainly there, albeit in a different framework than they are addressed in society. At this point, it is helpful to recall the notion of supervenience, with the reminder that although life is much more than our sexuality, our spirituality, our social practices, our attempts for doctrinal systematisation of theology, all supervene on our being organic, sexual creatures. Here, the church needs the theology of sexuality to be kept in a creative tension: on the one hand, acknowledging that sex is not the sum total of all things; nor can other aspects of our life be explained by sexual urges in a Freudian manner. Yet on the other hand, to act as if sexuality is insignificant will simply not hold: people are sexual beings whether they are married or not; and whether they engage in sexual acts or not.

Sexuality Minus Sexual Acts

Many theologians and Christian writers focusing on the issue of singleness realize the need for this tension, and suggest reflecting not on sexual acts *per se*, but on the ingrained sexuality of human beings. "Sexuality can have physical, psychological, emotional, intellectual, spiritual, personal, and social dimensions."[70] A characteristically evangelical way to explain it would be to suggest that "singleness was never meant to be a denial of sexuality, but simply another form of its expression."[71] Yet what on earth is it supposed to mean exactly, given that the author of this quotation, like many others, is clear that sexual acts should be reserved within the context of the marriage covenant? Further explanation does not really help: "For married people, their relationship with their spouse is where the primary expression of community, gender and sexuality occurs. For single people, their relationships within the church are the main arena for sexual expression."[72] If anything, such dualism not only does not make it any more concrete, but even more frightening: engaging in sexual expressions in the public arena of the church is hardly an encouraging prospect.

Another, more imaginative, suggestion (echoing some of the insights of chapter 6) comes from a New Testament scholar Stephen

---

70. Farley, *Just Love*, 159.
71. Aune, *Single Women*, 140.
72. Ibid., 140.

Barton, who proposes to see sexuality in the framework of "a theology of God's creation as God's play." Such a theology

> points us to a God who in the playfulness of divine grace has made us as embodied persons, who desires us with a holy desire, and who therefore makes us desirable and able to desire one another. It is in that desirability and ability to desire another which come from God as grace, which we are able to communicate through our bodies in a great variety of ways [including our relating to God].[73]

However, this still leaves a great deal of vagueness about how our sexuality is, or can be, actually expressed apart from genital activity. Such vagueness is not helped by the long-standing partitioning of the human being into body and soul, body and mind, or any other variations.[74] Once such separation is made, it becomes very difficult (if not impossible) to keep an equal balance between affirming the needs and potential of the soul *and* body. What would happen, however, if instead of such division into "bits," of dualist or tripartite notions of human nature, a different notion would be employed, which would see the body as the locus of all the activities which we consider spiritual?

To propose the abolition of the categories of soul and body is a dangerous move, for the "attack on soul" is commonly taken, consciously or subconsciously, as an attack on God. Thus clarification must be made concerning the word "soul" itself. Undoubtedly, it is part of the vocabulary both in the case of the Bible and of the church. The issue here, however, is what is implied as the word is used, and these usages can be radically different. Biblical scholars such as Joel Green would point out how current connotations of the term "soul" are quite different from the biblical world,[75] and that Scripture "points predominantly in the direction of a monist account of human nature."[76]

On this issue, the interests from fields as diverse as biblical studies, neuroscience, and philosophy converge. Whereas it may be argued that the absence of a separate substance which could be called "soul" means

---

73. Barton, *Life Together*, 80; emphasis original.

74. On a concise summary of these, see Murphy, *Theology in a Postmodern Age*, 24–32.

75. Green, "Scripture and the Human Person," 51–63.

76. Ibid., 52. Green's article provides a helpful but concise discussion on the subject.

that human beings are just an accumulation of cells, with their neurons functioning in a robotic fashion, my interest here is in the conceptual language which is often considered together with emergence and supervenience and is referred to as nonreductive physicalism. In contrast to reductionism, nonreductive physicalism

> takes account of what is known of the neurobiology of human nature and suggests that a nonreductive view of the relationship between human subjective mental life and neurobiology allows a key role for top-down causal influences. At the same time it presents a view of human soulishness as embodied in the capacity for the deepest and richest forms of personal relatedness, which recognize that it is God's sovereign choice to be in relationship to humankind in a manner that bestows ultimate and irreducible dignity to persons.[77]

A suggestion that there is no separate substance in the human being which can be called soul may not seem to be attractive: "Not many people will queue up to hear the message, 'You have no soul!'"[78] Perhaps a better way to put it is to point to the absolute inseparability of soul and what we consider to be a flesh-and-blood human being.[79] In the story of creation, "soul," or "nepheš," means God-given life, similar to the one given to all other creatures, and although the image of God in human beings, unique among all other creation, has been often (wrongly) associated with the possession of the soul, careful study of the first chapters of Genesis suggests that it has to be taken not in individual terms but in those of human community.[80] In such terms,

> our "soulishness" should be understood as our relatedness to God, to other humans, and to all of creation. The biblical idea is,

---

77. Jeeves, "Nature of Persons," 73–74. A note should be made here regarding the distinction between reductive and nonreductive physicalism. As noted earlier, reductive physicalism considers all processes to be ultimately reducible to the smallest physical building blocks of the universe. For it, all causation and its explanation goes bottom-up, whereas non-reductive physicalists would point out to the need for "hard sciences" to dialogue with disciplines such as philosophy and theology. The understanding of sexuality would be quite different depending on whether one takes up a reductive or nonreductive physicalist approach.

78. Green, "Scripture and the Human Person," 56.

79. For a brief summary of such a view, see Murphy, *Theology in a Postmodern Age*, 35–40.

80. For more on this, see Green, "Scripture and the Human Person," 53–54.

in this respect, remarkably similar to the neuroscience view that we are psychosomatic unities, not dualistic packages. I do not have a soul, I *am* a living being, or soul.[81]

Taking up such an understanding into different areas of Christian experience grounds the claims about sexuality being much more than sexual acts *per se*, and one's life with God being truly *embodied*. It is in this context that the broad definition of sexuality can begin to make sense.

> Sexuality involves how we respond to beauty in the world. Beauty gives me joy—whether it is the beauty of a visual display that represents a theological concept in worship, the sound of waves lapping against a shore-line, wheat sheaves waving in the wind, the ocean throwing up a storm that crashes against rock, a simple yellow gerbera daisy gracing my dining room table and bringing life into my home, or my cat lazily curled on her favourite chair and purring her contentment. Sexuality includes the depth of friendships forged over months and years; it includes levels of intimacy explored, pursued, and sometimes denied or rejected. It includes emotional intimacy, the secrets shared with a few people who know us well and whom we know well, a sense of safety within that unconditional love. Our sexuality is expressed through our intellect, through discussions and debates inspired by common interests or disparate experiences. It is expressed through our choice of life work, and in the compassion and hospitality we offer others.[82]

Or, as James B. Nelson puts it, sexuality "is who we are as body-selves who experience the emotional, cognitive, physical, and spiritual need for intimate communion, both creaturely and divine."[83]

To further the argument, the "sexuality" described above could be replaced by a more inclusive term of "bodiliness." The latter encompasses all sexual aspects, but more accurately points to the body as the necessary locus of any human experience. Importantly, it includes people who do not feel strong sexual urges, have intersex disorders (a

---

81. Jeeves, "Nature of Persons," 71; emphasis original.
82. Steinmann, "Singleness and Sexuality."
83. Nelson, *Between Two Gardens*, 6. To continue in Ronald Rolheiser's words, "Sexuality is the drive in us toward connection, community, family, friendship, affection, love, creativity and generativity. We are happy and whole when these things are in our lives, not on the basis of whether or not we sleep alone." Rolheiser, *Forgotten among the Lilies*, 52.

very challenging issue for the church),[84] or see themselves as completely asexual. Perhaps even more importantly, it points to the body being the locus of all our relationships with others, including God.

How could this celebration of bodiliness be encouraged in the believing community? Chapter 6 has already looked at some feminist considerations from an individual point of view. What about the church as the communal locus of such possibilities?

Bodiliness and the Church

Even though many voices, including those coming from feminist circles, have strong words of criticism of the church regarding its frequent derision of the body, the concern for embodiment of faith is not entirely new in the Christian tradition. Despite its prevailing tendencies of despising the body, it has had fathers such as Symeon the New Theologian (949–1022) who spoke of his whole body—even those considered the most embarrassing (though why should they be?) parts—being "Christ himself."[85] An intensely bodily approach was adopted by the Moravians, although it applied first of all to men, then to married women and mothers, then to the remaining women.[86]

As another example, consider the Ignatian Exercises. Their nature is such that they open up the practitioners to some hidden, subconscious corners of their psyche, including the depth of the desire for God which they have as God's creatures. That desire to *know* God—God in Jesus—"we feel . . . in the flesh":[87] "When God gazes at us and we gaze at God, something distressingly mutual passes between us."[88] Indeed, the yearning, particular, bodily love often associated with Eros can be "the kind of love proper to our being embodied."[89] Insights from Ignatian and similar exercises, including those coming from the male authors, are significant for the theme of this work as their context often involves

---

84. See Gudorf, "Erosion of Sexual Dimorphism."

85. Ware, "Body in Greek Christianity," 100.

86. Single women, however, were most clearly recognised as the brides of Christ, a living reminder for the whole community that this was the call of each believer. Atwood, "Sleeping in the Arms of Christ," 25–51.

87. Marsh, "Id Quod Volo," 10.

88. Ibid., 13.

89. Ibid., 13. Marsh also reflects on the risks and dangers of this erotic desiring after God.

the practice of celibacy.⁹⁰ Although some may suspect sublimation, the celibates can exhibit great sensitivity to the breadth of Love's calling:⁹¹

> O night that led'st me thus!
> O night more winsome than the rising sun!
> O night that madest us,
> Lover and lov'd, as one,
> Lover transform'd in lov'd, love's journey done!⁹²

A medieval French nun, Marguerite of Oingt, is said to have seen

> herself as a withered tree, which suddenly flowered when inundated by a great river of water (representing Christ). She then saw, written on the flowering branches of her self, the names of the five senses: sight, hearing, taste, smell and touch. It is hard to imagine a more pointed way of indicating that the effect of experiencing Christ is to "turn on," so to speak, the bodily senses of the receiving mystic.⁹³

There have been others asking whether God's inbreaking in the human story does not involve God's speaking through varied sensory mediums: "What if inspired speech is not the only means to bear witness to the wondrous works of God but is one of a plurality of sensory capacities through which God is present and active in our midst?"⁹⁴ Encouraging the same kind of a "Pentecostal spirituality of the wakened senses," Moltmann points out that the renewed interest in spirituality which we are presently witnessing involves "the new sensoriness."⁹⁵ For him, this "sensoriness" is intrinsically linked with the resurrection of the body proclaimed by the Risen Christ, which already affects our lives. The ministry of healing and loving attention to wounded, suffering bodies, so central to the life of Jesus, is one of the ways for the church to witness this richness of the experience of God's reality in the life of humans.⁹⁶

---

90. See, e.g., the work of Brother Ramon (originally a Baptist), *Flame of Sacred Love*.

91. Indeed it can be argued that a serious theology and practice of celibacy is a test case of the church's theology and practice of embodiment: without each other, they risk distortion and degeneration.

92. St. John of the Cross, Poem I, in *Counsels of Light and Love*, 74.

93. Bynum, *Fragmentation and Redemption*, 192. Bynum here refers to Marguerite of Oingt, *Les Oeuvres de Marguerite d'Oingt*, 147.

94. Yong, "Many Tongues, Many Senses," 177.

95. Moltmann, *Sun of Righteousness, Arise*, 65.

96. Moltmann-Wendel, *I Am My Body*, 36.

However, these have been isolated voices which have not had much impact on churchly practices. Sadly, joining a Christian community of faith often seems to run the risk of restricting, or even shutting off, the senses, rather than their development and blossoming. Although there are encouraging examples of communities open to different (and new) expressions of the Spirit's work, many churches do struggle with truly welcoming the *bodily* presence of people. However, it is here that the potential for changing the pattern lies. As an example, I take a practice central to the church's life: communal worship. Seeing how the body-selves and their relationships with others and God connect, the members—all of them, single and married—may well become better equipped to live out their faith in their daily routine. There are many new ways of being, communicating and worshipping to be discovered or rediscovered.[97] What follows are some initial considerations along the lines of Marguerite of Oingt's five senses.

A starting point in this may be hearing, a strong feature in worship and a dominant instrument for comprehending the sermon and listening to—or participating in—praying and singing. Yet, beside the preaching, praying or singing voices, the world of sounds offers so many other opportunities.[98] Employing silence in a more intentional way or an invitation to listen to something other than words as a part of congregational worship is one way to enhance the "soundscape";[99] so is a focus on less than usual sounds. I remember being struck once in a sermon delivered by a student on trusting God following the example of the birds of the air. It was a fresh spring morning when she preached;

---

97. Steve Taylor, a New Zealand Baptist, provides an overview reflecting on the initiatives of the emerging church in various places in the West (Taylor, *Out of Bounds Church*). For a daring proposal for the Roman Catholic tradition, see Empereur, "Physicality of Worship," 137–55. For a scientific study of embodied religiosity/spirituality, see Fuller, *Spirituality in the Flesh*. An insightful attempt from the Reformed perspective can be found in Shoop, *Let the Bones Dance*.

98. Among baptistic groupings, Pentecostalism has been prominent in the exploration of a greater variety of sonic expressions. Daniels, "'Gotta Moan Sometime,'" 5–32. Daniels argues that the array present in the early days of Pentecostalism has been curbed as the movement grew but that sound still plays an important role as "a way of knowing." For a fascinating reflection on the complex role of music and sound in general in the liturgical context of worship, see Morrill, "Liturgical Music," 157–72.

99. I take this word from Daniels, "Gotta Moan Sometime," 11.

and in the middle of her sermon, she opened the windows of the chapel and asked us to listen to the birds.[100]

Sight is another sense which on the one hand is much used in the church context, yet often is but a fraction of its potential. Belonging to the culture of reading (baptistic people are often called the "people of the Book," after all[101]) and the heirs of the Reformation, these communities tend to focus on simplicity of colors and structures, often over against the Catholic and Orthodox traditions.[102] Striving for simplicity might have good reasons, but it does not free the churches from the need to think it through. Moltmann helpfully reminds of the need to "learn to see"—to develop a child-like wonder of the world as if seen for the first time: "Adult people who no longer feel astonished at anything no longer understand anything."[103] As someone who grew up during the time of the Communist regime, I recall the severe limitation of available colors in clothing, interior decoration, etc. The repression of colors and their dullness was a sign to me as a child that there was something wrong with my immediate world. This feeling—this yearning for colors in their true richness—preceded the stories of occupation and oppression in which I was initiated when a little older. Although the availability of colors does not guarantee an occasion for astonishment of which Moltmann speaks, there is something to be said about the possibilities inherent in the spectrum of the rainbow.

The sense of taste is another key aspect of the realm of the organic. It would seem that tasting and eating is one of the least controversial ac-

100. It is also interesting to note the connection between the sense of hearing and that of smell, and their symbolic significance, in several episodes of Christian spirituality, especially of the medieval times. On this, see Saucier, "Sweet Sound of Sanctity," 10–27.

101. See, e.g., Jeffrey, *People of the Book*, xiii–xiv.

102. For a moving story of an interface between the Catholic and Baptist traditions in the context of a funeral and the wisdom with which a Catholic priest employed the colours (e.g., the white cover of the coffin symbolising the baptism of the deceased), ritual gestures, incense, bodily movements, etc., see Morrill, "Initial Consideration," 5–12. Although baptistic communities certainly would do well to take a careful look at the visual and olfactory elements in the traditions such as Catholic or Orthodox, as Moltmann-Wendel observes, there remains the issue as to whether these can speak sufficiently meaningfully to the contemporary needs of the person in search of God and a community of God's people. (Moltmann-Wendel, *I Am My Body*, 51. Thus, others have sought to experiment with new ways of incorporating visual and other signs. On this, see, e.g., Taylor, *Out of Bounds Church*.

103. Moltmann, *Sun of Righteousness, Arise*, 174.

tivities. However, from the removal of the actual meal from the practice of the Eucharist[104] to the scepticism of "time being wasted" on common meals in church instead of "concentrating on the central task of preaching the Word,"[105] much needs to be recovered for the church to be truly a community enjoying the gift of taste: "the mystery of God inhabiting our flesh and blood [which] sinks in as we chew and sip."[106] New ways need to be discovered to "taste and see that the Lord is good" (Ps 34:8).

Smell in the context of the baptistic community is more or less completely ignored, except for the smell of mould in older church buildings. Just as with other senses, some people may have very little of it, yet for others, smells are a very important part of life—of forming and bringing back memories, of inspiration, of creating emotions. Those communities which gather around a real meal rather than only the memory of its beginning and end, symbolized by the bread and wine, will also experience the smells of food. On the other hand, it is precisely because of the domesticity with which such smell can be associated, that some communities sadly tend to make a radical division between the smells appropriate for a sacred space in contrast to the profane.[107]

Tactile expressions are equally problematic, in spite of frequent metaphorical language that desires to "reach out and touch" Jesus.[108]

---

104. I owe this reminder to Keith G. Jones. As Shoop argues, the way the Protestant churches tend to celebrate the Lord's Supper is a paramount example of "dismembering" the body, rather than "re-membering" (*Let the Bones Dance*, 3, 168–70). Not only is the sense of taste brought to the minimum; the whole "communal experience in which we face one another, relate to one another, smell, hear, and touch one another is not a part of normal eucharistic practice" (ibid., 2).

105. I have personally encountered such objections in the post-communist regions of Europe. It is especially ironic that they are uttered in contexts which previously could survive only in the context of gatherings around meals: apart from perhaps agreed Sunday worship, other gatherings would often be forbidden by the Communist authorities. An excuse of gathering for celebrating a birthday, name-day or any other occasion which could be thought of, was the way to keep more frequent meetings: this was the church I grew up in as a child in Soviet Lithuania. See also Pilli, *Dance or Die*, 74, 209, for a similar description of Estonian baptistic communities.

106. Shoop, *Let the Bones Dance*, 170.

107. Moltmann-Wendel, noting on divorce in Western culture, as well as the church, from both taste and smell, observes: "With smell and taste we perceive life as renewal and death, as vitality and decay. We are stimulated but also repelled, and through our bodies we can experience reality and ourselves as part of this reality." Moltmann-Wendel, *I Am My Body*, 93.

108. Pentecostalism seems to have done a little better in this than most other baptistic groupings. For a consideration of somatic-sensory expressions of spiritual life

Beside contact with other bodies, touch, even if unacknowledged, happens all the time: of a pew, of a book, of a musical instrument. The skin is in contact with something else both in the most special moments of faith, such as when it meets the water of baptism, and in the most familiar of regular times. A faster movement would quickly remind the body that the skin, rather than existing in a vacuum, is in constant contact with the environment.

Then, surely, there is some contact between the members of a believing community: holding hands at the end of the celebration of the Lord's supper; a handshake; a hug; perhaps the laying on of hands; even a "holy kiss."[109] However, these bodily contacts can be very limited, failing to address the problem of "touch starvation" which many single people (and others) experience. By encouraging healthy, holistic ways of touching, a community of faith can demonstrate that intimacy is much more than sexual acts. Of course, fostering healthy touch involves risk. It is much safer to make sure touching is minimal as an insurance against any eruptions of a sexual nature. Yet for the community following the One for whom touch was an inseparable part of his ministry, there is a task of learning, and practicing, safe and healing ways of touching.[110]

Although it may be helpful to dwell on each of them separately, senses rarely work in isolation. The church is also presented with the challenge of disability, which both serves to creatively consider different sensorial expressions in the light of sense impairment, and to show that no one particular sense is required to communicate with God.[111] Yet all of them are an important outlet and expression of one's convictions, Indeed, at times they may be the best way of *understanding* one's convictions: the body can disclose what the mind is not ready to admit.[112]

---

among Pentecostals, see Yong, "Many Tongues, Many Senses," 181–83.

109. Jones, "Kiss of Peace," 290.

110. For a thoughtful study of touch in its non-sexual expression, see Autton, *Touch: An Exploration*. Moltmann-Wendel provides a theological reflection on the role of touch in the ministry of Jesus in *I Am My Body*, 60–65.

111. On this, see Yong, "Many Tongues, Many Senses," 167–88.

112. Walter Wink's *Transforming Bible Study* provides an inspiring illustration. Wink notes his own surprise when first realising, in the context of a creative, whole body-involving Bible study, that "the entire body is an instrument of consciousness, and needs to be involved in the struggle to integrate God-given insights prompted by Scripture into the total self" (19).

Intentional movement is one of the ways to employ several senses in helping the church to take bodiliness seriously:

> I once attended the most unusual Bible study. As the publicity said "wear loose clothing" it was obvious we were in for something different. The person leading it was a man who believed that the split between body and spirit in Western Christianity carried such profound and damaging consequences that he would not now lead a Bible study that did not include physical movement. For 40 minutes we were encouraged to move around the room in whatever way we chose, to a background of music and scripture reading. "And the word became flesh and dwelt among us."[113]

Some congregations would be familiar with activities such as liturgical dance,[114] which has seen an interest even in some rather rigid corners of Evangelical Christianity (even if sometimes it needs to be named "spiritually enhanced movement"[115]). The same can be said of various forms of theatre.

A personal account may be of help at this point. When sharing an embryonic version of the thoughts on non-reductive physicalism and spirituality in a gathering of a network[116] a few years ago, I combined it with a dance performed by my two colleagues. The dance was called "The Wings of Bodiliness" and recounted a story of two women learning to dance in their clothes for doing housework. The reaction after the session by the audience was that the dance was just as important a part of conveying the message as words. Unfortunately, I could not include the medium of dance in this book, and words will have to suffice, but may the reminder remain of these tremendously important, yet so frequently ignored, ways of celebrating the goodness of the body and its connection with its Creator.

---

113. Runcorn, *Spirituality Workbook*, 100.

114. As one contemporary example, see, e.g., "Liturgical Worship Dance Resources," http://www.celebrationofdance.com.

115. At the International Baptist Theological Seminary, such terminology was proposed, now some years ago, by Wesley Brown. Although used somewhat jokingly, at times it actually served as a bridge to introduce those coming from conservative backgrounds to dancing in the church context.

116. "The Web of Our Existence: Exploring Connectedness," organised by the Network of European Baptist Women in Ministries, Prague, 12–16 May 2008.

The next time the participants of the network met,[117] we engaged in creating a dance—or perhaps "movement" would be a more fitting word—as our exploration of the story of John 20:11–18: Mary Magdalene encountering the Risen Jesus.[118] For the final service of the network's meeting, we came to the conclusion that we wanted to explore this story—indeed, to relive the story—with all five senses.

Our service started in a cold dark cellar, with the beginning of the story retold and a prayer-song sung by candle-light, which then went out. Darkness—and silence—remained. We proceeded with prayers and songs of lament—for ourselves and others—and danced "a song of weeping." The flow of the service then made a bend, as a river does, and behind that bend there was a song of budding trust, flowing from the story of Mary finding Jesus in an unexpected place. A collage which part of the group had worked on, and which we now were all invited to take a piece of, was a reminder of being in the one body of Christ, even of Christ found in unexpected places. And so a dance of hope could start—danced by all; no spectators. Another participant then brought an invitation to taste God's goodness. We did not have much time in preparation, and the edible items we discovered to be available were chocolate Easter eggs—those with a crunchy sugary shell. A few sentences that accompanied the invitation to celebrate God's goodness by eating these Easter eggs—two for each, each egg with its own emphasis—are now always with me whenever I see or taste a chocolate egg. We concluded by singing a song of hope and celebration while also smelling a bunch of blooming lilacs which were collected from the bushes surrounding the Chapel and passed around to us as we sang. (Having a sensitive nose, it is the smell of those lilacs which I recall first of all when thinking of that service.)

Such an exploration and employment of all five senses requires a climate of trust and vulnerability (qualities explored in the next chapter).[119]

---

117. "Worship in the Seasons of Life," organised by the Network of European Baptist Women in Ministries. Prague, 17–20 May 2010.

118. The dance was coordinated by Gilija Žukauskienė, who uses dance and movement in an attempt to create a space for exploring the Christian faith both for committed Christians and others under the auspices of the School of Theology, Philosophy and Arts at Klaipėda and Vilnius Baptist churches, Lithuania. One of the tracks offered by the School constitutes an exploration of movement. More on this (in Lithuanian) can be found online at http://www.portikas.lt/Judesys.

119. Our network meeting was helped by the fact that only women were present.

The longing remains for the church to be a community which engages in wholeness-cultivating practices.

But? . . .

The intent of this exercise in exploring and interpreting issues of bodiliness, marital status, and the emergent community called the church was not to propose clear guidelines in regard to what sexual expressions (and how, and when) are allowed in the context of single believers. Disappointing as it may be, such an answer will not be provided, except to note that sexuality also contains pain—an ache which can also be present in the lives of those having genital sexual relationships, but perhaps especially for those who are acutely aware of missing one aspect of a human life fully expressed.

The place to work it out is in the context of particular intentional communities in their different contexts. Surely, reflections on "what should/should not be allowed" are at times needed (though first of all the questions would need to be overturned to enable a deeper analysis of assumptions present therein), but they should also lead into questions about what conditions (and how, and when) make sexual acts good or bad. That, surely, would be a task different from mine here. What can be said firmly, however, is that such questions become truly meaningful only in the context of a community which is serious about life embodied.

In this chapter, I have explored certain intersections of science and theology. Discussing the notions of emergence, supervenience, and non-reductive physicalism, I sought to test previously introduced ideas. The purpose was to point to the social level of reality and the role it plays—positive or negative—in the life of the persons who belong to specific communal entities. This runs contrary to the atomistic interpretation of reality as essentially based on the individual, a view that humans "are what they are apart from their relationships."[120]

Groups of one gender can make it easier to explore certain new experiences and ways of worship, yet this should not be a reason to assume that it could not also take place in a mixed congregation.

120. Quoted from Murphy's description of atomistic interpretation of reality, in *Theology in a Postmodern Age*, 54.

However, this is not to say that the level of the organic is less significant, or less real, than the communal. Both levels are real in the same way, as pointed out above; neither has a priority. Nevertheless, I started with the communal level because in discussions on singleness it is rather persistently taken as less important. Such an understanding of human beings not only suggests a new angle for discussing sexuality in particular and bodiliness more generally, but also insists, once again, on an inseparable connection of an ensouled body and a community of belonging.

I have also argued that, in spite of the negativity toward the body marking much of Christian history, the connection between the body and the community of belonging can be fostered with the sources present in the Christian tradition. Rodney Clapp tells a story of a little girl who was looking for a hippopotamus while standing on a rock in the water: what she did not realize is that she is standing on the thing she was looking for. Just as that girl went home disappointed for having not found a hippopotamus, Clapp argues, so the church at times seems incapable of seeing the resources available in its own home.[121] Yet the resources are there, and their playing out can be seen especially clearly when the bodily experience of different senses is given appropriate space and expression in the context of the emergent structure of Christian community.

---

121. Clapp, *Peculiar People*, 188.

8

I Have Called You Friends

A Theology of Friendship[1]

CONTINUING THE EXPLORATION OF the shape of the community of faith, I now look at one particular practice. Friendship has been repeatedly linked to happiness and a meaningful life, and is therefore significant for the discussion on the challenge of singleness. Hauerwas and Pinches once observed: "We are starved today for discussions on rich matters such as happiness, virtue, and friendship. Even more we lack the means to understand their interconnection."[2]

In contrast to the unfortunate synonymous use of "single" and "lonely," friendship suggests connection and companionship. Yet, just as with the issue of singleness, it has also been frequently neglected. At times friendship has been even strongly disapproved; this is also a part of the story of the church. On the other hand, there has been some genuine interest in friendship, including some recent theological writings. As Mother Mary Francis puts it, friendship is "about the oldest topic in the world," but "in our era it is also the newest topic."[3]

Friendship can also be seen as a vital mark of the moral life of a believing community; as such, it constitutes an essential test of the church's faithfulness. Although friendship can be highly personal, it is socially constructed and intrinsically connected to other communal practices, such as marriage or community formation: changes in one are likely to

---

1. Parts of the following chapter were first published as Andronoviene, "I Have Called You Friends," 115–29.

2. Hauerwas and Pinches, *Christians among the Virtues*, xiii–xiv.

3. Francis, *But I Have Called You Friends*, 11.

affect the others. So this chapter looks at the practice of friendship[4] and the way it supervenes upon the relationships of those who call themselves "friends" and specifically those who wish to call themselves the friends of Jesus.

Friendship Reconsidered

> Some friends play at friendship but a true friend sticks closer than one's nearest kin. (Prov 18:24)

Having grown up under a Communist regime, I recall the way relationships were labelled on the basis of the concept of *comradeship*. In my native language, Lithuanian, matters were complicated because there was only one word to describe amicable relationships: "friend," which covered personal friends as well as those "friends" who you dealt with at work, including those who could wreck your career in their speech in a party meeting by publicly shaming and blaming this "friend" or that "friend."

This was one of the versions of modification of the word, though the earlier, narrower meaning was not lost, and to be addressed as "friend" by a party member (even more so, a former fellow believer-turned-party member) never sounded quite natural. Another variety of the expansion of the meaning took place in the West where it became a synonym of any positive social contact—connection, acquaintance, associate—where "to have many friends" is part and parcel of an image of a successful life. The recent fad of collecting "friends" on social networking sites is a prime example.

Yet, whether we have been influenced by Communist or Western lifestyles, we still understand what Proverbs speaks about in the epigraph above.[5] Lucky are those who have a true friend, for that friend will indeed stick closer than one's nearest kin. This aspect of relationships has

---

4. It is particularly worth noting that friendship, as any other practice, is a powerful practice that can also be corrupt and abusive (McClendon, *Ethics*, 178–82).

5. One may also recall the classic description of the types of friendship by Aristotle as relationships based on their usefulness, the pleasure they bring, and finally, the virtues that they develop in those involved in the practice. For Aristotle, only the last type—a friendship based on and leading to goodness—can be truly named perfect and lasting (Aristotle, *Ethica Nicomachea*, 1156a9–20; 1156b4–12). On the other hand, see a discussion in Hauerwas and Pinches, *Christians among the Virtues*, 17.

recently become of interest to various thinkers as well as sociologists.⁶ The focus of the present discussion will be this particular meaning of "friend" and "friendship," signifying a term reserved for very few people in the lives of each of us.⁷ The cost of having a friend is such that one cannot afford to have too many of them, even if one may hope to be more optimistic than Michel de Montaigne who thought it impossible to have more than one.⁸

What Happened to Friendship

Of course, confusion and depreciation of the concept of "friend" did not start with Communism or Western consumerism. In the classical world of Greece and Rome, friendship was attributed a very significant role, as exemplified in the Greek philosophers' fascination with *philia*.⁹ However, in the Christian world, the notion of friendship-love soon became a significantly lesser motif, often relegated to the realm of the private, natural, or the feminine—which was to mean, not really a "seri-

---

6. Although, interestingly, not much research has been done on the friendships of single women past undergraduate college age. O'Connor, *Friendships between Women*, 115.

7. "People" is an important word here, too. Even though God is portrayed as a friend of certain persons in the Scriptures, I do not think it fair to include here a full-fledged discussion on being friends with God. The starting point of such discussion is Jesus of Nazareth who has called his disciples friends—and this is as far as I will go.
Even more stretched, it would seem, would it be to talk of the relationship with artifacts such as pieces of art as "friendship." Certainly one can be powerfully transformed by a book or a painting, yet terming it "friendship" makes the definition too broad to be meaningful.

8. Montaigne, *Of Friendship*, sec. 5. Cf. Meilaender, *Friendship*, 6.

9. Cf. Meilaender, *Friendship*, 1–2. As Meilaender notes, *philia* would be interpreted differently for Plato than for Aristotle. For the first, it starts with specific friendships widening into a universal love; for the latter, the other way around, friendship starts with a broad basis of positive relationships, then narrows to some particular friends chosen. "Plato grounds friendship in sentiment; Aristotle in choice." Ibid., 8.

ous subject."[10] Of course, there were exceptions, such as greater attention to the subject in monastic circles.[11] Otherwise, however,

> Christianity has pushed earthly love and friendship from the throne, the impulsive and preferential love, the partiality, in order to set spiritual love in its place, the love to one's neighbour, a love which in earnestness and truth and inwardness is more tender than any earthly love—in the union, and more faithfully sincere than the most celebrated friendship—in concord.[12]

The shadow of the reduction of friendship to the realm of temporary and, therefore, much less significant compared with things eternal is still present. Until recently, it had received very little attention in philosophy and theology. As Gilbert Meilaender has noted, "It would be difficult, if not impossible, to find a contemporary ethicist—whether philosophical or theological—who in writing a basic introduction to ethics would give friendship more than a passing glance."[13] As to fiction, it has also been dominated by romantic love: "Generally speaking, we simply do not find the ups and downs of friendship enough to sustain our interest in a story."[14] Perhaps this is because, until very recently,

---

10. O'Connor, *Friendships between Women*, 1. In the ancient world of Christianity, friendship was commonly regarded as a relationship between members of the same sex. Yet there are interesting and notable exceptions. Just to name a few, there were Perpetua and Saturus (2nd c.); Basil and Theodora (3rd c.); Gregory of Nazianzus and Theosebia (3rd c.). I will not spend much time on delineating the differences between same-sex and heterosexual friendships, which perhaps betrays a conviction of mine that gender differences, though existing, are not crucial when it comes to friendship.

11. Yet in the monastic tradition overall, close friendships were hardly encouraged for a variety of reasons, ranging from a theology of earthly things (which would include a suspicion toward particular friendships), the unity and homogeneity of the community, and the concern for the temptation of homosexual attraction. See Roby, "Doctrine of the *Spiritual Friendship*," 6–17. For an overview of the development of the ideas on love in friendship in the story of Christianity, see Carmichael, *Friendship: Interpreting Christian Love*.

12. Kierkegaard, *Works of Love*, 37.

13. Meilaender, *Friendship*, 1 (writing in 1981). However, there has been a resurgence of a kind in terms of the interest in friendship in recent years, as exemplified in Rouner, *Changing Face of Friendship*. In terms of individual works, Derrida's *Politics of Friendship* would be a ready example. MacIntyre's *After Virtue* presents an important consideration of Aristotle's interpretation of friendship. One field in which friendship has routinely received a serious treatment is feminist thought; for one notable example, see Hunt, *Fierce Tenderness: A Feminist Theology of Friendship*.

14. Allen, *Love*, 2.

friendship was seen as an accessory to leisure, rather than an essential aspect of a good life.[15] Such a perception is also reflected in the scarcity of *theological* discussion on friendship in relation to singleness: "One wonders . . . why much of what has been written is not really very useful. Instead of abstract treatises on 'spiritual friendship,' what we need now is a theological understanding of the very human experience of friendship, a theology of 'bodily friendship,' so to speak."[16]

The making of modernity has further qualified the problem of accounting for the place and the role of friendships.[17] One could note the growing importance of the work people do for a living as the major defining factor of their identity. This is further intensified by the lack of time to nurture friendships arising from the demand of the work place.[18] Then there is the issue of mobility that often precludes the nurture that lasting friendships require.

In addition, the focus on the erotic, whether in (Christian) marriage or in a sex-for-pleasure relationship, or the variations in between, has also pushed other non-family relationships to the margins. An erotically charged atmosphere in which daily life takes place has also impacted the physical expressions in friendships, be they same sex or not: one must be careful in the way physical affection is expressed. The fear arising from the problems shaking the institution of the family in the Western world also adds to the poverty of the practice of friendship. As noted earlier, friends can be perceived as detrimental to family life, taking away from the time which should be spent by the couple together.

On the other hand, there is some renewed interest in friendship in a recognition of the importance of relational aspects for a wholesome life.[19] Even when there is no space for friends in adult life, most parents

---

15. McFague, *Models of God*, 160.

16. Cardman, "Singleness and Spirituality." This is not to say that singleness and friendship are rarely connected. Almost any of the books or articles talking about singleness will address the importance of friends (see, e.g., Wilson, *Being Single*, passim, esp. 193–95.) Yet, most of the time, the discussion remains at a very general level. "Very little is known about adult friendships, especially those friendships that support unmarried and uncoupled individuals." Kaiser and Kashy, "Contextual Nature and Function of Singlism," 125.

17. On the diminishing quality of friendship in current times, see Anderson, *Losing Friends*.

18. Cf. Meilaender, *Friendship*, 2.

19. Pahl, *On Friendship*, 1. Pahl's work provides a good introduction to the notion and the practice of friendship.

care about the friends their children have, for they know too well that "through friendships we gain a sense of who we are and what the world is like—of the universe of the everyday."[20] Friendships are important for young people especially. Indeed, "today there is a whole repertoire of relational forms in modern society, and for young people there is a new, floating family network called friendship that seems to provide one of the few permanent elements in their lives."[21] There is a strong desire emerging for friendship, and it is perhaps for this reason that at times the practice is romanticized beyond recognition: a myth of a perfect friend suddenly appearing[22] is somewhat similar to the appearance of the knight on a white horse. Just as with romantic love, when the reality of the practice on the ground begins to look rather different from the icon glowing from the TV screen and billboards, disappointment follows.

There are differences in the dynamics of friendship in terms of gender in a local cultural context.[23] Some are more fortunate in having chances to be encouraged, throughout their life, to develop and nurture friendships. The depth and intensity expected in a "typical" friendship would somewhat vary from (sub-)culture to (sub-)culture. Keeping these differences in mind, however, there seems to be enough of a common basis to proceed in considering certain key pieces and parcels of the practice of friendship.

On the Assumed Inferiority of Friendship

In terms of Christian theology, the practice of friendship has been often considered to be morally inferior in contrast to perfect love of one's neighbor exemplified by the divine *agape*. At the heart of this superiority of Christian charity in relation to friendship is the problematic preferential nature of friendship which necessarily involves choices, intellectual, aesthetic, emotional or erotic attraction, and favoring of some people

---

20. McCarthy, *The Good Life*, 35.
21. Holloway, *Godless Morality*, 156.
22. O'Connor, *Friendships between Women*, 181.
23. Rather stereotypically, friendships of women are sometimes contrasted with the male type of friendships on the basis of the "sharing" as central for the former and "doing stuff" as the rationale of the latter (cf. ibid., 160). Yet "it is not clear whether this is a feature of nature or of socialization, or even whether these two 'causes' can be so easily divided." Humphrey, *Ecstasy and Intimacy*, 164.

(who are friends) over the others. Or, as Wadell sums up this view, "This does not mean friendship is bad, but it does mean that from a Christian perspective it is lacking . . . It is a powerful love, but it is not the love by which we imitate Christ."[24]

Contrasting the demands of a God-like life of *agape*, it is yet another example of the fascination with the Greek categories for love.[25] Wadell puts it aptly: "it [is] presumed that there was no intrinsic connection between friendship and Christian love, and that each could be given full definition apart from the other."[26] Yet, just as God's love can be seen to encompass the elements of the erotic and that of tender friendship, so the practice of friendship, while displaying many of the aspects typical of Greek *philia*, can also include features of selfless delight as well as passion.[27]

Wadell points to another reason for the tension and the snubbing of the practice of friendship within the Christian tradition: an abstract agape is always going to have an upper hand against an abstract friendship. Yet friendships never occur in a vacuum; they occur within some tradition which endows them with goals and sets them in a particular narrative out of which they draw their meaning.[28] It is for this reason that the classical texts on friendship such as Aristotle's *Nicomachean Ethics* can only be partially helpful for a discussion such as the one carried out here:[29] "What friendship sets out to achieve is one thing if the

24. Wadell, *Friendship and the Moral Life*, 71.

25. For the discussion of these categories, see chap. 4, sec. 3.

26. Wadell, *Friendship and the Moral Life*, 72.

27. Phillips observes that downplaying of (in his words, "saying less than we know" about) certain sorts of human love comes from our drive "to say more about a certain aspect of religious love, namely, love of the neighbour" (*Religion and Friendly Fire*, 161). It was love for the neighbor, or "Christian love," that was superior to all other kinds of love in Kierkegaard's thinking as well, as seen in the quote on the supremacy of the love to one's neighbor quoted above. All other kinds of love to him were but expressions of "merely blossoming" love, whereas, by contrast, "Christian love [was] eternal" (Kierkegaard, *Works of Love*, 7). Phillips notes, "Kierkegaard assumes, too quickly, that other loves necessarily come between us and love of God. In doing so, he says more than he knows about love of the neighbour, and less than he knows about the other loves" (Phillips, *Religion and Friendly Fire*, 168).

28. Wadell, *Friendship and the Moral Life*, 72.

29. As already explored in chap. 7, for the purposes of this work Aristotle's interest in virtues certainly provides a helpful framework for discussing practices such as friendship. The *substance* of a practice such as friendship, however (i.e., its particular virtues) may not be so similar given the difference between the guiding narrative ad-

friends aim to secure excellence in Athens, another thing if they aim for the Kingdom of God."[30]

In contrast, if friendship is seen as a practice in which Christians participate *as Christians*, the preferential love of friendship becomes a necessary good out of which love for non-friends and enemies can emerge. In her delightfully profound reflection on friendship, Mother Mary Francis contends that the love born in friendship is the starting point of "every kind of love there is ... There is no real love of any kind that is not rooted in friendship; and when love does not seem to be functioning properly, when it is not fruitful, it is always because there is not friendship in love."[31] This concerns practices such as marriage and child-rearing, but also the life of Christian communities. Addressing the members of her own walk of life, she warns: "If we do not call each other friends, then let us not pretend that we can call each other sisters. We cannot have real sisters who are not real friends. And so it goes with every human relationship."[32]

In the light of such understanding of friendship as a Christian practice, what can be said about the virtues of friendship? What kind of intrinsic qualities belong to the practice of friendship? I will attempt to respond to this question first by considering those special relationships with a few people known as close, special, "particular" friends. The last section of the chapter will discuss the implications of this practice for a Christian community as a whole.

Virtues of Friends

> What appears ... as the freest of all relationships, with no obligations except to delight, to play, carries a hidden but powerful responsibility of commitment to the other, a commitment to stay true, to stay trustworthy ... What one expects from a friend is, above all else, trust: reliability, constancy, loyalty.[33]

---

opted by Aristotle and that of the followers of Christ.
30. Wadell, *Friendship and the Moral Life*, 72–73.
31. Francis, *But I Have Called You Friends*, 12.
32. Ibid., 12–13.
33. McFague, *Models of God*, 162.

Friendship involves a range of virtues, or, in MacIntyrean language, 'standards of excellence' associated with being a friend. The virtue range is too broad to discuss fully here; thus it is given that friendship will require such qualities as trust, respect, patience, or truthfulness.[34] What I take below are four virtues that, I suggest, are especially important in the light of the disregard of friendship and the issues central to this book. I name them as follows: commitment, particularity, mutuality, and vulnerability.

Commitment

Although friendship may not be described as selfless, it requires commitment—or, as Aelred of Rievaulx would term it, "loyalty."[35] Commitment is often understood primarily in terms of readiness to give one's time and attention to a friend in need. It grows together with the practice, when friends discover each other's trustworthiness and faithfulness—not as a cold rational calculation and testing, but as a process of an ongoing growth of lives together. It is likely to be more assumed than spoken about, but commitment and the steadfastness it requires at times can be very costly. Crisis situations that demand such commitment are also the points where the endurance of a friendship is tested. Sociologists researching the costs involved in sustaining friendships list "emotional aggravation and time" as examples, also pointing out how the cost grows as the friendship develops and deepens.[36] Thus commitment is likely to be directly linked with the other virtues belonging to the practice of friendship: the more particular and trusting the friendship, the more space there is for commitment to grow.

Although friends can be those whom we like and with whom we naturally, without difficulties, become friends, there is another dimension of friendship in the conscious choosing to make and keep a friend. There are cases of friendships which have to start without any attraction, or in fact they even may have started with an antipathy. Nevertheless,

---

34. Francis would suggest three such virtues and the progression from the first to the second to the third: esteem, respect, and affection (*But I Have Called You Friends*, 16ff.). Or as Aelred of Rievaulx would suggest, "There are four qualities which must be tested in a friend: loyalty, right intention, discretion, and patience, that you may entrust yourself to him securely." Aelred of Rievaulx, *Spiritual Friendship*, 3:61.

35. E.g., ibid., 3:88.

36. See the report in O'Connor, *Friendships between Women*, 111–14.

with a conscious choice to start treating somebody as a friend; with a conscious choice to start loving somebody by *really knowing* them, a friendship can be born, the bonds of which can withstand violent storms of life.[37] Given that attraction and "naturalness" are likely to fluctuate as friends and the circumstances of friendship change, commitment will be an important ingredient for any friendship to endure.

Particularity

One of the results of the notion of commitment is that it necessarily limits the number of people one can be committed to. Drops of friendly behaviour distributed to all around equally render the notion of committed friendship meaningless. Therefore, at least for that reason, friendship is always particular. We choose friends because of the qualities of their character, or their experience, or common goals, etc. Even in a costly effort to make a friend, friendship grows as we begin to discover and appreciate particular qualities of the person.

> Friendship loves and prefers a particular person because of what that person is. That is why, when the person changes, friendship changes or fades. And though it may be good to know that we are loved with a love which never fades, it is doubtful whether anyone wishes to be loved in only that way—in spite of what we are, rather than because of what we are . . . It is not surprising that the words "I love you despite your failings" should as often be a subtle weapon as a genuine affirmation of the other person.[38]

The relationship between the particular and universal love becomes evident here. In Mother Mary Francis' words, "How can we have a universal love except by particularities?"[39] Particularity is the starting point; it is out of learning to love one, two, three friends that one can begin to get a grasp on how to befriend and love the fourth, the fifth, the sixth, who perhaps seem more difficult to love at the start. Thus Francis' advice for the nuns was, "We ought to have a particular relationship with every sister in the community."[40] What is important for the virtue of par-

---

37. This is Mother Mary Francis' insight: "Someone you really know, you cannot dislike. The trouble is that we think that we know people, and we really don't know them at all." *But I Have Called You Friends*, 15.

38. Meilaender, *Friendship*, 64.

39. Francis, *But I Have Called You Friends*, 18.

40. Ibid., 19. It would seem that she succeeded, as the testimony of the sisters of

ticularity not to turn into a vice is to keep the door open for new friendships that can yet be born.[41] A small number of these will be much more intense and intimate than others, but they all can reveal some aspect of what it really means to be a friend, and each will possess particular features, making every friendship unique. Something takes place once we are shown love toward us for who we are, which enables us to love others both for who they are and just as they are.

Mutuality

Friendship is inherently mutual; it "grows best in the soil of reciprocity."[42] Once again we are back to the "Christian" problem of seeing friendships as inferior and indeed inhibiting the true spirit of Christian relationships which should not expect to receive anything back. This needs to be considered seriously, it would seem, as contrasted with the call to (Christian) love which gives unconditionally.[43] However, as Meilaender notes incisively, such supposedly all-inclusive, unconditional love can be easily applied not so much to help the neighbor in need as it is to protect oneself while feeling so virtuous, so sacrificing, so Christian. "The focus is upon how such love protects the lover, secures the lover in an independence which absolutely nothing can shake."[44]

---

her monastery who collected and published her reflections on friendship described Mother Mary Francis as somebody in whose presence "each sister felt herself to be very personally known, appreciated and cherished . . . and each one felt herself to be one of Mother's dearest friends. And, wonderful to tell, each one was." Mother Mary Angela, foreword to Francis, *But I Have Called You Friends*, 10.

41. Francis, *But I Have Called You Friends*, 20–21.

42. Humphrey, *Ecstasy and Intimacy*, 161.

43. Another criticism for linking reciprocity to friendship comes from an entirely different source: in his *Politics of Friendship*, Jacques Derrida aims to deconstruct the "traditional" understanding of friendship ("the dominant schema of friendship" [240]) as he sees it to be "phallocentric" or "androcentric" in its (Greek, Christian, Arabo-Islamic) *fraternal* framework—i.e., excluding women, either in friendship between a man and a woman, or between women; those who are distant, those who are different, those, in other words, who cannot reciprocate in the strict sense of the word. Friendship, says Derrida, should be a gift; thus his interest in the possibility of coming "to call the friend by a name which is no longer that of the near one or the neighbour, and undoubtedly no longer the name of man" (292).

44. Meilaender, *Friendship*, 42. Meilaender is discussing and critiquing Kierkegaard's view of the superiority of unconditional love.

Of course, those who want to protect themselves from any "piercing" relationship may have a good reason to do so. There might have been a deep wound in the earliest relationships in the person's life. Yet it is in this mutuality that God can be seen in new eyes and, just as with healthy erotic love, love can be extended to others. Knowing reciprocal love means being enabled to love those who will not reciprocate it. It is a paradox similar to other paradoxes of the Gospel: those who give away are enabled to give away even more.

Another paradox follows: while without mutuality there cannot be real friendship, such reciprocity must remain unspoken and unreflected upon. As soon as there is a question—"What am I getting from this friendship?"—it is a likely sign that the friendship is less than genuine.[45] In the words of Meilaender: "Begin by taking reciprocity as our central concern and we will be ineluctably forced by the truth of this insight to retreat into the self, trusting no one and giving ourselves to no one."[46]

As to the specifics of mutuality, they are likely to vary in different relationships. Although people tend to become friends with people who have similar interests and capabilities, that sort of equality is not always straightforward. Friendship between sexes is sometimes argued against precisely on such grounds of difference. Yet while it may be easier to live by avoiding friendships across sexes, it robs humanity of some of the richness of God's gifts in others, and can be especially strongly felt by single women who have a limited access to a male perspective. In a perceptive insight of Ronald Rolheiser, "One of the deep wounds in Western culture is that men and women find it very hard to be friends. It's easy for them to be lovers, but not friends."[47]

There are friendships between very unlikely friends greatly differing in age, status, outlook, and purpose; as I shall argue later, this is the basis of the claim of the church as a community of the friends of Jesus. At some point, it might be argued it is not friendship anymore but some other relationship—that of a substitute grandfather-granddaughter, for example—yet it is not so clear-cut. What is clear is that the exchange has to be somehow mutual: friends need to be receivers and givers at the same time, even if the things given and received will be different for the

---

45. See Clapp's critique of the "managerial" approach to friendships in *A Peculiar People*, 207.

46. Meilaender, *Friendship*, 44.

47. Rolheiser, *Forgotten among the Lilies*, 36.

two parties.[48] For some, giving may turn out to be the more challenging part of mutuality, yet for others it will be their ability to accept the gifts of friendship that will be the test of its genuineness.[49]

Vulnerability

Mutuality leads to another virtue of a genuine friendship: vulnerability. Reminding of a real possibility of suffering, it is a crucial virtue of a friendship, both at its start, when one risks having his or her offer of friendship or one's exposure of a need or weakness snubbed, and later as friendship develops and the amount of trust risks great sorrow if betrayed. It is precisely such risk that can be too much to bear, with the result of various mechanisms of protection being built against the possibility of making oneself open to the impact of the other. Perhaps the most significant of such mechanisms for the present discussion is an imitation of friendship fuelled by unselfishness, loving kindness, and a concern which does not allow the other to reciprocate.

As personalities change over the course of time, as outlooks are adjusted and sometimes radically altered, friendship undergoes further tests.[50] What affects one's friend can affect one's own life. Even though there is the freedom and the requirement to be truthful to one's convictions, there is no safety of cutting oneself off from one's friend once the friend happens to be in some trouble. Such vulnerability will be expressed both in the inconvenient support of the friend as well as in the

---

48. For a concrete example, consider the insistence of Hauerwas and Pinches that their book is a result of such friendship which started as a significantly uneven relationship between an older teacher and a young student. *Christians among the Virtues*, xv–xvii.

49. Cf. Francis, *But I Have Called You Friends*, 52. As Francis observes, "It takes a certain depth of spirituality even to realize that receiving *is* a kind of giving, when the admission of my own inadequacies lets me give others the opportunity to help me or to supply for me. It requires humility to receive with graciousness" (ibid., 52–53).

50. One such test is represented by the relationships affected by the change of a friend's marital status—as when a friend who is single again is seen as someone who has changed "too much," or when marital bonds break and friends end up taking sides (either by their own choice or because the couple has divided not only former common property, but also common friends). For the report of studies on the proportion of friendship relationships which wither after a separation or divorce, see O'Connor, *Friendships between Women*, 103–4. At the same time, the presence of friends who remain faithful is particularly important in alleviating stress levels and restoring one to health and wholeness. Ibid., 106–11.

anguish of opposing him or her out of one's love for the person. What it will mean in either case will be that if one is committed to a particular friendship, that commitment will entail a certain readiness to be vulnerable in being affected by the changes the friend undergoes. And so, "no matter how many times we might be hurt, even betrayed, by those to whom we risked ourselves, we continue to take a chance with them because intuitively we know we cannot abide a self without them."[51]

At this point, it is hardly possible to abstain from noticing connections with other virtues. Friendship and the vulnerability that it demands would be unsustainable without forgiveness or hospitality, offering it as "the space that we have created for them."[52] Vulnerable hospitality will foster strength—just as contexts of acknowledged fear cultivate courage—and therefore will make it a space in which convictions can be scrutinized and refined.

For these virtues to flourish, they will require an intensity proper to a deepening relationship. Time devoted to such a relationship is an important factor here as people are learning creative ways to keep friendships alive over long distances. New developments in communication technology, enabling friends to hear and see one another, have improved such opportunities significantly, but have also facilitated the creation of imitations of friendly intimacies which make it possible to "friend" and "unfriend" somebody in an instant and to know of many minute details of one's "friend's" daily life without ever even being sure of her real name and other aspects of identity.[53]

That said, nurturing a friendship over distance is not new; for many a century people have maintained deep relationships through such means as letters.

> The cosmopolitan atmosphere of the time was also conducive to the formation of friendships all over the [Roman] Empire, with people often making friends during their student days when they came together from different countries, friendships which they managed to maintain for many years after, even when separated

---

51. Wadell, *Friendship and the Moral Life*, 148.
52. Cardman, "Singleness and Spirituality."
53. The way virtual social networks, still in their infancy, are affecting culture, including the perception and presentation of identity, is an important area of research and continuing discussion. Rosen's "Virtual Friendship and the New Narcisism" is a good example of such discussions.

by great distances on return to their homeland or on appointment to some administrative post in whatever corner of the Empire.[54]

This is a description not of one of the modern empires, but of Christians in the fourth century. However, not surprisingly, "in more despondent moments it was felt that letters were only a second best, unable to provide an adequate substitute for a friend's physical presence and conversation."[55] Such struggles remind of the importance of another virtue which McClendon has termed "presence"—"the quality of *being there* for and with the other."[56] This virtue is more readily evident in the actual, bodily encounter with the one to whom we are present; to be present for another who is physically distant requires even more commitment, effort and creativity.

Allowing for the virtue of presence, the door is also opened to consider "surprising" or "costly" friendships—those relationships which are almost "forced" upon us by the particular combination of circumstances where one has to rub shoulders with the other in such close proximity that they have to either come to hate each other or learn to love each other by learning to know each other in friendship. As Meilaender would say, bringing together different aspects of love, "in learning to take care of [friends] we may learn what it would mean to care for any human being. We may learn, that is, a love which is implicitly universal."[57]

A full discussion on the virtues of friendship would need to include an examination of the vices which can infest a particular relationship.[58] It is here that the interconnection with other practices can also be noted: just as the vices breeding in a particular practice bring degeneration into the whole framework or interrelated practices, fostering the virtues in one practice can have a positive effect on others. Commitment, particularity, reciprocity, and vulnerability—these are important virtues for other practices, and especially for the overarching Christian practice of witnessing to God's realm (Chapter 7, Section 2). Thus I now turn to the believing and witnessing community as a whole. How does friendship

---

54. White, *Christian Friendship in the Fourth Century*, 5.

55. Ibid., 8.

56. McClendon, *Ethics*, 115; emphasis original.

57. Meilaender, *Friendship*, 19–20.

58. Wadell describes a virtuous friendship as the one which "leads both persons to God" (*Friendship and the Moral Life*, 84), and points to two vices that can harm friendship—overdetachment and possessiveness (*Becoming Friends*, 49–51).

relate to the life of an intentional community that sustains and embodies the commitment to follow Jesus?

Friendships and Convictions

> From a theological angle ... good friendships and loving marriages are always incomplete, and are dependent on a wider company of friends.[59]

Chapter 7 has already explored the necessity of the communal framework—an intentional community of one sort or another—for sustaining the lives of the followers of Jesus. When it comes to friendship, however, a problem occurs. Friends in the sense used above are not usually seen as equivalent to intentional community. One's friend need not belong to one's community of faith. Those deep and personal friendships and their virtues explored in the previous section could be seen as a supporting network parallel to that of the community of faith in creating and sustaining a meaningful and wholesome life.

However, a rather different argument could also be made. Could not a reflection on small-scale, personal, close friendships suggest an enlargement of this practice to include a community focused on a particular task and, in the process, becoming a community of friends?[60] Such an inclusion should be done with care, and with an understanding that it does not obliterate those deep friendships discussed above. Yet very fact that personal friendships can be born not out of attraction, but of choice, points to the possibility of the growth of friendship of those who find themselves together around the Person they follow. This Person becomes the beginning of the process during which "we and others find ourselves through participation in a common activity that makes us faithful both to ourselves and the other."[61] In the words of a personal testimony, "It was through shared church—worship, work, fellowship—that I learned to love and came to be loved by many of my closest friends."[62]

---

59. McCarthy, *Sex and Love in the Home*, 172.

60. Here one may recall the aforementioned stereotype of women focusing on the relationship itself and the men on the task uniting the friendship. Although as stereotypes, these would need to be carefully unpacked, they do point to two important aspects of the life of the "community of Jesus' friends," and the need for a balance.

61. Hauerwas and Pinches, *Christians among the Virtues*, 49.

62. Clapp, *A Peculiar People*, 194. Diogenes Allen, on the other hand, would disagree with any equation of friendship with the *koinonia* of the church. Allen, *Love*, 56ff.

As sociologists and socio-psychologists have noted, a certain goal can bind unlikely people in friendship in context-specific relationships such as those formed at work.[63] Recalling a political theorist's Michael Walzer's description of participatory-communal polities,[64] Meilaender notes: "They are relatively small groups; they involve close, even intimate, relations; and they involve voluntary relations." "Polities of this sort," adds Meilaender, "begin to resemble a bond like personal friendship."[65] Behind the considerations of theorists, such as Walzer, stands the desire of "a political community worth living for, to be a member of which involves a kind of moral transformation: from self-serving pursuit of private purposes to other-regarding service of the common good."[66]

Meilaender finds such communities highly improbable, pointing out the impossibility of the ideal in the Greek polei and their subsequent replacement by the empire-state, as well as the problems inherent in the secular societies in which such friendships can disrupt the systems of justice and order. He goes on to say, "hesitantly but firmly, that a Christian ethic ought to recognize the ideal of civic friendship as essentially pagan, an example of inordinate and idolatrous love . . . Politics and ethics must always be distinguished. The comrade is not the friend."[67]

Compare this to the words of Jesus to his disciples, "I have called you friends, because I have made known to you everything that I have heard from my Father" (John 15:15). The disciples were in no way "natural" friends; rather, their being gathered into friendship presupposed a certain common purpose. Context-based, or purpose-oriented, friendships illustrate that friendship is more than just a private bond, but always a phenomenon dependent on its larger social context.[68] Keeping this in mind also helps to resist the temptation to assign to the practice an ideological role of something pure and perfect similar to that of the

---

63. O'Connor, *Friendships between Women*, 161. O'Connor reviews studies which demonstrate the importance of such friendships that often go unrecognised until they are faced with change, such as unemployment (ibid., 162). This is of special interest today when work often is the defining factor of one's identity but also when boundaries between work and leisure, or work and home life, are blurred.

64. Walzer, *Spheres of Justice*, passim, and esp. 318–21; *Obligations: Essays on Disobedience, War, and Citizenship*.

65. Meilaender, *Friendship*, 72.

66. Ibid., 73.

67. Ibid., 75, 78.

68. O'Connor, *Friendships between Women*, 171.

ideology of a romantic relationship. Even though "comrade," at least to my ears, may sound uncomfortable and remind of Communist propaganda, I have to admit that the distinction between friend and comrade is not as clear-cut as my experience of the grimaces of the Communist regime would suggest. The word itself may be currently spoiled, yet the connotation of comradeship in Jesus' "Society of Friends," as Quakers have put it, is certainly present.

Thus a believing community deserves another consideration of how it can be a place where, enabled by the Christian narrative and particular practices, the church can "embody a kind of friendship not otherwise available."[69] Mother Mary Francis would insist that it is only insofar as an intentional Christian community practices friendship does it grow into anything that can be genuinely called "love." Moreover, such community should be "the pattern of friendship for the world . . . We ought to be the ones to whom other people could look for the clear picture of how real friendships work: this is the way it functions, this is what it does, this is what it produces in people."[70]

MacIntyre has observed that friendship is essential for human flourishing because of the incredible human capacity to deceive ourselves. Without friends who are able to offer hard criticism, when such is needed, with the hopes that they will be heard, "one becomes the victim of one's hopes and fears, of wishful thinking and fantasy . . . Unless we are very careful, we tend not to see things as they are, but as our fantasies predispose us to see them. And we can only be rescued from this by a certain kind of friendship."[71] In an attempt to see that such a "certain kind of friendship" can be a Christian reality, I revisit the notion of convictional theology.[72] Theology of friendship can be understood as an exploration of three convictional spheres: organic, communal, and eschatological, as they relate to one friend's version of their convictional set compared to the other's. The quality of friendship can be evaluated in terms of the extent to which the compatibility of these convictional spheres in various issues that arise, are argued, and have to be dealt with,

---

69. Clapp, *A Peculiar People*, 204.

70. Francis, *But I Have Called You Friends*, 13.

71. MacIntyre, "Illusion of Self-Sufficiency," 120.

72. See chap. 5, sec. 1. I am indebted to Parush Parushev for his willingness to share his insights which were so helpful in organising the argument of this section.

allowing for an assessment of progression from acquaintance to partnership to friendship.

To what extent can differing convictional sets be tolerated for friendship to start, and to continue? The nature of friendship will be quite different depending on where the greatest amount of overlap takes place: the social/communal, in terms of sharing time and common activities; organic, in terms of an intimate attachment of some sort; or the visionary, in terms of striving for the same eschatological purpose, perceiving the ultimate reality in a comparable way.[73] These convictional sets will not be necessarily evident to all involved, including those to whom they belong; and it will often be only through tension that they become apparent. "How much do we learn about ourselves from our reactions to other people! . . . But when we find out by this action and interaction with others what we are really like and what our own weaknesses are, we also learn what our strength is."[74] Care will be needed in discerning the nature of the clash, as it may be that the real conflict is not about the convictions which have been presented on the surface, but about deeper insecurities, passions, and conflicting loyalties.[75]

A sufficient overlap of convictions will be especially significant for those sufficiently close to the "core" of a particular believing community. Here I am borrowing Keith Jones' notion of a "porous," still "gathering" (as opposed to "gathered") community, open for new people to join as well as leaving the freedom for others to leave if they so wish.[76] Considering such "porousness" leads to various practical questions which would certainly include the issue of a manageable size of such a particular community. As Jones and Parushev argue, it should be "small enough for real *koinonia*":[77] it presupposes "communities of the street corners, of the side streets and apartment blocks, of the corner shop

---

73. This, of course, would be true to any vision which is capable of binding people together to work for the common purpose, but here I focus on the Christian vision of God's realm.

74. Francis, *But I Have Called You Friends*, 23–24.

75. Stassen and Gushee provide an insightful outline of the factors involved in the formation and display of one's character which carry an important role in the case of a convictional clash: beside what they call "basic convictions," these include "way of seeing," "way of reasoning," and "loyalties, trusts, interests, passions." *Kingdom Ethics*, 59ff.

76. Jones, "On Abandoning Public Worship."

77. Ibid., 10–11; cf. Aristotle's insistence that the number of one's friends should not exceed the "number with whom one can live together" (*Ethica Nicomachea* 1171a1).

and the corner pub."[78] Following the biblical witness, the deepening of the friendship—the getting to know ourselves and our friends—would certainly take place "in the breaking of the bread"—that is, the context of a meal shared by those who do it because of the One who called them friends.[79] What happens in the church, meeting in and meeting out, is exactly the work of discerning, defending, clarifying, challenging, and transforming such convictions, especially their visionary dimension. Thus the church's reaction to singleness I described earlier can be seen as symptomatic of the lack of such convictional refinement arising out of the thin practice of friendship, or alternatively because it has become a vicious, toxic friendship which is not "porous" and open to new friends.

Yet no matter how tightly overlapping the convictional sets of two or more friends are, they will never be identical, not the least because we as persons carry conflicting convictions in ourselves. Such discrepancies are bound to create tensions, resulting in struggle and, at certain times, in suffering. This will be the focus of the next chapter, but here I would like to stop for one moment at the dynamics that are involved in such convictional tension, particularly in relation to the visionary sphere of convictions. In some sense, such tension will be almost mandatory for such a community of friends to remain missionally and ecclesiologically porous if it is to be faithful to the One who was known as a friend of sinners and tax collectors. As Clapp puts it, "Christian friendship is not a matter of managing or controlling others, but of genuinely accepting their differences and standing open to surprises—surprises that, whether joyful or demanding, extend our powers to achieve greater excellence in the practice of friendship epitomized on the cross."[80]

How far can the discovery and interpretation of several conflicting convictional sets help with bringing them into line? It is helpful to recall the practice of communal discernment, or the rule of Christ, based on Matthew 18:15–20.[81] The attempt to understand one's convictions runs

---

78. Jones, "On Abandoning Public Worship," 11.
79. Ibid., 15–23.
80. Clapp, *A Peculiar People*, 209.
81. See Yoder, "Practicing the Rule of Christ," 132ff. Such discernment is tightly connected with the virtue of love that forgives, for it is such love that enables the relationship to go on. As Wadell says, "Every marriage, every friendship, any communal life together, when we look at any of these, we know there are points when we could easily say 'It could have ended here.' We need the life-giving love of forgiveness because it is the only power we have against the bumps and bruises of life" (*Becoming Friends*, 162).

a rather high probability of facing the need to reshape and transform those convictions. If the rule of Christ, or the communal discernment, is taken seriously, then the outcome of such struggle might include more than the parting of ways, or unconditional repentance; or even a compromise between the disagreeing parties, but a creativity of new actions, a new approach, an unexpected angle: a new creation *in Christ*.[82]

Such moments of tension, or convictional struggles, among friends illustrate how difficult loving friends may sometimes be. Yet, just as we ourselves can feel cherished and valued because God has loved us, "your love will make [your fellow believers] lovable."[83] In recognising in others the potential they cannot yet see in themselves, new doors into avenues of transformation and growth can be opened.[84] Indeed, "perhaps the crucial test for Christian friendship is our willingness to nurture for another a self they never were allowed to believe they had."[85]

Thus, whereas complementarity on the level of the organic and communal will be rather limited in protecting from the dangers of possible conflict among friends, a tension occurring on the level of the rapport with the divine, if resolved in a transformative way, has momentous potential.[86] The narrative pointing to the common vision, larger than ourselves or our interrelationships, can cohere differing convictional sets and, given the time and the virtues, such as commitment, particularity, mutuality, and vulnerability, align them so that these friendships can withstand times of testing. Through such moments of test and transformation, new insights and new embodiments of the meaning of life become possible as these friends of Jesus learn both how to live well and how to die well, practicing both happy life and happy death.[87]

Aelred of Rievaulx speaks of "great happiness" of "true and eternal friendship, which begins in this life and is perfected in the next, which here belongs to the few where few are good, but there belongs to all

---

82. For a similar argument of the church as a community of friends and of biblical interpretation which happen in its midst as a "persuasive testimony" in which truth is sought together, see Winter, "Persuading Friends."

83. Francis, *But I Have Called You Friends*, 27.

84. Wadell, *Friendship and the Moral Life*, 161.

85. Ibid., 162–63.

86. I owe this insight to Parush Parushev.

87. On the role of friendship in learning how to die, see Hauerwas and Yordy, "Captured in Time," 183.

where all are good."[88] In Aelred's vision, "this friendship, to which here we admit but few, will be outpoured upon all and by all outpoured upon God, and God shall be all in all."[89] Indeed, our best and most treasured moments in this life can be seen as but a foretaste of life to come. The moments we are able to experience with particular people, such as in parent-child, lover-lover, friend-friend relationship, are indeed the signs of the presence of God and of the fullness of life that only God can bring if those relationships are to be healthy and fulfilling. The hope for the future, then, is not the extinction of such relationships, but their healing, transformation, and expansion through the costly journey of learning to be a church of the friends of Jesus. In the visionary words of Aelred of Rievaulx, "Let us now grieve together over the miseries of the world, now rejoice together in the hope of future happiness. Let us now refresh one another by confiding our mutual secrets, now long together for the blessed vision of Jesus, and for heavenly wellbeing."[90]

In this chapter I looked at one of the (sub-)practices of Christian community, friendship. I have argued for the significance of this practice not only for questions related to happiness and the meaning of life, but also for its role in community formation and the sharpening of its convictions. I treated non-preferential love and preferential friendship not as mutually exclusive, but as two necessary elements of the Christian experience of growing into the likeness of Christ.

Next, I turned to a discussion of the virtues appropriate to the practice of friendship. The virtue list is certainly not exhaustive, but for the purposes of the present discussion I chose to focus on commitment, particularity, mutuality, and vulnerability. I sought to show how these virtues of the practice of friendship work as the "standards of excellence" according to which personal friendships can be appraised.

Finally, I opened up the implications of such an understanding of the practice of friendship in the context of the church. Not everybody

---

88. Aelred of Rievaulx, *Spiritual Friendship*, 3:80.

89. Ibid., 3:134. Hauerwas and Yordy also remind us of the dual meaning of the practice of friendship—"both in the sense of rehearsal and of habit" as the process of discipleship. Hauerwas and Yordy, "Captured in Time," 178.

90. Aelred of Rievaulx, *Mirror of Charity*, 300.

may agree that the relationships between the members of a believing community are best termed as "friendship," but I take a view that the practice of friendship is an inseparable element of the practice of Christian community formation and relates to the formation and transformation of the convictional sets of believing communities. Friendship is one of the central practices of the believing community set in a culture which yearns for connection but often is unable to practice healthy bonds of intimacy and love. In this, I concur with Wadell who claims that the church "should be a befriending community that not only welcomes all who come to it but also offers them a place where the grammar of intimacy and friendship can be learned."[91] In the process of such learning, both personal and communal transformations can take place.

---

91. Wadell, *Becoming Friends*, 53.

9

The Grain That Dies

Creative Growth of Suffering-Love

For the formative power of Christ lies in the formlessness of the grain of wheat that dies and wastes away [*ver-wesen*] in the humus, the grain that rises again, not in its own form but in that of the stalk of wheat . . . But the Christian grain of wheat possesses a genuine formative fruitfulness only if it does not encapsulate itself within a particular form set alongside all the forms of the world, an illusory form that thus condemns itself to sterility, but in imitation of the Founder's archetype squanders itself and offers itself up as a particular form—without being afraid of the dread [*Angst von der Angst*] of being abandoned and of letting go of oneself. Indeed, for the world, love alone is credible.[1]

ALTHOUGH IN SOME SENSE it may be surprising, the explorations of the previous chapters inevitably lead to the suffering aspect of love. It is impossible to address issues such as the struggle of involuntary singleness, meaning-making, community life, and the love it requires without attending to the pain involved in the process. I already touched upon such reality of suffering in the description of the experiences of involuntary singleness and encounters with indifference, being treated as inferior, or rejection. This is a suffering which in many cases has been made worse by the embodied convictions of the believing community. This is a suffering which the church has the responsibility to alleviate and eradicate.

---

1. Von Balthasar, *Love Alone Is Credible*, 136–38.

Yet even in a supportive environment, suffering will still be present, and the presence of such suffering will point to its mysterious role in the unfolding of life, especially life in relationship to others. Love, whether in friendship, in erotic attraction, or in the dedicated care for the other, often involves a measure of pain. Thus the purpose of this final chapter is to explore the realities of suffering and a particular virtue of love which blossoms in the context of suffering. As the guiding word for expressing this reality of suffering intrinsic to love, I will use the term 'suffering-love'.[2]

"Suffering" is a loaded and uncomfortable word. The discussion on suffering, altruism, or renunciation of one's needs can easily provoke an uncomfortable silence followed by a quick change of subject. Yet there is no way to quickly change the subject in an honest discussion of life in general and Christian life in particular. The epigraph for this chapter included Balthasar's reflection on Jesus' metaphor of the grain of wheat that must die for the new life to come. Such an observation is true on the literal level as well as in its implication for the life of following Jesus. Pain and sacrifice seem to be ingrained in the very life of this planet, so that without suffering there can be no new beginnings. It is also the condition for new spiritual beginnings. The one "that seeks not the Cross of Christ seeks not the glory of Christ," warned St. John of the Cross.[3] Suffering-love is central to the Christian web of practices; and its transformative power points to its proper interconnections with other aspects of a wholesome, meaningful, and truly happy life.[4] So now I reflect on how and when suffering can become part of love and become a testimony to its transformative, or redemptive, qualities.

---

2. I am grateful to Nancey Murphy for the suggestion of this term. Cf. McClendon's use of "grace-love" and "delight-love" in *Ethics* (2nd ed.), 154; Nicholas Wolterstorff's usage of *suffering*-Love (*Lament for a Son*, 90); and Kallistos Ware's discussion of God's suffering love as a victory, sacrifice, and example, in *Orthodox Way*, 80–83.

3. St. John of the Cross, *Counsels of Light and Love*, 57.

4. Human beings seem to have been granted an incredible ability to endure and redeem hardships, even such which in anticipation or retrospect might seem to have been unendurable. I reflect on the story of my own family who, at the height of Soviet repression, were deported to Siberia. Although the experience certainly involved physical and mental anguish, the way the stories have been told to me illustrate how such suffering was woven into a colourful fabric of some very warm memories and my family's sense of identity. (A theological reflection of the story of my family and particularly my grandfather can be found in Andronovienė, "Jonas Inkenas and Forgiveness Lived Out.")

Delineating Suffering

Yet how does one pinpoint "suffering"? After all, it can refer to such varying and differing experiences. Not only does it vary in degree and kind, but it also depends on circumstances and personality: what seems a horrifying experience to some may be considered a nuisance to others, although, of course, there are experiences that are horrific for anybody undergoing them, even if the sufferers still react to them with varying degrees of anguish. In the broadest sense, suffering could be said to be a result of sensing, in one way or another, a significant limitation to something necessary, or good, or desirable. Reasons for those limitations, as well as the perception of their extent, will differ. Suffering takes place when one experiences an acute physical pain, but also when someone feels oneself to be utterly alone in the world, deserted by all (and the two may well represent one affliction). It happens when one experiences anguish for another sufferer, or is deeply distressed about a particularly destructive situation. Suffering can take place when an older single woman is separated from the couples of her age and asked to go to a Bible study with young people "for singles." It is there in an abusive or difficult marriage. It can be born out of the dashed hopes of giving birth to a child, or when one's child travels a desctructive road. It can take place in the form of sexual frustration, in singleness as well as in marriage; or by being unable to find ways that would seem appropriate to express and channel care and affection to those around who are not one's spouse; or by being let down by those one has called friends. Suffering is there when rightful safety is given up and risk is taken for the sake of something greater than one's own avoidance of suffering. Suffering concerns all three spheres of human existence explored in this book—the organic, the social, and the visionary. For the Christian life-orientation, the ultimate story of suffering in all these spheres is that of the crucified Jesus—beaten and tortured, abandoned by both the closest and the crowd, and experiencing God-forsakenness.

Suffering is commonly associated with the conditions in which "the poor" live—the multitudes in the Majority World barely fighting for their own, and their loved ones', survival, working for meagre salaries, often in dangerous and life-threatening conditions, continually destroyed by unjust practices sustained by the Minority—"the developed world." Yet the common surprise of those from affluent societies visiting the poorest of the poor is that the latter often seem so joyous. The paradox of celebrating the exuberance of life alongside that very life being at a constant risk is difficult to fathom for those who are well-off.

One can also reflect on a very different situation which, inconceivably, seems to be colored by suffering in an utterly different way—the suffering of those who are the "misfits" of affluent society, unable to conform to expected standards. There are also those who suffer from physical or mental illness and sense their own "uselessness" in an extremely painful way. Even more depressingly, there are those who seem to have everything to prevent any suffering, and in that abundance, are left with excruciating emptiness. In the words of a Norwegian poet and artist Ole Paus, "We've got all, but that is all we've got."[5]

Whichever way it is experienced, suffering can rarely be described as "sheer suffering." Most of the time, it cannot be so easily pinpointed or isolated from other experiences. It can become precious when it becomes a significant part of our identity, or when its familiarity is preferred to the prospect of a different kind of suffering brought about by our changing selves. However, suffering can also enhance one's sensitivity to the occasions for joy—life deeply immersed in joy.[6] Indeed, for much of the time, life is a mixture of excitement and frustration in varying and ever-shifting degrees. Yet, no matter how seemingly small or significant, suffering is likely to be present. As Frankl has observed, it seems to possess gas-like qualities: if gas is in the room, it fills the whole room, no matter how much or how little gas is released. In the same way, suffering fills the mind evenly, no matter how severe or light it is.[7]

Not only does the suffering vary in nature and degree, it also has ghost imitations. How much of our perception of suffering is a result of the pictures we have grown up with, the language we have learned, the ways we have been taught to live? In other words, how much is suffering dependent on our interpretative world?[8] When am I making a sacrifice, and when is it a clever, even if subconscious, way of receiving a subtle reward, such as social recognition, a future repayment, or a chance to

5. "Vi har alt, men det er også alt vi har" in Norwegian. I am grateful to Håkon Sigland for bringing my attention to this quote. This line was used by the then Norwegian Prime Minister, Jen Stoltemberg, in his "Address to the Nation" for the New Year 2001.

6. Sydney Callahan provides a thoughtful reflection on the intricate relationship between suffering and joy in her *Created for Joy*.

7. Frankl, *Man's Search for Meaning*, 64.

8. Cf. Stanley Hauerwas' insightful essay on suffering, "Reflections on Suffering, Death, and Medicine": "In a sense . . . we must be taught that and how we suffer" (28).

manipulate? If I am single, how much of my suffering is that of missing a significant type of human relationship, and how much of it is being told that I should be miserable because I am a spinster? If I am a busy pastor, does my sacrifice of any free time mean suffering, or does it help me to avoid certain questions that start pressing on me whenever I am alone or with people who know me too well? If my community of faith has undergone persecution, what is it saying when, after the persecution ceases, the community emigrates in order to enjoy greater financial benefits and sees such emigration as God's reward for the suffering endured?[9]

Suffering can also be misinterpreted to become the basis for an unjust expectation of others—a point made by many a feminist thinker in regard to a woman's role as that of a sufferer.[10] In reaction to such abuse, some have rejected any notion of a positive interpretation of suffering. Criticising theologies that extol suffering as a Christian mark, Joanne Carlson Brown and Rebecca Parker resist the "piety" which

> sanctions suffering as imitation of the holy one. Because God suffers and God is good, we are good if we suffer. If we are not suffering, we are not good. To be like God is to take on the pain of all . . . The glorification of anyone's suffering allows the glorification of all suffering.[11]

Thus suffering-love is possibly the most contested virtue both within the Christian tradition and the secular discourses of today's Western societies. Perversions of this virtue need to be carefully looked at, and different safeguards are needed to address the various distortions. Suffering itself is not redemptive, or necessarily leads to wisdom and maturity. However, as suffering is an integral part of human life as we know it, it requires some thought on how it is to be faced. In other words, given that suffering is a reality—at times inevitable, at times chosen as a price for one's integrity—how can it be best met, so that it is woven into the fabric of love, rather than bitterness and retaliation?

---

9. Andronoviene and Parushev, "Church, State, and Culture." For another case study of the Ukrainian communities which moved to the United States after the end of persecution, see Wanner, *Communities of the Converted*, chap. 3, the title of which is telling: "The Rewards of Suffering: The Last Soviet Refugees."

10. For a sharply critical view, see Magli, *Women and Self-Sacrifice*.

11. Brown and Parker, "For God So Loved the World?" 19.

Suffering-Love in the Moral Universe: Science, Religion, and Altruism

> For the creation waits with eager longing for the revealing of the children of God; for the creation was subjected to futility, not of its own will but by the will of the one who subjected it, in hope that the creation itself will be set free from its bondage to decay and will obtain the freedom of the glory of the children of God. We know that the whole creation has been groaning in labour pains until now. (Rom 8:19–22)

For a fuller definition of suffering-love, I turn first to the resources arising from the intersection of science and theology. I do so in order to make a point that although there is something very particular in the suffering-love to which the followers of Christ are invited, foregoing one's benefit for the sake of the other(s) is more common than has often been thought. A common understanding of suffering has been heavily formatted by a modern thought pattern. It is often assumed, for example, that aggression is the underlying principle of natural life,[12] or that what may appear as altruism is actually the result of genetic programming ensuring the survival of the particular animal's genes through the survival of the group, or an anticipation of a favor returned (reciprocal altruism).[13] As Kristen Monroe argues, scientists "need to recognize that individual self-interest is neither universally nor necessarily the dominant force behind human behavior."[14]

Such a discussion is connected with a synonymous concept of suffering-love which is often employed in relevant literature: altruistic love.[15] The extent of such love and its underlying motives is vigorously

---

12. De Waal, *Good Natured*. Also see the criticism of such interpretation of the natural world to justify human violence and war issued by a group of scientists from various relevant fields on the occasion of Unesco's International Year of Peace (1986) in the Seville Statement on Violence (http://www.unesco.org/cpp/uk/declarations/seville.pdf). This is not to negate the aggression present in the natural world, but to question what has become the interpretive framework for construing (human) ethics.

13. Post et al., "General Introduction," 118–19.

14. Monroe, "Explicating Altruism," 115.

15. Stephen G. Post defines altruistic love as a "uniquely human" quality which represents "an intentional affirmation of the other, grounded in biologically given emotional capacities that are elevated by worldview (including principles, symbol, and myth) and imitation into the sphere of consistency and abiding loyalty." Post then refers to other virtues tightly linked with such altruistic love: care, compassion, sympathy,

contested, but the topic currently receives much attention. It has been suggested that although selfishness is certainly an important key in the way humans organize their lives, altruistic attitudes outside of the pool of one's own genes, one's own kin, or the promise of a favor returned, are also present, and at times extraordinarily so. Such altruistic behavior can be interpreted as emergent capacities observable in human beings. Various research projects have been undertaken, both from a Christian as well as other perspectives, to explore the human potential of altruism in various situations of life, challenging some settled assumptions in such fields as economics, psychology, biology, or sociology.[16]

One set of factors in the emergence of suffering-love is the importance of practices: "just as our identities influence our actions, so our acts shape and change us."[17] As discussed in chapters 7 and 8, these observations prompt a consideration of the community of belonging where such practices can take place. It is here that the difference between humans, who can reflect upon such communities, and the rest of the natural world, become important. While altruism is observable in the non-human world, when it comes to people, the most profitable way to speak about altruism is not so much an inherent quality as a skill acquired through practice.[18] "Beyond any human capacity to actualize a self . . . humans are distinguished by their capacity to see others, to oversee a world."[19] Such capacity to "see others," or the sense of the self as "[connected] to others and to a common whole,"[20] seems to be directly related to the emergence of suffering-love. The evidence of the research on such connection has prompted Monroe to suggest that "it may be that what I called an altruistic worldview might also be called spirituality."[21]

---

and the sense of justice. "Tradition of Agape," in Post, *Altruism and Altruistic Love*, 51.

16. See Grant, *Altruism and Christian Ethics*, chap. 1. For an overview of the interest in altruism among humans in social and biological sciences as well as cosmologists, see Oord, *Defining Love*, 65–172.

17. Monroe, "Explicating Altruism," 117.

18. Flescher and Worthen observe that as altruism is "more a matter of skill than talent, and therefore largely the result of hard work, it is something we should regard as contingent on our moral development." *Altruistic Species*, 239.

19. Rolston, "Kenosis and Nature," 64.

20. Monroe, "Explicating Altruism," 113.

21. Ibid., 112. Monroe points out that it is not spirituality/religion *per se* that seems to foster an altruistic worldview, but its particular content: for example, the Nazis interviewed by her described themselves as Christians or adherents of Germanic pagan-

This has direct links to the Christian worldview, but it also points out the significance of the convictional framework of human behaviour. As Collin Grant observes, it "is ultimately a matter of vision."[22] Thus George F. R. Ellis, overviewing the evidence for the enormity of expressions of letting go and giving up in the social, natural, and religious realms chooses to interpret the constant lending of chemical elements in the biosphere in the following way:

> Indeed, we are made of materials that are lent to us for the period of our lives, incorporating in our bodies atoms that have been utilized again by many thousands of living beings before us, and that will be utilized again by many thousands more after our death.[23]

Ellis, together with his coauthor Murphy, proposes a kenotic interpretation of the natural world.[24] Their claim is that such moral vision is confirmed both "from below," meaning "social and applied sciences," as well as "from above" by the discipline of researching an account of ultimate reality, i.e., theology of one or another kind.[25] Their argument is that ethics is always more than, but not free from, either the research taking place on the plane of social sciences, or from theology (whichever that theology may be—including any atheistic account of ultimate reality) from which it infers its presuppositions as to what a moral vision should entail.[26] In the same way, the argument applies to scientific research on altruistic or suffering-love: it is also not free from convictions and their expressions in the researcher's behaviour and articulated or unspoken attitudes. Without an awareness of such interlinking, any

---

ism and "genuinely seemed to believe they were doing something fine for the world by engaging in genocide" (113).

22. See his discussion on sociological research and the psychological, moral, and religious paradoxes of altruism in Grant, *Altruism and Christian Ethics*, 242–50. "The fact that there is not more altruism in the world than there is may be an indication of how superficial much of our religion is" (250). For the purposes of this work, I am only concerned here with the Christian vision, although some other religious traditions—Buddhism perhaps most notably—offer alternative proposals.

23. Ellis, "Kenosis as a Unifying Theme," 120.

24. See chaps. 1–3 in Dueck and Lee, *Why Psychology Needs Theology*, 3–76, which follow Murphy's work; as well as Murphy and Ellis, *On the Moral Nature of the Universe*, chap. 6ff. What is meant by "kenotic" will be clarified in the next section.

25. Murphy and Ellis, *On the Moral Nature of the Universe*, 1.

26. Ibid.

discipline—whether it be theology or socio-biology—risks unacknowledged fundamentalism.

An objection to this kind of reading of the nature of life on planet Earth is to observe that apart from humans, the rest of nature cannot be, strictly speaking, "moral," as actions in nature are not intentionally self-sacrificial. However, the opposite must also hold true: nature then equally cannot be seen as "cruel." Yet it has been persistently read in such a way for the last few centuries, and such persistence once again points to the inescapability of a convictional perspective of one sort or another. A morally neutral interpretation of the natural world is simply not viable. Holding to such an understanding, Murphy and Ellis therefore argue for an interpretation of the "moral nature of the universe" which sees suffering as nothing short of a transformative necessity.[27] Elaborating on the research on the morality of nature and the presence of pain and struggle, they observe:

> Pain seems to be necessary in any universe that involves freedom, since it protects the higher organisms from self-destructive behavior. In short, all living things must participate not only in the taking of life in order to live but also in the painful *giving* of their lives that others might live.[28]

How does such view inform a theological account for suffering-love? On the one hand, it could be argued that such an account need not be dependent on the evidence of altruism in the natural world. After all, the Gospel invitation to deny oneself and carry the cross is of a radical nature and stands regardless of, and in contrast to, "the way things are" either in the biblical domain of the "world" or in the scientific account of evolutionary realities. As Murphy notes, "Christian morality is different not only in motive but in content from kin-preserving altruism."[29] However, the gleanings from the world of science suggest that suffering-love may not be as rare as it has sometimes been thought of, and therefore significantly enriches an argument for and a theological appreciation of suffering-love.[30] To put it very bluntly, if even science is researching the reality of suffering-love, how much more so should Christian theology.

27. Ibid., passim. Or as Pierre Teilhard de Chardin phrases it: "Everything that *becomes* suffers or sins." *On Suffering*, 2.

28. Murphy and Ellis, *On the Moral Nature of the Universe*, 213.

29. Murphy, *Bodies and Souls*, 120.

30. It is important to keep in mind here that I am following a discussion on non-

Moreover, such kenotic interpretation of the natural world points to a variety of ways suffering-love is expressed in the Christian practice. As Holmes Rolston III puts it, when such a perspective is appropriated instead of the non-altruistic interpretations such as the theory of the "selfish gene,"[31] the following picture emerges:

> Life on earth is not a paradise of hedonistic ease, but a theater where life is earned by toil and sweat. We do not really have available to us any coherent alternative models by which, in a hurtless, painless world, there might have come to pass anything like these dramas in botanical and zoological nature and that have happened, events that in their central thrusts we greatly treasure . . .
>
> The abundant life that Jesus exemplifies and offers to his disciples is that of a sacrificial suffering through to something higher. The Spirit of God is the genius that makes alive, that redeems life from its evils. The cruciform creation is, in the end, deiform, godly, just because of this element of struggle, not in spite of it. There is a great divine "yes" hidden behind and within every "no" of crushing nature.[32]

Even taking into the account that "nature" as such does not make moral choices, either selfish or altruistic, it transpires that "far from making the world absurd, suffering is a key to the whole, not intrinsically, not as an end in itself, but as a transformative principle, transvalued into its opposite. *The capacity to suffer through to joy is a supreme emergent and an essence of Christianity.*"[33] Is it indeed the case? How might theology see the shape of the virtue required for enduring such suffering through to joy? This is what I now turn to.

---

reductive physicalism which would claim that human behavior is more than what takes place on the level of chemistry and physics. If human uniqueness in terms of the capacity for kenotic behavior is understood, not in terms of the existence of soul, but of the capacity to communicate with the created order and the Creator, then kenotic behavior can be enhanced by the means of top-down causation, or "participation in a kenotic community" (Jeeves, "Nature of Persons," 74)—the topic to which I turn in the second section of this chapter.

31. As represented by Dawkins' *Selfish Gene*.
32. Rolston, "Kenosis and Nature," 59.
33. Ibid., 60; emphasis mine.

Kenosis: A Theological Account of Suffering-Love

> If real, self-giving, others-centered love is not possible, why would anyone risk connecting with imperfect people who will inevitably mess you up?[34]

> Our brokenness reveals something about who we are. Our sufferings and pains are not simply bothersome interruptions of our lives; rather, they touch us in our uniqueness and our most intimate individuality.[35]

Whereas scientists most often referred to words such as altruism or benevolence, switching now to theological terminology I turn attention to the word commonly used in this field, "kenosis." This will be an important working term for this section before I move to the use of suffering-love, my preferred term.

Numerous voices have argued for the importance of the notion of kenosis for Christian theology.[36] Briefly put, kenotic theology involves an exploration of the self-giving and suffering of God, especially, though not exclusively, in the suffering of Jesus on the cross.[37] As Tillich notes, "The suffering of God, universally and in the Christ, is the power which overcomes creaturely self-destruction by participation and transformation."[38] I will be referring to some of the theological enquiries into the phenomenon of suffering and its reasons, but my main focus is on the response of love.which it can generate.

I return now to the work undergone by Murphy and Ellis who elaborate on their own, that is, Anabaptist (or in the terms I use, baptistic) tradition. They describe this tradition—in their terms, "theological research programme"—as centered around the practice of kenosis: "The moral character of God is revealed in Jesus' vulnerable enemy love and renunciation of dominion. Imitation of Jesus in this regard constitutes a social ethic."[39] In another work, Ellis elaborates on this further:

---

34. Gilliam, *Revelations of a Single Woman*, 194.
35. Nouwen, *Life of the Beloved*, 71.
36. See, e.g., Evans, *Exploring Kenotic Christology*.
37. In its Christian use, the term "kenosis" derives from Phil 2:7 where it is used in reference to the self-emptying of Christ. The concept of kenosis as an important theme in Christology for both Eastern Orthodox and Western theologies has appeared in a variety of forms but has come to the fore especially during the course of the last two centuries.
38. Tillich, *Systematic Theology*, 2:176.
39. Murphy and Ellis, *On the Moral Nature*, 178. Murphy and Ellis conclude that

> Kenosis is understood not just as a letting go or giving up, but as being prepared to do so in a creative and positive way for a positive purpose in tune with the nature of God. Thus it is seen, when given a theological grounding, as follows:
>
>> *Kenosis:* a joyous, kind, and loving attitude that is willing to give up selfish desires and to make sacrifices on behalf of others for the common good and the glory of God, doing this in a generous and creative way, avoiding the pitfall of pride, and guided and inspired by the love of God and the gift of grace.[40]

As Murphy suggests elsewhere, such "'kenotic' ethic of self-renunciation . . . [includes] detachment from material possessions, renunciation of one's rights to rewards and to retaliation, non-violence, acceptance of suffering, and submission to God."[41] The essence of Christ-like ethics then can be seen as "self-renunciation for the sake of the other."[42] Furthermore, the goal of Murphy and Ellis is to demonstrate that such ethics is possible and in existence in many more instances than it is usually recognized.[43] It is precisely these kinds of demonstrations that, in Murphy and Ellis' understanding, make such an ethical stance legitimate, for "an ethic as a whole can be refuted if it can be shown that it calls for a form of life that is simply incapable of social embodiment."[44]

---

there is significant disagreement on the way human nature is viewed by theologians coming from different theological traditions. This has to do with the way the life of Jesus is appropriated theologically and specifically to such references as Phil 2:7 and Christ's "emptying of himself." If the "emptying" is considered not in the framework of the discussion of the preexistence of Jesus and his incarnation, but submission, such as especially exemplified in facing the cross, then the issue becomes a moral one rather than a reflection on the nature of God. For a succinct overview of the differences of reading the Phillipians in these two distinct ways, see Coakley, "Kenosis: Theological Meanings and Gender Connotations," 194.

40. Ellis, "Kenosis as a Unifying Theme," 108.

41. Murphy, "Theological Resources for Integration," 29.

42. Ibid., 42.

43. Murphy and Ellis, *On the Moral Nature*, passim, but see esp. chaps. 6 and 7. They also provide an extensive bibliography on other works researching the feasibility of a non-violent (and thus kenotic) way of life in terms of empirical evaluation.

44. Ibid., 141.

Attention to the notion of suffering as a corporate task of the church can be argued to constitute an important baptistic feature.[45] In the "baptistic heritage" explored by authors such as McClendon or Stassen and Gushee, or Parushev, suffering (and, at some points of history, martyrdom) is "not a marginal but central part" of the Christian life,[46] the vehicle of delivering others from their affliction,[47] and an element germane to the emergence of the baptistic Christian witness.[48] Of course, such an emphasis is also met in the work of theologians of other traditions and perspectives in their dealing with the implications of Jesus' suffering on the cross, and therefore also the suffering of God. Thus, for example, a feminist theologian McFague states:

> Kenosis is a unifying theme in Christian thought, extending beyond God's actions in creation and the incarnation to include the discipleship of followers. As Paul reminds his flock, "Let each of you look not to your own interests, but to the interests of others. Let the same mind be in you that was in Christ Jesus" (Phil 2:4); namely, follow the self-emptying Christ. *Kenosis—self-limitation so that others may have place and space to grow and flourish—is the way God acts toward the world and the way people should act toward one another and toward creation.*[49]

Yet there is another point to consider, and it has to do with the undertones that at least partly may be related to gendered experience. As Coakley points out, a typical understanding of what kenosis entails is to take God's voluntary foregoing of his power and freedom in order to make "space" for the world, and more concretely, for human beings. Here is the word picture Coakley draws to illustrate this sort of understanding: "The visual picture here . . . is of a (very big) divine figure backing out of the scene, or restraining his influence, in order that other (little) figures may exercise completely independent thinking and acting."[50] Given the danger present in such an image becoming a tool in sustaining systems of domination and victimisation, it is no wonder that feminist theologians have repeatedly expressed scepticism and even rejection of

---

45. See, e.g., Fiddes, "Prophecy, Corporate Personality, and Suffering," 72–94.
46. McClendon, *Witness*, 347.
47. Stassen and Gushee, *Kingdom Ethics*, 333ff.
48. Parushev, "Knowing the Risen Christ," 53–54.
49. McFague, *New Climate for Theology*, 136; emphasis original.
50. Coakley, "Kenosis: Theological Meanings and Gender Connotations," 205.

self-emptying as the core of Christian ethics. For example, attending to the issues of body and sexuality, Isherwood and Steward state: "We are called to change the world not through self-emptying sacrifice as with *agape*, but rather through mutual, interactive, self-affirming sensuous love. How far this is from the Christ of the power brokers and yet how close to the man of the gospels who sought relationality."[51]

However, as Coakley suggests, an alternative appropriation of the kenotic love of God could be considered as "nurturing and sustaining us into freedom."[52] In this case, God's freedom and ours, or God's power and ours, is not in competition but "is emptied" by an unexpected, empowering movement enabling the birth of new things. I will return to both the distortions of kenotic emphasis and the imagery of birth further on in the chapter; here it may be noted that such understanding of kenotic love as Coakley's has to do with a dynamic understanding of the self as becoming—in Daniel Day Williams' words, "a career" of its own, or in Soelle's, suffering itself understood as "a mode of becoming."[53] Thus it is always not only saying a "no" to something that is, but a "yes" to what will be.

Yet even if intellectually consented to, the kenotic rendering of the core of Christian ethics is an uncomfortable one. If one has any integrity, it immediately calls for an investigation of one's life and the extent of self-giving, suffering-love. I am forced to think about it while writing this paragraph. I am also reminded of the many times the church has been unable to embody such a kenotic attitude, as well as the times when, at least on the surface, kenotic acts seem to have "failed" in terms of their effect (although one must remember that Jesus' crucifixion and death looked a failure to the watching world). Indeed, "Christians cannot prove that self-emptying will be met eventually by increased infilling. . . . They can only testify to their and the Christian tradition's experience of this—and their belief that God is faithful."[54]

This becomes an impossibility when there is no personal kenotic testimony to offer. Moreover, the witness of the larger Christian tradition—including its baptistic stream—points to a multivalent nature of kenotic experiences. One of the first objections would seem to be the

---

51. Isherwood and Stuart, *Introducing Body Theology*, 50.
52. Coakley, "Kenosis: Theological Meanings and Gender Connotations," 205.
53. Williams, *Spirit and the Forms of Love*, 203; Soelle, *Suffering*, 98.
54. Finger, *Self, Earth & Society*, 293.

unqualified nature of self-renunciation. As noted above, does not such an ethic run a great danger of glorifying suffering for its own sake, or legitimizing the abuse of others? These are serious concerns. Whenever self-renunciation becomes an end in itself or a calculated move, serious distortions take place. Sacrificial appearance can be used as a mask, become an ideology, or a fake passport to God's realm, thereby losing its redemptive quality.

These concerns are apparent to those reflecting on kenosis. Ellis is careful to underline that "[sacrificial kinds of acts] are appropriate when they have the potential to transform the nature of the situation to a higher level," thus calling for a discernment.[55] Ellis makes clear qualification to kenotic behavior. First, it means willingness or preparedness to act kenotically when required and when appropriate; and appropriateness is judged by the transformative potential of the situation.[56] Second, therefore, the requirement is expressed in the creativity of treating all parties in the conflict not equally in a simplistic way, but taking into account their intentions, which thereby legitimizes such actions as standing against aggressors in order to protect innocent victims.[57]

Ellis acknowledges that this view, in fact, could lead to a variant of the just-war theory and, given the inventiveness with which human beings find moral justification for their actions, to becoming not much different from the perpetrator(s). He thus suggests that in order to be viable and sustainable as an option, such kenotic action has to be the norm "for some people, all the time," and for the rest, at least "some of

55. Ellis, "Kenosis as a Unifying Theme," 122. Stassen and Gushee similarly would be keen to emphasise the "delivering" intent of such suffering-love. *Kingdom Ethics*, 333–44.

56. Ellis notes that the doubt if self-sacrifice works in the case of mass murder has not been confirmed because such kenotic behaviour has not been practiced enough. On the other hand, testimonies abound of the power of kenotic behaviour in the face of seeming hopelessness and pointlessness. As a Lithuanian, I witnessed the buds of such behavior in the armless opposition to the Soviet forces in the so-called January events of 1991, when the crowds stood to protect the parliament and media buildings with their own bodies, staying there even in the face of the tanks. This was an extremely risky behaviour, without any guarantee of success. Moreover, it was not regulated from above; in fact, given the grave danger the leaders of the independence movement repeatedly urged people to go home. Instead, the spirit of the nation was seen clearly embodied in the people's resolve to stay, to attempt to engage the Soviet soldiers in a discussion of what they were about to do, and to carry food and wood to keep those standing from hunger and cold.

57. Ellis, "Kenosis as a Unifying Theme," 121–23.

the time."[58] (Even though the ideal would be all the people all the time, Ellis recognizes this is not simply true, and thus calls for the "idealists" who do believe in kenosis to be witnesses to the possibility of a different kind of life.)

Building on these insights, it may be more valuable to approach kenosis not as action but as a virtue—the virtue of suffering-love. Such an understanding allows for an appropriation of practices and acts which could be described in kenotic terms as particular expressions of this virtue. In this fashion, the discussion turns away from the focus on the problematic issue of discovering how, when the "right" time comes, a person willing to act kenotically could actually recognize the moment (with all the requirements of "potential for transformation") and, will that action really be sacrificial as far as intentions go. Rather, the key concern becomes the fertility of the setting in which the virtue of suffering-love can flourish.

I will once again employ a three-stranded hermeneutics of human existence: bodily experience, social setting and the guiding vision which arises from the first two but also enables their transformation.[59] As indicated earlier, these three spheres will always remain interconnected; in some sense their separation is both artificial and partial. Yet considering them separately for a moment allows for the emphases in terms of the role that suffering-love can play in each.

Suffering-Love: Persons, Communities, Visions

> Part of the power of healing lies in discovering another who can hear my story, experience my feeling, and not be destroyed by it.[60]

> We thank you for this strange, terrible, marvellous power of our body, power which makes it spiritual and image of your love, power to feel pity

---

58. Ibid., 123–26.

59. Even though I explore these realms chiefly from a theological perspective, similar insights can be made from the viewpoint of other fields too. Thus, reflecting on the medical ethics involved in dealing with patients, William F. May observes that a bodily suffering involves a crisis in how "the patient identifies with her body, with her community, and with the ultimate. The self . . . identifies in all sorts of ways, wittingly and unwittingly, with these three, depending heavily and daily upon each. Whatever separates the self from these identities imposes upon the self the shudder of death." May, *Patient's Ordeal*, 9.

60. Williams, "Suffering and Being in Empirical Theology," 188.

and compassion, so that the sufferings of other bodies are felt as if they were our own.[61]

The tone of the fortitude shown by the tortured is very different when they think of themselves only as poor, or brave, lonely wretches, and when they think of themselves as members of the mystical body of Christ. Only the latter are likely to come through without succumbing to hatred. Moreover it is only they who can pool their terrible experiences with the redemptive work of others.[62]

Suffering-Love and Bodily Tenderness

When the body is in pain, it easily demands the sole focus of the sufferer. The task of meaning-making may feel too painful, the vision may seem dimmed, the social setting perceived as an insignificant background, or even a source of irritation or anger: "they do not care nor understand what I am going through." Thus the circumstances that generate suffering also produce, as D. D. Williams terms it, a "hightened self-consciousness."[63] Here lies both the possibility of the rejection of suffering-love and its healing potential. In terms of the latter, if suffering is to become a transformative feature, it needs to be woven into the fabric of one's identity. The story of sufferer's self is thus enriched and, as I shall argue later, capable of identifying with other sufferers. On the other hand, as Williams warns, there is a danger of being attached to the present sufferings so that they become a static aspect of one's identity, so that there is no willingness to move beyond them even when given a chance to do so. "We cling to our sufferings," says Williams, "as guaranteeing our identity. Our sufferings are ourselves."[64] Such clinging represents a danger of the disintegration of the self as a whole. Suffering-love in such case can be compared to a muscle that never had a chance to develop or has atrophied: the sufferer's world is shrinking, the interest in the lives of those around her or him is increasingly diminishing, and the disappearing vital links of the self reveal the disappearance of the self. For, as Hauerwas aptly notes, "we depend upon others not only for our survival but also for our identity. Suffering is built into our condition because it

---

61. Alves, *I Believe in the Resurrection of the Body*, 58.
62. De Beausobre, *Creative Suffering*, 24.
63. Williams, "Suffering and Being," 182.
64. Ibid., 184.

is literally true that we exist only to the extent that we sustain, or 'suffer,' the existence of others and the others include not just others like us, but mountains, trees, animals, and so on."[65]

This is not to say that such disappearance of the self is the sufferer's own choice and fault. The distress caused by a limitation of one sort or another—especially of a chronic and highly physical nature—can cause the sufferer to feel utterly cut off from the world around. There is a sense of isolation and abandonment that may seem like a wall impossible to break without an initiative of those on the other side of it. But with such initiatives, the muscle of suffering-love can be put to use in order to break out of the static identification with suffering and its isolation. The self can be empowered to transform the sense of loneliness into solitude of a sort, something which is essential for a deep knowledge of oneself, and which then enables the self to reach out in communion.

The work of suffering-love includes embracing and reintegrating the frustrated, ailing, agonising, or even dying bodies. Encouraging such integration is one of the tasks of the believing community, perhaps notably in its intercessory prayer. Particular faith communities will have varying attitudes toward prayer for healing. Some will be enthusiastic and, in their enthusiasm, can even escalate the pain if no physical healing takes place. Others, weary of this danger and in reaction to the abuses of "praying in faith," can adopt a stance which concentrates on the sufferer's "soul" and can further alienate her or him from her or his bodily sensations.

Both distortions need to be avoided. Prayers for healing need to be centered on an understanding of the virtue of suffering-love as both bestowing and inviting a blessing. The language of blessing returns me to the discussion on happiness. In the context of suffering, the happiness of the Beatitudes can come to life when the sufferer is helped to see in the prayers offered not only the blessing of consolation but also an invitation to respond with a blessing. Such an invitation holds in itself an energy for meaning-making out of which an offer of blessing can emerge.

To illustrate what I mean, I take a few thoughts of Henri Nouwen as he reflects on the brokenness of personal longings: "The first response . . . to our brokenness is to face it squarely and befriend it. It may seem quite unnatural . . . My own pain in life has taught me that the first step to healing is not a step away from the pain, but a step toward

---

65. Hauerwas, *Suffering Presence*, 169.

it."⁶⁶ This is the mystery of the happiness—blessedness—promised in the Beatitudes: "The deep truth is that our human suffering need not be an obstacle to the joy and peace we so desire, but can become, instead, the means *to* it."⁶⁷ To explore this deep truth will require a fuller discussion on the visionary realm of suffering, but here I note the mystery and the gift of coming to embrace an affliction as a surprising blessing.

The second response to suffering, as Nouwen suggests, involves becoming aware of how the blessing of suffering can spring out as a blessing for others: "When we keep listening attentively to the voice calling us the Beloved, it becomes possible to live our brokenness, not as a confirmation of our fear that we are worthless, but as an opportunity to purify and deepen the blessing that rests upon us."⁶⁸ Those who have been cared or prayed for or given a blessing by someone severely ill or dying would probably agree that it is a strongly moving, and sometimes life-changing, experience.⁶⁹ In such a way, using Nouwen's phrase, the sufferers themselves become the "wounded healers."⁷⁰

It is perhaps more obvious how this double-direction of the blessing works in more extraordinary cases. However, it would also be true of what might be thought of as less challenging examples of bodily frustrations: here, also, the suffering-love can grow as the blessing is both given and received. Rather than attempting to describe it, it may be best to present a particular account of a single woman:

> There have been moments, such as a particularly languid summer night at the beach or the evening after a long weekend of speaking, when my heart and body feel a longing for some greater connection, some greater release; a part of me suddenly aches to curl up with my man, to have warm flesh touch warm flesh. Sitting in that unfulfilled moment, there is an undeniable ache, almost physical in nature. I used to fear that ache—that if left unfulfilled, it would make me crazy or barren or a social misfit. But I don't fear the ache anymore. Yes, it feels bad, but I know that in the

---

66. Nouwen, *Life of the Beloved*, 75.
67. Ibid., 77; emphasis original.
68. Ibid., 79.
69. Writing these words, I recall various sufferers whose life has left a deep impact on me, but especially on the life of my own grandmother, a person who was confined to a wheelchair and bed for more than fifty years, yet who has been considered as a blessing by many who have been enriched by an encounter with her.
70. Nouwen, *Wounded Healer*.

end, the ache does not have to destroy me. Rather, I have slowly been discovering that the disease to be feared is not—contrary to so many of the voices that surround me—*not gettin' it*, but rather, it's *not givin' it*. So my hope has become that I will grow in my capacity to give it, give myself—whether that takes the form of my body, my heart, my time, my energy, or my dreams—in ways that give life to others.[71]

Suffering-love's buds will be visible whenever such gift of giving—freely and perhaps unexpectedly for others—emerges out of sorrow and torment. Such giving can be free from the contemporary hang-ups on productivity and effectiveness, and as such, present a prophetic reminder of the real value of the gift of the human person. And so, somewhere in the recognition of one's own suffering as an unexpected, uneasy blessing, healing can begin. Yet the full story of healing and integration cannot be told without the other two elements necessary for a transformative interpretation of the suffering within the body. To these I now turn.

The Social Setting of Suffering-Love

So much suffering in today's Western societies has a marked social emphasis: broken links, withered friendships, commodified relationships, superficial contacts. It can be especially painful to see such marks in ecclesial life, when the vision of the Christian story is presented without its social embodiment; where one is told to go and figure out the meaning of her or his life in Jesus on one's own. In such settings, one is not likely to experience genuine care regarding her or his organic anguish (shallow promises to pray notwithstanding), and this may only sharpen the ache. Such experience can be widespread, and its repercussions may be much more momentous than a sudden loss of one vital social connection such as the death of a close friend, spouse, or a relative. The descriptions presented earlier give a clear indication of such danger for the communities of faith.

At the same time, I have been making an argument that the communal realm has a crucial role to play in bringing about healing and transformation. The reality of the chuch's expressions of suffering-love pertains both to its ability to absorb the pain of the particular, suffering, members, and to the experience of the community suffering as a

---

71. Gilliam, *Revelations of a Single Woman*, 69–70.

corporate body—certainly in times of persecution, but not only then.[72] Conditions enabling the growth of suffering-love involve not a community that could be described as perfect, but a community which, while it proclaims the vision of healing and restoration, is sufficiently immersed in community-forming practices, such as friendship. It is through such practices that the church can create the "catalytic effect"[73] for fostering Christ-like suffering-love. The stories of personal anguish can be woven together and in the process, their interpretation will be enlarged, enriched, and transformed. As D. D. Williams puts it, "Either we share suffering in love or outside of love . . . Suffering with the other in love becomes a sacrament of the possibility of love in all being and is the deepest source of the transmutation of suffering."[74]

Reflecting on the dynamics involved in such transmutation of suffering, Soelle has suggested that it brings about an expression of solidarity with others who suffer. It takes place, she contends, when suffering is verbalized and the isolation of its muteness is broken. As one becomes able to express what one is going through, such communication has a potential to lead one into solidarity with others, and thus, the possibility of true transformation.[75] Such solidarity would need to be reflected in the concentric circles of the believer's social setting: not only solidarity within the Christian community, but in the ecumenical circle also, then those outside of the Christian community of faith, and, in most challenging cases, even among enemies who are no longer viewed as such but as fellow humans in pain.

How can the church enable such expression, communication, and sharing of pain? In exploring the answer to this question, I turn to one of the essential church practices: worship. Here, the public reading of Scripture will be of special importance in its ability to provide a language for articulating the reality of suffering. Psalms, the prayer book of the church, represent a particularly powerful resource. Although often reduced to the "nice" bits that can survive "the polite hermeneutic of the church,"[76] the Psalms, read, sung, or retold by the community, represent

---

72. For a moving personal account of the community's care for a sufferer, see Goldingay, *Walk On*, esp. 48–61.

73. Jeeves, "Nature of Persons," 88.

74. Williams, "Suffering and Being," 189.

75. Soelle, *Suffering*, 70–74.

76. Brueggemann, *Message of the Psalms*, 16. Brueggemann aptly voices the prob-

a vital piece and parcel of the church's task of "teaching to speak" for all of its members.[77] As such language-learning begins to take place, not only one's own suffering finds an expression in a complaint, but an awareness of others' suffering grows, links begin to be formed to the experiences of others, and out of that, solidarity with their suffering. Such solidarity unites suffering with love so that it becomes an active force, transforming not only one's own, but also the suffering of others.

The Psalms point to another significant element of the practice of worship: prayer. Prayer provides a natural space for both communication of suffering and solidarity with the suffering of others, "in order to look at things not just from our own self-centered perspective but from the perspective of the vision we are seeking together."[78] A strongly communal dimension is necessary for prayer to be able to foster and express suffering-love. To talk of the communal nature of common prayer may seem strange: after all, prayer is naturally associated with the life of the believing community. However, prayers prayed in the presence of others can nevertheless lack any real sense of community. They can be exclusively concentrated on individual needs and offered in reference to the vision commonly professed, yet without the space for honesty which is required for genuine communication of one's suffering and without any communal effort at meaning-making.[79]

This exploration of the practice of worship and two of its elements, prayer and the reading of Scripture, serves to illustrate the role of suffering-love in approaching the theme of suffering within the life of the believing community. Other elements, and other practices, could be explored in a similar fashion, but I hope I have already made the intended point: by resisting the urge to shy away from the presence of suffering,

---

lem: "Much Christian piety and spirituality is romantic and unreal in its positiveness. As children of the Enlightenment, we have censored and selected around the voice of darkness and disorientation, seeking to go from strength to strength, from victory to victory. But such a way not only ignores the Psalms; it is a lie in terms of our experience" (ibid., 11).

77. The idea of the church's task of "teaching people to speak" is taken from Soelle, *Suffering*, 74.

78. Vanier, *Becoming Human*, 31.

79. I assume that for Vanier, writing out of an experience of l'Arche communities, this would be an aspect much more readily present and therefore not necessarily needing a special mention. It is significantly more difficult to hide behind a façade of self-sufficiency in a setting such as l'Arche, where life is shared by both the so-called "healthy" and severely handicapped people.

the church trains itself to embrace suffering with love, thereby opening a door to its transformation. At the same time, the church is also engaged in *preparing* for suffering that is still to come, both corporate and personal. In worship, the community of God's people learns to read the world and their experience of the world kenotically, and in such learning, discerns its own situation and the kenotic actions which it calls for. However, as I will discuss next, such kenotic reading is possible only in the framework of a guiding vision which enables the community to make sense out of the specific situations of affliction.

The Vision of Suffering-Love

Such vision is articulated through a story capable of conferring a meaning to the particular experience of suffering.[80] For those committed to the way of Christ, the contours of such story emerge and take shape around the way the believing community reiterates the story of God in Christ. As with the bodily and communal spheres, the visionary domain of life may also be severely damaged, for example, when the vision is reduced to a comfortable interpretation of Christian life that does not require facing the costly call to follow the One who chose to suffer for others' sake.

Yet, as reviewed earlier, suffering-love is a disturbingly essential element of the Christian vision, impossible to miss if one is genuinely approaching it with a desire to understand. Following such a vision, all suffering—that which can be more or less explained or felt as deserved as well as the inexplicable, Job-like suffering—is to gain meaning as it is woven into the Christian narrative. Learning to reiterate the Christian narrative has to do with learning and practicing a language that allows for multiform expressions of anguish.

I have already referred to that resource for the vocabulary of lament, the book of Psalms, discovered by many who have turned to it— and specifically the less-than-happy portions—in their own anguish. As pain is verbalized, it can then be placed into the larger story of faith. Just

---

80. Fiddes, *Creative Suffering of God*, 146. As noted earlier, the story which enables meaning-making (including situations of pain and suffering) may not be explicitly religious. In May's description, it involves "those connections which the self makes, whether conventionally religious or not, with those patterns and powers that go beyond, yet sustain, his life, perhaps unreflected upon, not prayed to, but that keep his life on a firm footing and that put a spring into his step." May, *Patient's Ordeal*, 12.

as many psalms move from putting affliction into words to the pleading, anticipation, and experience of reintegration and healing, so it is with other exercises of articulating suffering; and most notably, with telling the story of Christ, both his suffering and his resurrection. In the words of Hauerwas and Pinches, "We learn to inhabit the narrative of God's work in Jesus Christ and so to see all existence as trustworthy."[81] This conviction becomes a place where hope can live even in the most pressing and depressing encounters of senseless suffering, and leads to a faith in God for who all time is present, and in whom all suffering is taken up to gain meaning and be enveloped in love.[82] As Teilhard puts it, "Not everything is immediately good to those who seek God; but everything is capable of becoming good."[83] The suffering of Christ, and the ending of his suffering in resurrection, gives meaning for our own experience.

Such apparent simplicity of identifying with the sufferings of Christ must be at the same time taken with care and subtlety. Here Psalms provide an important reminder again. In their multiplicity of voices, moods and attitudes, in their fluctuation from firm convictions to pleading for mere survival, they offer multiple hermeneutical perspectives for interpreting suffering.[84] They also reflect the nature of biblical faith which does not shy away from complaints and laments addressed to God, but seems to require them for that faith to be genuine.[85] As the suffering-love gropes for meaning, it must find it as a gift, rather than a forced explanation in the fashion of Job's friends.

When such gift is recognized and gratefully received, one is again reminded of the paradox deeply ingrained into the experience of suffering-love: in expending oneself, one's own self is enhanced—or in biblical words, life is found by losing it.

> We always become more truly ourselves when we give ourselves away, and we sacrifice ourselves only to find that we receive our selves back. We find ourselves as a mysterious by-product of los-

---

81. Hauerwas and Pinches, *Christians among the Virtues*, 126.

82. Here I am taking the "eternalist position" in relation to God and time, i.e., that, as Charles E. Gutenson puts it, God is "temporally omnipresent." See his "Time, Eternity, and Personal Identity," 117–32. Cf. also Moltmann, *Coming of God*, 292–95.

83. Teilhard, *On Suffering*, 74.

84. Swenson, *Living through Pain*, 66.

85. Hauerwas notes: "Ironically, the act of unbelief turns out to be committed by those who refuse to address God in their pain, thinking that God just might not be up to such confrontation." *Naming the Silences*, 84.

ing ourselves; that is the pattern of the divine love itself, and is nothing to do with selfishness, which is a matter of setting out deliberately to realize ourselves as the main goal.[86]

These insights are reverberated in the studies of happiness I have reviewed earlier. If, as it has been suggested, happiness has to do with forgetting ourselves in an activity focused on something other than ourselves, this demonstrates a tight link between suffering, meaning, and deep happiness. Shaped by the virtue of suffering-love, the pain and the struggle move away from the center of one's attention and preoccupation. What emerges is the paradox that suffering—suffering endowed with meaning—becomes the source of deep joy for its transformative capabilities.[87]

I can now reattend to Murphy and Ellis' insights on kenotic ethics. A vision which looks for the growth of suffering love calls the church to have its eyes open to various injustices that require change, and to do something about them in ways consistent with the kenotic ethic. This task includes recognising, in the experience of the suffering of others and in the response to such suffering, the seeds of love which can be grown into living out the story of Jesus. "The word of God which became flesh in Jesus Christ moves in human life, often secretly, often unrecognized, yet persistently becoming the luminous word through which we begin to understand what every love really is."[88]

Suffering-love is capable of such recognition, and such determination, because of the creative nature of its guiding vision. The link between suffering and creativity has been noted repeatedly.[89] As pointed out by Ellis, it involves creative treatment of those experiencing a particular

---

86. Fiddes, *Creative Suffering of God*, 171–72.

87. Yet care must be taken not to reverse the argument: if suffering love is seen to be automatically rewarding, then we arrive at "the sophisticated self-interest of 'virtue ethics'" (Ellis, "Kenosis as a Unifying Theme," 110).

88. Williams, *Spirit and the Forms of Love*, 212.

89. It was Martin Luther King Jr. who in his "I Have a Dream" called those suffering from racist oppression "the veterans of creative suffering." Three other significant Christian thinkers who have written on the subject of creative suffering are Iulia de Beausobre (*Creative Suffering*), Paul Tournier (*Creative Suffering*), and Paul S. Fiddes (*Creative Suffering of God*). The work by Tournier, a Christian physician whose passion was a holistic approach to people, is especially notable due to his frequent references to involuntary singleness (especially that of women) as an important experience to reflect on creative suffering.

struggle (much echoing the precepts of the Sermon on the Mount). What is more, creativity is inextricably linked to the very nature of suffering-love. Although sometimes creativity is equated with ease and play, the creativity of suffering-love can be extremely costly. Reflecting on the agony of Jesus, Teilhard talks about "[abandoning] oneself with faith and love, to the divine future (the becoming) which is '*the* most real' of all, '*the* most living'—whose most terrifying aspect is that of being the most renewing (and hence the most creative, the most precious of all)."[90]

In the face of resistance, such creativity can be expressed subversively, confronting, confusing, and possibly transforming the inflictors of suffering. Subversion of suffering-love's creativity is also evident in humor, that rather unexpected, but extremely powerful resource for neutralising the source of suffering and transforming the experience of sufferers. Human beings can laugh and cry at the same time; as recalled by many of those who have survived horrific forms of suffering, humor is a powerful companion of creative suffering.[91] It is tragic that the church often forgets its gift and power. However, there are both biblical and historical examples for the church to use as inspiration. As Wink points out, there are various instances of humor undermining and sabotaging the seemingly overpowering shackles of oppression and despair.[92]

I complete my reflections with one of the most powerful metaphors of love's creativity in suffering: that of giving birth. Given the concerns I have been exploring in this work, it is a particularly fitting way of conveying the "mysterious fecundity" of suffering.[93] It is fitting not only for the sake of those who have longed, but were unable, to experience giving birth to a child, but also as an encouragement for the faith community

---

90. Teilhard, *On Suffering*, 30–31; emphasis original.

91. See, e.g., Frankl, *Man's Search for Meaning*, 63–64.

92. Wink, *Engaging the Powers*, 190–91. My favorite story is one from Poland in the period of Solidarity's struggles: "One group dressed in Santa Claus outfits distributed scarce sanitary napkins to women as a way of dramatizing the difficulty of obtaining essentials. When these Santas were arrested, other Santas showed up at jail insisting that the others were frauds, that they were the *real* Santas" (191; emphasis original). I have not been able to verify the facts of this story, but even if it is fictional, it ought to happen, somewhere, someday.

93. This is the phrase used by Vanier, *Man and Woman He Made Them*, 147. The element of the "mysterious" here lies not only in its metaphorical usage, but also in the necessarily unknown outcomes of such fecundity: "All acts of 'self-sacrifice' have the poignant element of 'not knowing' the end. Love does not demand to know" (Williams, *Spirit and the Forms of Love*, 212).

as a whole to expand the concept and to learn to see itself as a mother enduring the mysterious travail of bringing new creation into being.[94] Employing the metaphor of birthing is one way to describe the task of the church in keeping the vision and inviting everybody into its embodiment, each with their particular sufferings. Proclaiming the Good News involves preaching such fecundity, present even in the greatest pain and frailty.[95] The practice of witnessing to God's realm[96] itself can be seen as the process of birthing. It is a long, difficult task, but one that ends with an immense joy: "When her child is born, she no longer remembers the anguish . . . So you have pain now; but I will see you again, and your hearts will rejoice, and no one will take your joy from you" (John 16:21–22).

"Suffering runs through the whole texture of human life."[97] This is the premise on which this chapter was built. By considering the theology of suffering-love I did not regard it as an "explanation" for the struggles of single believers, and even less as an attempt to legitimize the failing of the believing communities to be such reflections and embodiments of God's realm preached by Jesus which would embrace the life of singleness as well as the life of marriage. Rather, I addressed the believing community as a whole and sought to explore suffering-love as a key virtue for several of its shared practices. Yet the very idea of suffering often brings discomfort among those who claim to follow Christ; thus they neither know how to express their own struggles and agonies nor help others to embrace the calling of Jesus to deny themselves. My interest was to re-

---

94. See an earlier discussion on enlarging the concept of mothering in chap. 7. Of course, the church as a mother is a familiar theme in the sacramental communities such as the Orthodox and the Catholic. As Cyprian of Carthage so famously put, "He can no longer have God for his Father who has not the Church for his mother" (*Writings of Cyprian, Bishop of Carthage*, 382). For baptistic communities, however, the motherhood of the church is largely an alien, if not heretical, concept.

95. Vanier observes: "Suffering people are often totally unaware that their distress can bear fruit. Perhaps the community, in living with them and their cries, can offer this suffering on their behalf to the Father in the belief that their cries are heard; that the Father makes them fruitful in union with the Passion of his Son." *Man and Woman He Made Them*, 148.

96. See chap. 7, sec. 2.

97. Beausobre, *Creative Suffering*, 1.

flect on suffering chiefly from the angle of its redemptive and life-giving qualities. With Tournier, I put an emphasis on love as the transformative power of suffering: "Love applies a positive coefficient" to the experience of suffering.[98] This requires paying close attention to the development of the virtue of suffering-love.

I began by considering the setting of the natural world as a background for interpreting suffering-love, and specifically focused on the concept of altruism. Although much of modern science, biology particularly, has not been inclined to acknowledge genuine altruism in the natural world, there are voices arguing for a much more subtle account of the nature which, put theologically, sees life on earth as "a passion play."[99] Next, I turned to the theological concept of kenosis as an action central to Christian identity, engaging with the voices which see the self-emptying of Christ as the core of Christian theology and ethics. Lastly, I considered the creative powers of suffering-love in its bodily, communal and visionary framework. I explored such a framework as a venue for meaning-making, creativity, and fecundity, suggesting that in the light of the potential for transformation, of oneself and others, differences of various experiences of suffering are no longer important. Both long-term and short term, cursory and chronic, physical and emotional, lonely and communal, suffering can be redemptive when enveloped in love.

---

98. Tournier, *Creative Suffering*, 34.
99. Nancey Murphy, "Science and Society," in McClendon, *Witness*, 123.

Conclusion

THE PURPOSE OF THIS book was to explore the challenge which involuntary singleness poses for Christian (and in particular, baptistic) communities. How does the negative experience of involuntarily single women believers critique the current theology and practices of these communities? While single women are configuring ways for meaningful, happy lives, society in general also witnesses an unprecedented fragility of the nuclear family structure. Baptistic faith communities are often greatly concerned about the latter issue and suspicious, or ignorant, about the former.

My goal was, first, to describe the challenge of involuntary singleness among women, then provide its theological interpretation and, lastly, to proceed with suggestions for bringing about a change. Such change, I argued, is possible; in spite of a significant failure to address involuntary singleness, Christian tradition offers sufficient resources to turn the tide. However, this requires a holistic framework which draws together the personal, communal, and visionary spheres of human existence. Taken together, they offer a possibility of a more fulfilling personal existence, communal life, and visionary development than each of them separately.

I started with some introductory descriptions of the problem which has prompted me to make it the theme of this book. Thus in chapter 1 I reviewed the difficulty encountered by many Christian women in finding a marriage partner, particularly due to the much higher ratio of women to men in church membership. I also observed the much lesser, but growing, ratio of single to married members. Lastly I suggested four broad sketches describing how singleness is perceived and lived out by single women in the church. I termed these four different types of singleness as temporary, unexpected, regretted, and taken on.

Chapter 2 provided an account and preliminary analysis of the response of churches to the single way of life. Building upon the notion of the church as culture, I introduced one of the tools employed throughout this work: the lens of the communal interpretive web of practices and beliefs. Such a web necessarily borrows and adapts aspects of the surrounding culture(s)—the evidence for which was provided further in chapters 3 to 6. The borrowing becomes especially extensive when the cultural dimension of religion is missed, ignored, or denied. Understanding how such borrowing takes place requires looking at how the doctrine taught is actually embodied in the way a church leads its life, including its attitudes to singleness. I suggested three dominant patterns of how singles are being treated by the rest of the church. They are the overall sense of many single believers of being ignored or overlooked; the rational justifications which the church offers for singleness; and the wished-for and real cases of singles genuinely valued for who they were. The final section of the chapter explored the clash between the claims that singleness does represent a fulfilling way of life in God's will, and the enormous weight the churches put on the institution of marriage as the ultimate source of a happy and fulfilled life.

Chapter 3 pointed to the fact that the currently dominant motifs of happiness in the church context closely resemble the way happiness is popularly perceived in the secular world. Acknowledging the inescapable religiousness of culture, I argued that it can be expected to be a source of influence and yet clash with the convictions proper to the realm of God. Either subversively or explicitly, cultural perceptions are reflected in the church's views toward singleness. I observed a tension between the increasing numbers of single people on the one hand, and the lingering economic and social discrimination against singles on the other. The latter relates to a strong emphasis on coupledom which frequently acquires the taste of an ideology. In this context, I suggested three dominant themes representing the singles' attitudes toward their non-marital status: singleness as a discouraging and despondent state; singleness as an aspect of some larger purpose of one's life; and singleness as a preferred lifestyle. In order to understand the origins of these attitudes, I explored the perceptions of the goodness of life and happiness in society at large. Although the recent explosion of interest in happiness studies marks different routes to a happy and fulfilled life, coupledom, or the nuclear family, still seem to be consistently perceived as the most significant factor contributing to happiness.

Chapter 4 sought to uncover the reasons for such a high regard for coupledom in the theology and practice of the believing communities. This required an acknowledgment of the seriousness of the current difficulties besetting the institution of family, reflected in the rapidly dwindling numbers of marriages. The difficulties affecting the so-called "traditional," coupledom-based nuclear family are notably often perceived in connection with the diminishing social role of the church in contemporary society. I reviewed some of the factors which have brought about the current shape of the nuclear family, and considered several theological insights arising from the New Testament insistence that for the followers of Christ, the church is the primary family in relation to which all other structures—including the biological family—should be aligned. If the current practice of marriage and family is undergoing a significant change, this itself presents an opportunity to rethink family in terms of faithfulness to the Christian story and the reflection on, and practice of, love. This led me to an exploration of the interpretations of love and, specifically, the two guiding myths of the nature of love: the view of love as a libidinal drive and the myth of romantic love. Focusing especially on the latter and its powerful grip on much of today's appropriation of love, I reflected on the danger of making such love the object of one's ultimate loyalty.

Chapter 5 prompted a review of the theological perspective guiding this book. I have argued that a careful examination of deeply held convictions of persons and communities in relation to their professed, or wished-for, theology allows one to consider possibilities for a better alignment of these convictions. Prevalent perceptions of happiness encountered in the church context represent a prime case of a convictional clash, with significant implications for the way in which singleness is viewed. A serious clash appears between what the churches feel they ought to be saying (and may believe they are saying) on the subject of happiness, and what they actually convey about the purpose and goodness of life. I looked at some reflections on happiness both outside and inside theology and Christian practice, and noted that although these findings are enlightening, they are rarely embodied in practice. In seeking to understand how these proposals could become a reality, I explored their interconnection with the visionary, organic, and social spheres of human life, and introduced another synonym of happiness: that of "meaning-making." Beyond the basic call to follow Jesus, I suggested, such meaning-making is to be necessarily polymorphous.

In chapter 6, I explored how the interconnectedness of these three spheres (visionary, organic, and social) and the polymorphousness of happiness can be discerned. I listened to the voices from a particular domain of critical theory—that of feminist thought—which is also interested in the investigation of routes to wholeness and flourishing *apart* from the concept and the practice of coupledom. I attended to three significant motifs. First, there was a recognition of alternative notions of human personhood arising from women's studies. Such perspectives allow for a reweaving of personal identity and reenvisioning the meaning of personal existence. As all accounts of the self, they shape the perceptions of what counts as a happy life. Second, I looked at the feminist emphasis on the "community of connections" and the dynamics of such connectedness. I shared the claim that "authentic community is the prerequisite both for the blossoming of the connected self as well as the recovery of healing connection in every area of society."[1] The discussion lastly turned to the organic sphere and its role in building a meaningful existence by highlighting the importance of the role of the body in transcendent intimations and Christian community life.

In chapter 7, I began to work out the particular shape of my proposed route to the transformation of the current attitude and practices related to singleness in community. I turned to the conceptual language of emergence, supervenience, and metaphysical holism. I looked at the implications of viewing community as an emergent structure and, employing the concept of supervenience, underscored that claims of the reality of God's presence in the community of faith must supervene on descriptions of the form of life practiced by a community of faith. Placing a particular emphasis on the reality of life in an intentional community of faith, I have concurred with McClendon that "for Christians the connecting link between the embodied ethics of each disciple and the communal ethics of the church confronting society, between the moral self and the morals of society, is to be found in the body of Christ that is the gathering church."[2] On this premise, I explored the dynamics of practices and their alignment in intentional Christian communal living. Taking the concept of metaphysical holism, I suggested that it provides a valuable angle for discussing sexuality and a wider concept of bodiliness. This led me to explore how, given the strong baptistic emphasis on

1. Grey, *Wisdom of Fools*, 120.
2. McClendon, *Ethics*, 214.

the visionary dimension of faith and the necessity of a relationship with God through Jesus, these could be expressed organically.

Chapter 8 took the case of friendship as one of the complex and largely overlooked practices in Christian communities. I argued for the significance of this practice, not only for a wholesome life, but also for its role in community formation and the sharpening of its convictions. I highlighted four virtues which I took to be particularly important for this practice: commitment, particularity, mutuality, and vulnerability. I sought to show how these virtues work as standards of excellence according to which friendships are appraised. This led me to an exploration of friendship as an inseparable element in the life of believing communities, particularly in the formation and transformation of their convictional sets. Beside the most intimate or personal friendships, then, the practice of friendship in the context of the church involves a task of becoming a community of friends in which individual convictional sets are nurtured, honed, and aligned with those of other friends.

Given the struggle involved not only in the practice of friendship, but in all human experience, chapter 9 brought me to an exploration of suffering and the virtue that it calls for, which I have termed "suffering-love." This in no way implied an "explanation" for the struggles of single believers, or an attempt to legitimize the failings of the believing communities in regard to their single members. Rather, my interest was to reflect on suffering from the angle of its redemptive and life-giving qualities in regard to all the believers, as all of them experience suffering of one kind or another. I turned to the concept of altruism as it is used in the philosophy of science, and explored the significance of altruism in the natural world. Such an interpretation shares links with the theological concept of kenosis as an action central to Christian identity. Yet the very idea of suffering frequently presents those who claim to follow Christ with another case of a convictional clash. Not knowing how to express their own struggles and agonies, they are even less able to help others. This, I suggested, requires paying close attention to the development of the virtue of suffering-love. Thus I considered the creative powers of suffering-love in its bodily, communal and visionary setting as a venue for meaning-making, creativity, and fecundity.

The situation reflected in the unprecedented growth in the numbers of singles is in many ways unique and is likely to present major challenges for the life of human societies in the coming years. It calls for a further investigation of involuntary singleness, in terms of the numbers and their dynamics in different communities of faith as well as in the settings different from those explored here. One such example would be the study of involuntary singleness of men and a comparison of similarities and differences with the involuntary singleness of women from the same context and the same or similar faith communities. The same would apply for exploring interconnections with other, non-Western, contexts. China, for example, is experiencing an exceptional situation of millions of men facing involuntary singleness resulting from the one-child policy combined with traditional preference for male progeny. In many ways, their plight parallels what many single women have gone through over several recent decades in the West.[3] The numbers of these involuntarily single men are likely to explode over the next decade, and it is conceivable that the two groups—single European women and single Chinese men—will come together in significant ways, hopefully not only through mail-order bridegroom business ventures.

This book has touched upon many different areas of human life. Although primarily a work of theological ethics, it drew from several disciplines, including cultural studies and sociology as well as intersections of the philosophy of science and theology. These different areas needed to be brought into the discussion, I believe, as they help to understand the extent of the challenge as well as the potential for the transformation of the attitudes and practices of the church. Thus, although concern for the difficulties faced by single women was the starting point, the book's scope and aim go much further. As Yoder has aptly observed, singleness represents "a test of method in thinking about ethics in the Christian community."[4] That the church should address the issue for the sake of these single women should go without saying; yet the failure to address this issue is symptomatic of the lack of health in a believing community as a whole.

By taking their own communal claims more seriously, the churches can experience signs of wholesomeness, not only on a personal level among their members, but also in their communal life and their vision-

3. For a human face on the issue, see, e.g., *The Guardian*'s feature of Duan Biansheng: "Duan worries about growing old with no one to care for him. He chafes at the unhelpful pressure to wed from his parents and neighbours. The worst thing of all is the loneliness." Branigan, "China's Village of the Bachelors," 9. For a recent study of male singleness in China, see Li Shuzhuo et al., "Male Singlehood," 679–94.

4. Yoder, *Singleness in Ethical and Pastoral Perspective*, 10.

ary aspirations. In seeking to identify some routes to wholesomeness, I hope to have demonstrated the validity of convictional theology as a method. Moreover, I hope that I have provided some inspiration that a similar approach can be applied to other issues faced by any type of intentional community, but especially by the one which calls itself a church.

Bibliography

Abramsky, Sasha. "Defining the Indefinable West." *Chronicle of Higher Education* 53 (2007) B6–B8.
Acuff, Jonathan. "Surviving Church as a Single." http://www.jonacuff.com/stuffchristians like/2009/06/550-surviving-church-as-a-single/.
Aelred of Rievaulx. *The Mirror of Charity*. Kalamazoo, MI: Cistercian, 1990.
———. *Spiritual Friendship*. Kalamazoo, MI: Cistercian, 1977.
Ahmed, Sara. "The Happiness Turn." *New Formations* 63 (2007/2008) 7–14.
Ajdacic-Gross, V., et al. "Suicide after Bereavement: An Overlooked Problem." *Psychological Medicine* 38 (2008) 673–76.
Allen, Diogenes. *Love: Christian Romance, Marriage, Friendship*. Cambridge, MA: Cowley, 1987.
Althaus-Reid, Marcella, and Lisa Isherwood, eds. *Controversies in Feminist Theology*. Controversies in Contextual Theology series. London: SCM, 2007.
Altman Irwin, and Joseph Ginat. *Polygamous Families in Contemporary Society*. Cambridge: Cambridge University Press, 1996.
Alves, Rubem. *I Believe in the Resurrection of the Body*. Philadelphia: Fortress, 1986.
Anderson, Digby C. *Losing Friends*. London: Social Affairs Unit, 2001.
Andronovienė, Lina. "As Songs Turn into Life and Life into Songs: On the First-Order Theology of Baptist Hymnody." In *Currents in Baptistic Theology of Worship*, edited by Keith G. Jones and Parush R. Parushev, 129–41. Prague: International Baptist Theological Seminary, 2007.
———. "'I Have Called You Friends': On a Theology of Friendship." In *Ethical Thinking at the Crossroads of European Reasoning*, edited by Parush R Parushev et al., 115–29. Prague: International Baptist Theological Seminary, 2007.
———. "I Sing Life." For Šárka Valley Community Church in Prague, Czech Republic. *Colours of Grace*. Song album. Prague: Šárka Valley Community Church, 2002.
———. *Involuntarily Free or Voluntarily Bound: Singleness in the Baptistic Churches of Post-communist Europe*. Prague: International Baptist Theological Seminary, 2003.
———. "Involuntarily Free: Single Women in the Believing Community." *Journal of European Baptist Studies* 3 (2002) 5–18.
———. "Jonas Inkenas and Forgiveness Lived Out: An Experiment in Biography as Narrative Theology." *American Baptist Quarterly* 22 (2003) 247–61.
Ariel, David. "Ancient Lovers to Be Kept Together." Associated Press release, quoted in *Toronto Star*, 13 February 2007. http://www.thestar.com/news/2007/02/13/ancient_lovers_to_be_kept_together.html.

Bibliography

Aristotle. *Ethica Nicomachea*. Translated by W. D. Ross. London: Oxford University Press, 1915.

Arnault, Larissa. "Living in the In-Between." *Christian Single*, November 2009, 6.

Ashworth, Jacinta, and Ian Farthing. *Churchgoing in the UK: A Research Report from Tearfund on Church Attendance in the UK*. Teddington, UK: Tearfund, 2007.

Atwood, Craig D. "Sleeping in the Arms of Christ: Sanctifying Sexuality in the Eighteenth-Century Moravian Church." *Journal of the History of Sexuality* 8 (1997) 25–51.

Aune, Kristin. *Single Women: Challenge to the Church?* Carlisle: Paternoster, 2002.

———. "Singleness and Secularization: British Evangelical Women and Church (Dis)affiliation." In *Women and Religion in the West: Challenging Secularization*, edited by Kristin Aune et al., 57–70. Aldershot, UK: Ashgate, 2008.

"Australian Passports to Have Third Gender Option." World News. *Guardian.com*, September 15, 2011. http://www.theguardian.com/world/2011/sep/15/australian-passports-third-gender-option.

Autton, Norman. *Touch: An Exploration*. London: Darton, Longman & Todd, 1989.

Balswick, Jack O., and Judith K. Balswick. *The Family: A Christian Perspective on the Contemporary Home*. 3rd ed. Grand Rapids: Baker Academic, 2007.

Balthasar, Hans Urs von. *Love Alone Is Credible*. San Francisco: Ignatius, 2004. Original German ed., *Glaubhaft ist nur Liebe*. Einsiedeln: Johannes Verlag, 1963.

Baptist World Alliance Information Service. "A BWA reflection on the family." 3 May 2011.

Barger, Lilian Calles. *Chasing Sophia: Reclaiming the Lost Wisdom of Jesus*. San Francisco: Jossey-Bass, 2007.

Barton, Stephen C. *Life Together: Family, Sexuality and Community in the New Testament and Today*. Edinburgh: T. & T. Clark, 2001.

———. "Living as Families in the Light of the New Testament." *Interpretation* 52 (1998) 130–44.

Beasley-Murray, George R. *Jesus and the Kingdom of God*. Grand Rapids: Eerdmans, 1986.

Beasley-Murray, Paul. *Power for God's Sake: Power and Abuse in the Local Church*. Carlisle: Paternoster, 1998.

Beausobre, Iulia de. *Creative Suffering*. Oxford: SLG Press, 1984.

Bedell, Geraldine. "What Makes Women Happy?" *Observer*, 11 June 2006. http://www.guardian.co.uk/lifeandstyle/2006/jun/11/familyandrelationships6.

Belenky, Mary Field, et al. *Women's Ways of Knowing*. New York: Basic Books, 1986.

Belozerskaya, Nina. "Otvet moyey sestre" [A response to my sister]. In Russian. http://www.lio.ru/archive/vera/03/02/article12.html.

Berger, Peter, et al. *Religious America, Secular Europe? A Theme and Variations*. Aldershot, UK: Ashgate, 2008.

Bergsma, Ad. "The Advice of the Wise." *Journal of Happiness Studies* 9 (2008) 331–40.

Bjørnskov, Christian. "How Comparable Are the Gallup World Poll Life Satisfaction Data?" *Journal of Happiness Studies* 11 (2010) 41–60.

Bonke, Jens, et al. "Time and Money: A Simultaneous Analysis of Men's and Women's Domain Satisfactions." *Journal of Happiness Studies* 10 (2009) 113–31.

Bos, Johanna W. H. "Out of the Shadows: Genesis 38; Judges 4:17–22; Ruth 3." *Semeia* 42 (1988) 37–67.

Boyce-Tillman, June. "Unconventional Wisdom—Theologizing the Margins." *Feminist Theology* 13 (2005) 317–41.

Branigan, Tania. "China's Village of the Bachelors: No Wives in Sight in Remote Settlement." *The Guardian*, 2 September 2011, 9. http://www.guardian.co.uk/world/2011/sep/02/china-village-of-bachelors.

Briggs, John H. Y. "Divorce and Remarriage." In *A Dictionary of European Baptist Life and Thought*, edited by John H. Y. Briggs, 148. Milton Keynes, UK: Paternoster/International Baptist Theological Seminary, 2009.

Brown, Jonathan. "Isolated: Single Christians Feel Unsupported by Family-Focused Churches." *Independent*, 25 August 2013. http://www.independent.co.uk/news/uk/home-news/isolated-single-christians-feel-unsupported-by-familyfocused-churches-8586640.html.

Brown, Malcolm. "Happiness Isn't Working, but It Should Be." In *The Practices of Happiness: Political Economy, Religion and Wellbeing*, edited by John Atherton et al., 75–85. London: Routledge, 2011.

Bruce, Deborah A., et al. "An International Survey of Congregations and Worshipers: Methodology and Basic Comparisons." *Journal of Beliefs & Values* 27 (2006) 3–12.

Brueggemann, Walter. *Genesis*. Atlanta: John Knox, 1982.

———. *The Message of the Psalms: A Theological Commentary*. Minneapolis: Augsburg, 1984.

Brunner, Brenda. "Low-Sex Marriages." PhD diss., Texas Woman's University, 2008.

Bynum, Caroline Walker. *Fragmentation and Redemption: Essays on Gender and the Human Body in Medieval Religion*. New York: Zone, 1992.

Byrne, Anne and Deborah Carr. "Caught in the Cultural Lag: The Stigma of Singlehood." *Psychological Inquiry* 16 (2005) 84–91.

Cahill, Lisa Sowle. "A Christian Social Perspective on the Family." *Mennonite Quarterly Review* 75 (2001) 161–71.

———. "Sexuality, Christian Theology, and the Defence of Moral Practices." *Modern Theology* 16 (2000) 347–52.

Callahan, Sidney. *Created for Joy: A Christian View of Suffering*. New York: Crossroad, 2007.

Cardenal, Violeta, et al. "Impact on Personality Loss or Separation from Loved Ones." *Journal of Loss and Trauma* 10 (2005) 267–92.

Cardman, Francine. "Singleness and Spirituality." *Spirituality Today* 35 (1983). http://spiritualitytoday.org/spir2day/833542cardman.html.

Carmichael, Liz. *Friendship: Interpreting Christian Love*. London: T. & T. Clark, 2004.

Carroll, Michael P. "Give Me that Ol' Time Hormonal Religion." *Journal of the Scientific Study of Religion* 43 (2004) 275–78.

Charles, Tyler. "(Almost) Everyone's Doing It." *Relevant*, Sept/Oct 2011, 65–69.

Chilcraft, Steve. *One of Us: Single People as Part of the Church*. Milton Keynes, UK: Word, 1993.

Chilcraft, Steve, et al. *Single Issues: A Whole-Church Approach to Singleness*. Warwick: CPAS, 1997.

Chopp, Rebecca. "Eve's Knowing: Feminist Theology's Resistance to Malestream Epistemological Frameworks." *Concilium* 1 (1996) 116–23.

Clapp, Rodney. *Families at the Crossroads: Beyond Tradition and Modern Options*. Downers Grove: InterVarsity, 1993.

———. "From Family Values to Family Virtues." In *Virtues and Practices in the Christian Tradition*, edited by Nancey Murphy et al., 186–201. Harrisburg, PA: Trinity, 1997.

———. *A Peculiar People: The Church as Culture in a Post-Christian Society.* Downers Grove: InterVarsity, 1996.
Clark, Margaret S., and Steven M. Graham. "Do Relationship Researchers Neglect Singles? Can We Do Better?" *Psychological Inquiry* 16 (2005) 131–36.
Clayton, Philip. "Conceptual Foundations of Emergence Theory." In *The Re-emergence of Emergence*, edited by Philip Clayton and Paul Davies, 1–31. Oxford: Oxford University Press, 2006.
Clements, Marcelle. *The Improvised Woman: Single Women Reinventing Single Life.* New York: Norton, 1998.
Cline, Sally. *Women, Celibacy and Passion.* London: Optima, 1994.
Coakley, Sarah. "Introduction: Religion and the Body." In *Religion and the Body*, edited by Sarah Coakley, 1–12. Cambridge: Cambridge University Press, 1997.
———. "Kenosis: Theological Meanings and Gender Connotations." In *The Works of Love: Creation as Kenosis*, edited by John Polkinghorne, 192–210. Grand Rapids: Eerdmans, 2001.
Cobb, Kelton. *The Blackwell Guide to Theology and Popular Culture.* Malden: Blackwell, 2005.
"Commentaries On: Singles in Society and in Science." *Psychological Inquiry* 16 (2005) 84–141.
Copeland, M. Shawn. "Difference as a Category in Critical Theologies for the Liberation of Women." *Concilium* 1 (1996) 141–51.
Cossman, Brenda. *Sexual Citizens: The Legal and Cultural Regulation of Sex and Belonging.* Stanford: Stanford University Press, 2007.
Croly, Jennifer. *Missing Being Mrs: Surviving Divorce without Losing Your Friends, Your Faith, or Your Mind.* Oxford: Monarch, 2004.
Csikszentmihalyi, Mihaly. *Flow: The Classic Work on How to Achieve Happiness.* London: Rider, 2002.
Cyprian, Bishop of Carthage. *The Writings of Cyprian, Bishop of Carthage.* Translated by Robert Ernest Wallis. Edinburgh: T. & T. Clark, 1932.
Daly, Mary. *Beyond God the Father: Toward a Philosophy of Women's Liberation.* Boston: Beacon, 1973.
Daniels, David Douglas, III. "'Gotta Moan Sometime': A Sonic Exploration of Earwitnesses to Early Pentecostal Sound in North America." *Pneuma: Journal of the Society for Pentecostal Studies* 30 (2008) 5–32.
Dawkins, Richard. *The Selfish Gene.* New York: Oxford University Press, 1989.
Deacon, Terrence W. "Emergence: The Hole at the Wheel's Hub." In *The Re-emergence of Emergence*, edited by Philip Clayton and Paul Davies, 111–50. Oxford: Oxford University Press, 2006.
Deci, Edward L., and Richard M. Ryan. "Hedonia, Eudaimonia, and Well-Being: An Introduction." *Journal of Happiness Studies* 9 (2008) 1–11.
Demir, Meliksah, and Metin Özdemir. "Friendship, Need Satisfaction and Happiness." *Journal of Happiness Studies* 11 (2010) 243–59.
DePaulo, Bella, comp. Singles Research and Writing. http://belladepaulo.com/singles-research-and-writing.
DePaulo, Bella M., and Wendy L Morris. "Should Singles and the Scholars Who Study Them Make Their Mark or Stay in Their Place?" *Psychological Inquiry* 16 (2005) 142–49.
———. "Singles in Society and in Science." *Psychological Inquiry* 16 (2005) 57–83.

Derrida, Jacques. *The Politics of Friendship.* Translated by George Collins. London: Verso, 2005.
Deshpande, Lakshmi. *Singled Out of One in the Body? An Exploration of Singleness in the Church Today.* Grove Pastoral Series 87. Cambridge: Grove, 2001.
Dietrich, Gabrielle. "The Blood of a Woman." In *One Day I Shall Be Like a Banyan Tree: Poems in Two Languages*, 31–35. Belgaum, India: Dileep S. Kamat, 1985.
Distercheft, Vilhelm. "Kogda traditsiya gubit nas i nashikh detey" [When tradition is destroying us and our children]. In Russian. *Vera i zhyzn'*, June 2010. http://www.lio.ru/archive/vera/10/06/article04.html.
Dixon, Marcia. "Why Are So Many Christian Women Single?" http://www.voice-online.co.uk/content.php?show=17076. Accessed 10 May 2010. Article no longer accessible.
Drotován, Michal, and Branislav Bleha. "Analýza fenoménu singles v Európe a na Slovensku" [Analysis of the phenomenon of singles in Europe and Slovakia]. In Slovak. *Sociológia—Slovak Sociological Review* 40 (2008) 62–81.
Dueck, Alvin, and Cameron Lee, eds. *Why Psychology Needs Theology: A Radical-Reformation Perspective.* Grand Rapids: Eerdmans, 2005.
Eaton, B. Curtis, and Mukesh Eswaran. "Well-Being and Affluence in the Presence of a Veblen Good." *Economic Journal* 119 (2009) 1088–104.
Ellis, George F. R. "Kenosis as a Unifying Theme for Life and Cosmology." In *The Work of Love: Creation as Kenosis*, edited by John Polkinghorne, 107–26. London: SPCK, 2001.
———. "On the Nature of Emergent Reality." In *The Re-emergence of Emergence*, edited by Philip Clayton and Paul Davies, 79–107. Oxford: Oxford University Press, 2006.
Empereur, James L. "The Physicality of Worship." In *Bodies of Worship: Explorations in Theory and Practice*, edited by Bruce T. Morrill, 137–55. Colegeville: Liturgical, 1999.
Eurostat. *Demography Report 2010: Older, More Numerous and Diverse Europeans.* Report. Luxembourg: Publications Office of the European Union, 2011. http://epp.eurostat.ec.europa.eu/portal/page/portal/product_details/publication?p_product_code=KE-ET-10-001.
———. "8 March 2011: International Women's Day; Women and Men in the EU Seen through Figures." Press release. Eurostat Press Office, March 4, 2011. http://europa.eu/rapid/press-release_STAT-11-36_en.htm.
———. *Europe in Figures—Eurostat Yearbook 2010.* Report. Chap. 2, "Population." Luxembourg: Publications Office of the European Union, 2010. http://epp.eurostat.ec.europa.eu/portal/page/portal/product_details/publication?p_product_code=CH_02_2010.
———. *Europe in Figures—Eurostat Yearbook 2010.* Report. Chap. 6, "Living Conditions and Welfare." Luxembourg: Publications Office of the European Union, 2010. http://epp.eurostat.ec.europa.eu/portal/page/portal/product_details/publication?p_product_code=CH_6_2010.
———. *The Life of Men and Women in Europe: A Statistical Portrait of Women and Men in All Stages of Life.* Report. Luxembourg: Eurostat, 2002. http://epp.eurostat.ec.europa.eu/portal/page/portal/product_details/publication?p_product_code=3-08102002-AP.
———. "Marriage and Divorce Statistics." Luxembourg: Eurostat, 2011. http://epp.eurostat.ec.europa.eu/statistics_explained/index.php/Marriage_and_divorce_statistics.

———. *Social Values, Science & Technology*. Survey and report. Requested by Directorate General Research, coordinated by Directorate General Press and Communication, 2005. http://ec.europa.eu/public_opinion/archives/ebs/ebs_225_report_en.pdf.

Evans, C. Stephen, ed. *Exploring Kenotic Christology: The Self-Emptying of God*. Oxford: Oxford University Press, 2006.

Evans, Stephen. "Germany Allows 'Indeterminate' Gender at Birth." November 1, 2013. http://www.bbc.co.uk/news/world-europe-24767225.

Eržerskytė, Kornelija. "R. Parafinavičius į žurnalistų darbą pažvelgė per skaudžią istoriją" [R. Parafinavičius considers the reporters' work through the lens of a painful story]. In Lithuanian. September 29, 2010. http://www.lzs.lt/lt/naujienos/zurnalistu_kuryba/archive/p15/r.parafinavicius_i_zurnalistu_darba_pazvelge_per_skaudzia_istorija.html.

Fanestil, John. "Graveside hope." *Christian Century* 124 (2007) 24–27.

Farley, Margaret A. *Just Love: A Framework for Christian Sexual Ethics*. New York: Continuum, 2006.

Farley, Wendy. *The Wounding and Healing of Desire: Weaving Heaven and Earth*. Louisville: Westminster John Knox, 2005.

Fiddes, Paul S. "Creation Out of Love." In *The Works of Love: Creation as Kenosis*, edited by John Polkinghorne, 168–84. Grand Rapids: Eerdmans, 2001.

———. *The Creative Suffering of God*. Oxford: Clarendon, 1988.

———. "Prophecy, Corporate Personality, and Suffering: Some Themes and Methods in Baptist Old Testament Scholarship." In *The "Plainly Revealed" Word of God? Baptist Hermeneutics in Theory and Practice*, edited by Helen Dare and Simon Woodman, 72–94. Macon, GA: Mercer University Press, 2011.

Finger, Thomas N. *Self, Earth & Society: Alienation & Trinitarian Transformation*. Downers Grove: InterVarsity, 1997.

Fishburn, Janet. *Confronting the Idolatry of Family: A New Vision for the Household of God*. Nashville: Abingdon, 1991.

Flescher, Andrew Michael, and Daniel L. Worthen. *The Altruistic Species: Scientific, Philosophical, and Religious Perspectives of Human Benevolence*. Philadelphia: Templeton, 2007.

Forgeard, Marie J. C., et al. "Doing the Right Thing: Measuring Wellbeing for Public Policy." *International Journal of Wellbeing* 1 (2011) 79–106.

Francis, Mother Mary. *But I Have Called You Friends: Reflections on the Art of Christian Friendship*. San Francisco: Ignatius, 2006.

Frank, S. L. *The Meaning of Life*. Translated by Boris Jakim. Grand Rapids: Eerdmans, 2010.

Frankl, Viktor E. *Man's Search for Meaning*, Rev. ed. New York: Washington Square, 1984.

Freeman, Curtis W., et al. *Baptist Roots: A Reader in the Theology of a Christian People*. Valley Forge, PA: Judson, 1999.

Fuchs, Esther. *Sexual Politics in the Biblical Narrative: Reading the Hebrew Bible as a Woman*. Sheffield: Sheffield Academic, 2000.

Fuller, Robert C. *Spirituality in the Flesh: Bodily Sources of Religious Experience*. New York: Oxford University Press, 2008.

Fulton, E. Margaret. Foreword to *Single Women: Affirming Our Spiritual Journeys*, edited by Mary O'Brien and Clare Christie, xi–xii. Westport, CT: Bergin & Garvey, 1993.

"Geidžiamas vienišius ieško ištikimos draugės" [The desired groom is looking for a faithful girlfriend]. In Lithuanian. Gyvenimo būdas section, *Lietuvos Rytas*, December 22, 2007.

Generace Singles. Directed by Jana Počtová. Czech Republic: HBO, 2011.

Giddens, Anthony. *Transformation of Intimacy: Sexuality, Love and Eroticism in Modern Societies*. Cambridge: Polity, 1992.

Gilbert, Daniel. *Stumbling on Happiness*. New York: Kopf, 2006.

Gilliam, Connally. *Revelations of a Single Woman: Loving the Life I Didn't Expect*. Carol Stream, IL: Tyndale, 2006.

Gilligan, Carol. *In a Different Voice: Psychological Theory and Women's Development*. Cambridge: Harvard University Press, 1982.

Gillis, John R. *A World of Their Own Making: Myth, Ritual, and the Quest for Family Values*. Cambridge: Harvard University Press, 1997.

Gitari, David. "The Church and Polygamy." *Transformation* 1 (1984) 3–10.

Goering, Elizabeth M., and Andrea Krause. "Odd Wo/Man Out: The Systematic Marginalization of Mennonite Singles by the Church's Focus on Family." *Mennonite Quarterly Review* 75 (2001) 211–30.

Goldingay, John. *Walk On: Life, Loss, Trust, and Other Realities*. Grand Rapids: Baker Academic, 2002.

Gombis, Timothy G. "A Radically New Humanity: The Function of the *Haustafel* in Ephesians." *Journal of the Evangelical Theological Society* 48 (2005) 317–30.

Gottschall, Jonathan, and Marcus Nordlund. "Romantic Love: A Literary Universal?" *Philosophy and Literature* 30 (2006) 432–52.

Götz, Ignacio L. *Conceptions of Happiness*. Rev. ed. Lanham: Unversity Press of America, 2010.

Graham, Billy. *The Secret of Happiness*. Rev. ed. Milton Keynes, UK: Word, 1986. First published 1955.

Graham, Carol. "Happiness and Health: Lessons—and Questions—for Public Policy." *Health Affairs* 27 (2008) 72–87.

Graham, Elaine. *Making the Difference: Gender, Personhood and Theology*. London: Mowbray, 1995.

———. "The 'Virtuous Circle': Religion and the Practices of Happiness." In *The Practices of Happiness: Political Economy, Religion and Wellbeing*, edited by John Atherton et al., 224–34. London: Routledge, 2011.

———. *Words Made Flesh: Writings in Pastoral and Practical Theology*. London: SCM, 2009.

Grams, Rollin G., and Parush R. Parushev, eds. "A Comparative Mapping of Baptist Moral Concerns and Identity in Six Regions of Europe and Central Asia." *Journal of European Baptist Studies* 6 (2006) 41–60.

———. *Towards an Understanding of European Baptist Identity: Listening to the Churches in Armenia, Bulgaria, Central Asia, Moldova, North Caucasus, Omsk and Poland*. Prague: International Baptist Theological Seminary, 2006.

Grant, Colin. *Altruism and Christian Ethics*. Cambridge: Cambridge University Press, 2001.

Green, Joel B. "Scripture and the Human Person: Further Reflections." *Science and Christian Belief* 11 (1999) 51–63.

———, ed. *What about the Soul? Neuroscience and Christian Anthropology*. Nashville: Abingdon, 2004.

Grey, Mary C. *Beyond the Dark Night: A Way Forward for the Church?* London: Cassell, 1997.

———. "Feminist Images of Redemption in Education." In *Theological Perspectives on Christian Formation: A Reader of Theology and Christian Education*, edited by Jeff Astley et al., 216–26. Grand Rapids: Eerdmans, 1996.

———. *Prophecy and Mysticism: The Heart of the Postmodern Church.* Edinburgh: T. & T. Clark, 1997.

———. *Redeeming the Dream: Feminism, Redemption and Christian Tradition.* London: SPCK, 1989.

———. *The Wisdom of Fools? Seeking Revelation for Today.* London: SPCK, 1993.

Griffin, James. "What Do Happiness Studies Study?" *Journal of Happiness Studies* 8 (2007) 139–48.

Griswold, Charles L., Jr. "Happiness, Tranquillity, and Philosophy." In *In Pursuit of Happiness*, edited by Leroy S. Rouner, 13–37. Notre Dame: University of Notre Dame Press, 1995.

Grubbs, Judith Evans. *Women and the Law in the Roman Empire: A Sourcebook on Marriage, Divorce and Widowhood.* London: Routledge, 2002.

Guder, Darrell L. *The Continuing Conversion of the Church.* Grand Rapids: Eerdmans, 2000.

Gudorf, Christine E. *Body, Sex, and Pleasure: Reconstructing Christian Sexual Ethics.* Cleveland: Pilgrim, 1994.

———. "The Erosion of Sexual Dimorphism: Challenges to Religion and Religious Ethics." In *Sexuality and the Sacred: Sources for Theological Reflection*, edited by Marvin M. Ellison and Kelly Brown Douglas, 141–64. 2nd ed. Louisville: Westminster John Knox, 2010.

Gunderson, Gary R. "Emergent Wholeness: Congregations in Community." *Word & World* 20 (2000) 360–67.

Gutenson, Charles E. "Time, Eternity, and Personal Identity: The Implications of Trinitarian Theology." In *What about the Soul? Neuroscience and Christian Anthropology*, edited by Joel B. Green, 117–32. Nashville: Abingdon, 2004.

Harding, Linda. *Better Than or Equal To? A Look at Singleness.* Milton Keynes, UK: Word, 1993.

Harrison, Beverley. "Human Sexuality and Mutuality." In *Christian Feminism: Visions of a New Humanity*, edited by Judith Weidman, 141–57. New York: Harper & Row, 1984.

Hart, Julian. *Christian Critique of American Culture.* New York: Harper & Row, 1967.

Haude, Sigrun. *In the Shadow of Savage Wolves: Anabaptist Münster and the German Reformation during the 1530s.* Boston: Humanities, 2000.

Hauerwas, Stanley. *A Community of Character: Toward a Constructive Christian Social Ethic.* Notre Dame: University of Notre Dame Press, 1981.

———. *Naming the Silences: God, Medicine, and the Problem of Suffering.* Grand Rapids: Eerdmans, 1990.

———. *Suffering Presence: Theological Reflections on Medicine, the Mentally Handicapped, and the Church.* Notre Dame: University of Notre Dame Press, 1986.

Hauerwas, Stanley, and Charles Pinches. *Christians among the Virtues: Theological Conversations with Ancient and Modern Ethics.* Notre Dame: University of Notre Dame Press, 1997.

Hauerwas, Stanley, and William H. Willimon. *Where Resident Aliens Live: Exercises for Christian Practice*. Nashville: Abingdon, 1996.
Hauerwas, Stanley, and Laura Yordy. "Captured in Time: Friendship and Aging." In *Growing Old in Christ*, edited by Stanley Hauerwas et al., 169–84. Grand Rapids: Eerdmans, 2003.
Haybron, Dan. "Life Satisfaction, Ethical Reflection, and the Science of Happiness." *Journal of Happiness Studies* 8 (2007) 99–138.
———. *The Pursuit of Unhappiness: The Elusive Psychology of Well-Being*. Oxford: Oxford University Press, 2010.
Heyward, Carter. "Notes on Historical Grounding: Beyond Sexual Essentialism." In *Sexuality and the Sacred: Sources for Theological Reflection*, edited by Marvin M. Ellison and Kelly Brown Douglas, 6–15. 2nd ed. Louisville: Westminster John Knox, 2010.
———. *The Redemption of God: A Theology of Mutual Relation*. Washington: University Press of America, 1982.
Hick, John. "The Religious Meaning of Life." In *The Meaning of Life in the World Religions*, edited by Joseph Runzo and Nancy M. Martins, 268–86. Oxford: Oneworld, 2000.
Hiebert, Paul G. *The Gospel in Human Contexts: Anthropological Explorations for Contemporary Mission*. Grand Rapids: Baker Academic, 2009.
Hillis, Marjorie. *Live Alone and Like It: A Guide for the Extra Woman*. London: Duckworth, 1936. Reprint, New York: 5 Spot, 2008.
Hird, Myra J., and Kimberly Abshoff. "Women without Children: A Contradiction in Terms?" *Journal of Comparative Family Studies* 31 (2000) 347–66.
Hodgson, An. "One Person Households: Opportunities for Consumer Goods Companies." *Euromonitor International*. September 27, 2007. http://www.euromonitor.com/one-person-households-opportunities-for-consumer-goods-companies/article.
Holden, Katherine, and Helen Kendall. First Person section. *The Guardian*, November 21, 2008. http://www.guardian.co.uk/lifeandstyle/2008/nov/22/single-marriage-asexual.
Holloway, Richard. *Godless Morality: Keeping Religion Out of Ethics*. Edinburgh: Canongate, 1999.
Hsu, Al. *The Single Issue*. Leicester: InterVarsity, 1998.
Humphrey, Edith M. *Ecstasy and Intimacy: When the Holy Spirit Meets the Human Spirit*. Grand Rapids: Eerdmans, 2006.
Hunt, Mary E. *Fierce Tenderness: A Feminist Theology of Friendship*. New York: Crossroad, 1991.
Hymas, Lisa. "The GINK Manifesto. Say It Loud: I'm Childfree and I'm Proud." *Grist.org*. March 31, 2010. http://www.grist.org/article/2010-03-30-gink-manifesto-say-it-loud-im-childfree-and-im-proud.
Isherwood, Lisa, and Elizabeth Stuart. *Introducing Body Theology*. Introductions in Feminist Theology 2. Sheffield: Sheffield Academic, 1998.
"Izpovedaniye. Pis'mo bez obratnogo adresa. Zachem zhyvu? Zachem dishu?" [A confession. A letter without the sender's address. Why do I live? Why do I breathe?]. In Russian. *Vera i zhyzn'*, February 2003. http://www.lio.ru/index.php/arkhiv-zhurnala/podpiska-2/arkhiv-v-formate-html.
Jackson, Melissa. "Lot's Daughters and Tamar as Tricksters and the Patriarchal Narratives as Feminist Theology." *Journal for the Study of the Old Testament* 98 (2002) 29–46.

Jankowiak, William R., and Edward F. Fisher. "A Cross-Cultural Perspective on Romantic Love." *Ethnology* 31 (1992) 149–56.
Jeeves, Malcolm. "The Nature of Persons and the Emergence of Kenotic Behaviour." In *The Work of Love: Creation as Kenosis*, edited by John Polkinghorne, 66–89. London: SPCK, 2001.
Jeffrey, David L. *People of the Book: Christian Identity and Literary Culture*. Grand Rapids: Eerdmans, 1996.
Jelsma, Auke. *Frontiers of the Reformation: Dissidence and Orthodoxy in Sixteenth-Century Europe*. Aldershot, UK: Ashgate, 1998.
John of the Cross. *Counsels of Light and Love*. Mahwah, NJ: HiddenSpring, 2007.
Johnson, Robert A. "Beyond Romance to Human Love." In *Perspectives on Marriage: A Reader*, edited by Kieran Scott and Michael Warren, 222–29. 3rd ed. Oxford: Oxford University Press, 2007.
Jones, Ann Rosalind. "Writing the Body: Toward an Understanding of *l'écriture feminine*." *Feminist Studies* 7 (1981) 247–63.
Jones, Keith G. "Kiss of Peace." In *A Dictionary of European Baptist Life and Thought*, edited by John H. Y. Briggs, 290. Milton Keynes, UK: Paternoster, 2009.
———. "On Abandoning Public Worship." In *Currents in Baptistic Theology of Worship Today*, edited by Keith G Jones and Parush R Parushev, 7–23. Prague: International Baptist Theological Seminary, 2007.
Jones, Serene. Afterword to *The Embrace of Eros: Bodies, Desires, and Sexuality in Christianity*, edited by Margaret D. Kamitsuka, 297–302. Minneapolis: Fortress, 2010.
Jordan, Judith V., et al. *Women's Growth in Connection: Writings from the Stone Center*. New York: Guilford, 1991.
Kaiser, Cheryl R., and Deborah A. Kashy. "The Contextual Nature and Function of Singlism." *Psychological Inquiry* 16 (2005) 122–26.
Kallenberg, Brad J. "All Suffer the Affliction of the One: Metaphysical Holism and the Presence of the Spirit." www.thomerica.com/essays/kallenberg_sufferaffliction.pdf. Also published in *Christian Scholar's Review* 31 (2002) 217–34.
Kalmijn, Matthijs, and Marjolein Broese van Groenou. "Differential Effects of Divorce on Social Integration." *Journal of Social and Personal Relationships* 22 (2005) 455–76.
Keay, Kathy. *Letters from a Solo Survivor*. London: Hodder & Stoughton, 1991.
Kekes, John. *The Art of Life*. New York: Cornell University Press, 2002.
———. *Enjoyment: The Moral Significance of Styles of Life*. Oxford: Clarendon, 2008.
Kierkegaard, Søren. *Works of Love*. Translated by David F. Swenson and Lillian Marvin Swenson. Princeton: Princeton University Press, 1946.
King, Martin Luther, Jr. "I Have a Dream." http://www.americanrhetoric.com/speeches/mlkihaveadream.htm.
"Kodėl mes norime išteketi?" [Why do we want to get married?]. In Lithuanian. 12 January 2009. http://gyvenimas.delfi.lt/love/article.php?id=20037881.
Kontorovich, Sergey. "Tochka zreniya" [A point of view]. In Russian. *Vera i zhyzn'*, March 2004. http://www.lio.ru/archive/vera/03/02/article06.html.
Kotter-Grühn, Dana, et al. "What Is It We Are Longing For? Psychological and Demographic Factors Influencing the Contents of Sehnsucht (Life Longings)." *Journal of Research in Personality* 43 (2009) 428–37.
Kreider, Eleanor. *Communion Shapes Character*. Scottdale: Herald, 1997.

Krueger, Roberta L. "Questions of Gender in Old French Romance." In *The Cambridge Compation to Medieval Romance*, edited by Roberta L. Krueger, 132-49. Cambridge: Cambridge University Press, 2000.

Langton, Sherri. "A Woman's Worth." *Mutuality* 11 (2004) 8-9. A reprint from *Today's Christian Woman*, March/April 2003.

Lawrence, Raymond J., Jr. *Sexual Liberation: The Scandal of Christendom*. Westport, CT: Praeger, 2007.

Layard, Richard. *Happiness: Lessons from a New Science*. Rev. 2nd ed. Kindle ed. New York: Penguin, 2011.

Lazarova, Daniela. "Have Young Czechs Given Up on Marriage?" Radio Prague. http://www.radio.cz/en/article/87079.

Lee, Cameron. *Beyond Family Values: A Call to Christian Virtue*. Downers Grove: InterVarsity, 1998.

Li Shuzhuo, Zhang Qunlin, et al. "Male Singlehood, Poverty and Sexuality in Rural China: An Exploratory Survey." *Population-E* 65 (2010) 679-94.

Lindbeck, George A. *The Nature of Doctrine: Religion and Theology in a Postliberal Age*. 25th anniv. ed. Louisville: Westminster John Knox, 2009.

Lorde, Audre. *Uses of the Erotic: The Erotic as Power*. Tucson: Kore, 2000.

Love, Heather. "Compulsory Happiness and Queer Existence." *New Formations* 63 (2007/2008) 52-64.

Lucas, Richard E., and Andrew E. Clark. "Do People Really Adapt to Marriage?" *Journal of Happiness Studies* 7 (2006) 405-26.

Lucas, Richard E., et al. "Reexamining Adaptation and the Set Point Model of Happiness: Reactions to Changes in Marital Status." *Journal of Personality and Social Psychology* 84 (2003) 527-39.

Lynch, Katherine A. *Individuals, Families, and Communities in Europe, 1200-1800: The Urban Foundations of Western Society*. Cambridge: Cambridge University Press, 2003.

MacIntyre, Alasdair. *After Virtue*. 2nd ed. Notre Dame: University of Notre Dame Press, 1984.

———. "The Illusion of Self-Sufficiency." Interview by Alex Voorhoeve, in *Conversations on Ethics*, edited by Alex Voorhoeve, 110-31. Oxford: Oxford University Press, 2009.

———. *A Short History of Ethics: A History of Moral Philosophy from the Homeric Age to the Twentieth Century*. 2nd ed. Notre Dame: University of Notre Dame Press, 1998.

Mackin, Theodore. "The Primitive Christian Understanding of Marriage." In *Perspectives on Marriage: A Reader*, edited by Kieran Scott and Michael Warren, 22-28. 3rd ed. Oxford: Oxford University Press, 2007.

Maeckelberghe, Els. "Across the Generations in Feminist Theology: From Second to Third Wave Feminisms." *Feminist Theology* 23 (2000) 63-69.

Magli, Ida. *Women and Self-Sacrifice in the Christian Church: A Cultural History from the First to the Nineteenth Century*. Jefferson: McFarland, 2003.

Malone, Mary T. *Women and Christianity*. Vol. 3, *From the Reformation to the 21st Century*. New York: Orbis, 2003.

Margolis, Rachel, and Mikko Myrskylä. "A Global Perspective on Happiness and Fertility." *Population and Development Review* 37 (2001) 29-56.

Marguerite of Oingt. *Les oeuvres de Marguerite d'Oingt*. Edited and translated by Antonin Duraffour et al. Paris: Belles Lettres, 1965.

Marin, Peter. "A Revolution's Broken Promises." In *Perspectives on Marriage: A Reader*, edited by Kieran Scott and Michael Warren, 168–75. 3rd ed. Oxford: Oxford University Press, 2007.

Marler, Penny Long. "Religious Change in the West: Watch the Women." In *Women and Religion in the West: Challenging Secularization*, edited by Kristin Aune et al., 23–56. Aldershot, UK: Ashgate, 2008.

Marsh, Robert R. "Id Quod Volo: The Erotic Grace of the Second Week." *The Way* 45 (2006) 7–20.

Martin, Mike W. "Paradoxes of Happiness." *Journal of Happiness Studies* 9 (2008) 171–84.

May, William F. "Four Mischievous Theories of Sex: Demonic, Divine, Casual, and Nuisance." In *Perspectives on Marriage: A Reader*, edited by Kieran Scott and Michael Warren, 186–95. 3rd ed. Oxford: Oxford University Press, 2007.

———. *The Patient's Ordeal*. Bloomington: Indiana University Press, 1994.

McCarthy, David Matzko. *The Good Life: Genuine Christianity for the Middle Class*. Grand Rapids: Brazos, 2004.

———. *Sex and Love in the Home: A Theology of the Household*. London: SCM, 2004.

McClendon, James Wm., Jr. *Biography as Theology: How Life Stories Can Remake Today's Theology*. 1974. Reprint, Philadelphia: Trinity, 1990.

———. *Doctrine: Systematic Theology*. Vol. 2. Nashville: Abingdon, 1994.

———. *Ethics: Systematic Theology*. Vol. 1. 2nd ed. Nashville: Abingdon, 2002.

———. *Witness: Systematic Theology*. With Nancey Murphy. Vol. 3. Nashville: Abingdon, 2000.

McClendon, James Wm., Jr., and James M. Smith. *Convictions: Defusing Religious Relativism*. Valley Forge: Trinity, 1994. Originally *Understanding Religious Convictions*. Notre Dame: University of Notre Dame Press, 1975.

McDonald, Skip. *And She Lived Happily Ever After: Finding Fulfillment As a Single Woman*. Downers Grove: InterVarsity, 2005.

McFague, Sallie. *Models of God: Theology for an Ecological, Nuclear Age*. London: SCM, 1987.

———. *A New Climate for Theology: God, the World, and Global Warming*. Minneapolis: Fortress, 2008.

McGrath, Alister E., and Darren C. Marks. "Protestantism—the Problem of Identity." Introduction to *The Blackwell Companion to Protestantism*, edited by Allister E. McGrath and Darren C. Marks, 1–19. Oxford: Blackwell, 2004.

Mckee, Alan. "Views on Happiness in the Television Series *Ally McBeal*: The Philosophy of David E Kelley." *Journal of Happiness Studies* 5 (2004) 385–411.

Meilaender, Gilbert. *Friendship: A Study in Theological Ethics*. Notre Dame: University of Notre Dame Press, 1981.

Meyers, Diana. "Feminist Perspectives on the Self." In *Stanford Encyclopedia of Philosophy*, edited by Edward N. Zalta. Spring 2010 ed. http://plato.stanford.edu/entries/feminism-self/.

Michaelson, Juliet, et al. *National Accounts of Wellbeing: Bringing Real Wealth Onto the Balance*. London: New Economics Foundation, 2009. http://www.nationalaccountsofwellbeing.org/learn/download-report.html.

Mikula, Jelena. "Pochemu v tserkvah bol'she zhenshchin, chem muzhchin (nenauchnaya gipoteza" [Why are there more women than men in the churches: A non-scientific hypothesis]. In Russian. *Vera i zhyzn'*, March 2004. http://www.lio.ru/archive/vera/03/02/article06.html.

Miller, Alan S., and John P. Hoffman. "Risk and Religion: An Explanation of Gender Differences in Religiosity." *Journal for the Scientific Study of Religion* 34 (1995) 63–75.

Miller, Alan S., and Rodney Stark. "Gender and Religiousness: Can Socialization Explanations Be Saved?" *American Journal of Sociology* 107 (2002) 1399–423.

Miller, Jean Baker. *Toward a New Psychology of Women*. Boston: Beacon, 1986.

Miller, Kevin. "What Pastors Are Saying." *Leadership Journal*, December 2001. http://www.christianitytoday.com/le/2001/december-online-only/cln11205.html.

"Mitai apie santuoką arba nutekėjimo laimė" [Myths about marriage or the happiness of becoming a wife]. In Lithuanian. 5 August 2009. http://www.soso3.lt/Sveikas_gyvenimas/Psichine_sveikata/Mitai_apie_santuoka_arba_nutekejimo_laime.

Moltmann, Jürgen. *The Coming of God: Christian Eschatology*. London: SCM, 1996.

———. *Sun of Righteousness, Arise! God's Future for Humanity and the Earth*. Translated by Margaret Kohl. Minneapolis: Fortress, 2010.

Moltmann-Wendel, Elisabeth. *I Am My Body*. Translated by John Bowden. London: SCM, 1994.

Monroe, Kristen Renwick. "Explicating Altruism." In *Altruism and Altruistic Love*, edited by Stephen G. Post et al., 106–22. Oxford: Oxford University Press, 2002.

Morrill, Bruce T. "Initial Consideration: Theory and Practice of the Body in Liturgy Today." In *Bodies of Worship: Explorations in Theory and Practice*, edited by Bruce T. Morrill, 1–15. Colegeville: Liturgical, 1999.

———. "Liturgical Music: Bodies Proclaiming and Responding to the Word of God." In *Bodies of Worship: Explorations in Theory and Practice*, edited by Bruce T. Morrill, 157–72. Colegeville: Liturgical, 1999.

Moss, Brigid, ed. "Real Happiness Starts Here." *Red*, February 2010, 155.

Mudure, Mihaela. "Zeugmatic Spaces: Eastern/Central European Feminisms." *Human Rights Review* 8 (2007) 137–56.

Murk-Jansen, Saskia. *Brides in the Desert: The Spirituality of the Beguines*. Maryknoll: Orbis, 1998.

Murphy, Nancey. *Bodies and Souls, or Spirited Bodies?* Cambridge: Cambridge University Press, 2006.

———. *Reasoning and Rhetoric in Religion*. Valley Forge: Trinity, 1994.

———. "Reductionism: How Did We Fall into It and Can We Emerge from It?" In *Evolution and Emergence: Systems, Organisms, Persons*, edited by William R. Stoeger and Nancey Murphy, 19–39. Oxford: Oxford University Press, 2007.

———. *Theology in a Postmodern Age*. Nordenhaug Lectures 2003. Prague: International Baptist Theological Seminary, 2004.

———. "Using MacIntyre's Method in Christian Ethics." In *Virtues and Practices in the Christian Tradition: Christian Ethics after MacIntyre*, edited by Nancey Murphy et al., 30–44. Notre Dame: University of Notre Dame Press, 1997.

Murphy, Nancey, and Warren S. Brown. *Did My Neurons Make Me Do It? Philosophical and Neurobiological Perspectives on Moral Responsibility and Free Will*. Oxford: Oxford University Press, 2007.

Murphy, Nancey, and George F. R. Ellis. *On the Moral Nature of the Universe: Theology, Cosmology, and Ethics*. Minneapolis: Fortress, 1996.

Murphy, Nancey, Brad J. Kallenberg, and Mark Thiessen Nation, eds. *Virtues and Practices in the Christian Tradition: Christian Ethics after MacIntyre*. Notre Dame: University of Notre Dame Press, 2003.

Murrow, David. *Why Men Hate Going to Church*. Nashville: Nelson, 2005.
Naugle, David K. *Reordered Love, Reordered Lives: Learning the Deep Meaning of Happiness*. Grand Rapids: Eerdmans, 2008.
Nelson, James B. *Between Two Gardens: Reflections on Sexuality and Religious Experience*. New York: Pilgrim, 1983.
New Economics Foundation. "The Happy Planet Index 2.0: Why Good Lives Don't Have to Cost the Earth." 2009. http://www.researchgate.net/publication/47529286_The_Happy_Planet_Index_2.0_Why_good_lives_dont_have_to_cost_the_Earth.
Newbigin, Leslie. *The Household of God*. New York: Friendship, 1959.
Nouwen, Henri J. M. *Clowning in Rome: Reflections on Solitude, Celibacy, Prayer and Contemplation*. New York: Image, 2000.
———. *Life of the Beloved: Spiritual Living in a Secular World*. New York: Crossroad, 2000.
———. *The Wounded Healer: Ministry in Contemporary Society*. New York: Doubleday, 1972.
Nowacka, Keiko. "Reflections on Christine de Pizan's 'Feminism.'" *Australian Feminist Studies* 17 (2002) 81–97.
"Ob itogah Vserosiyskoy perepisi naseleniya 2010 goda" [On the results of the all-Russia population census of 2010]. In Russian. *Rossiyskaya Gazeta*, December 16, 2011. http://www.rg.ru/2011/12/16/stat.html.
O'Connor, Pat. *Friendships Between Women: A Critical Review*. London: Harverster Wheatsheaf, 1992.
Office for National Statistics (UK). "Population Estimates by Marital Status: Married Population Continues to Decline." http://www.statistics.gov.uk/CCI/nugget.asp?ID=2312. Accessed 8 March 2010. Link no longer accessible.
Ogloblina, Svetlana. "Nepolnotsennaya zhenshchina?" [An inferior woman?]. *Klub odinokih i nezavisimyh zhenshchin* [Single and independent women's club]. In Russian. 25 September 2000. http://newwoman.ru/club1.html.
Oord, Thomas Jay. *Defining Love: A Philosophical, Scientific, and Theological Engagement*. Grand Rapids: Brazos, 2010.
Osborn, Ronald E. Review of *The Secret of Happiness: Jesus' Teaching on Happiness as Expressed in the Beatitudes*, by Billy Graham. *Encounter* 17 (1956) 200–202.
Osiek, Carolyn. "The Family in Early Christianity: 'Family Values' Revisited." *Catholic Biblical Quarterly* 58 (1996) 1–24.
———. "The New Testament and the Family." *Concilium* 4 (1995) 1–9.
Owen, Thomas C. "Beatrice or Iseult? The Debate About Romantic Love." *Anglican Theological Review* 79 (1997) 571.
Pahl, Ray. *On Friendship*. Cambridge: Polity, 2000.
Parushev, Parush R. "Baptistic Theological Hermeneutics." In *The Plainly Revealed Word of God? Baptist Hermeneutics in Theory and Practice*, edited by Helen Dare and Simon Woodman, 172–90. Macon: Mercer University Press, 2011.
———. "Convictions and the Shape of Moral Reasoning." In *Ethical Thinking at the Crossroads of European Reasoning*, edited by Parush R. Parushev et al., 27–45. Prague: International Baptist Theological Seminary, 2007.
———. "Doing Theology in a Baptist Way." In *Doing Theology in a Baptist Way*, edited by Teun van der Leer, 8–10. Amsterdam: Vrije Universiteit, 2009. http://www.baptisten.nl/upload/ParushevEng.pdf.

———. "Knowing the Risen Christ: The Anabaptist Holistic Missiona as Witness." *Baptistic Theologies* 3 (2011) 46–63.
Parushev, Parush R., and Lina Andronovenė. "McClendon's Concept of Mission as Witness." In *Anabaptism and Mission*, edited by Wilbert R. Shenk and Peter F. Penner, 247–64. Erlangen: Neufeld, 2007.
Patterson, Sheron C. "Singles and the Church." *Quarterly Review* 12 (1992) 45–56.
Peacocke, Arthur. "The Cost of New Life." In *The Work of Love: Creation as Kenosis*, edited by John Polkinghorne, 21–42. Grand Rapids: Eerdmans, 2001.
———. "Emergence, Mind, and Divine Action: The Hierarchy of the Sciences in Relation to the Human Mind-Brain-Body." In *The Re-emergence of Emergence*, edited by Philip Clayton and Paul Davies, 277–87. Oxford: Oxford University Press, 2006.
Percy, Martyn. "Sweet Rapture: Subliminal Eroticism in Contemporary Charismatic Worship." *Theology and Sexuality* 6 (1997) 71–106.
Peterson, Anna L. *Seeds of the Kingdom: Utopian Communities in the Americas*. New York: Oxford University Press, 2005.
Phillips, D. Z. *Religion and Friendly Fire: Examining Assumptions in Contemporary Philosophy of Religion*. Hants, UK: Ashgate, 2004.
Pilli, Toivo. *Dance or Die: The Shaping of Estonian Baptist Identity under Communism*. Milton Keynes, UK: Paternoster/International Baptist Theological Seminary, 2008.
Pillsworth, Elizabeth G., and Martie G. Haselton. "The Evolution of Coupling." *Psychological Inquiry* 16 (2005) 98–104.
Pirogov, Aleksey. "Stradayushchim" [To those who suffer]. In Russian. *Vera i zhyzn'*, February 2003. http://www.lio.ru/archive/vera/03/02/article06.html.
Plagnol, Anke. "Subjective Well-Being Over the Life Course: Conceptualizations and Evaluations." *Social Research* 77 (2010) 749–68.
Plato. *Symposium*. Translated by Benjamin Jowett. Project Gutenberg. http://www.gutenberg.org/dirs/etext99/symp010.txt.
"Po sledam publikacii. Tema odinochestva" [Follow-up on previous articles: The topic of loneliness (or *singleness*—L.A.)]. In Russian. *Vera i zhyzn'*, June 2003. http://www.lio.ru/archive/vera/03/06/article12.html.
Podles, Leon J. *The Church Impotent: The Feminization of Christianity*. Dallas: Spence, 1999.
Polivy, Janet, and C. Peter Herman. "Sociocultural Idealization of Thin Female Body Shapes: An Introduction to the Special Issue on Body Image and Eating Disorders." *Journal of Social and Clinical Psychology* 23 (2004) 1–6.
Post, Stephen G. "The Tradition of Agape." In *Altruism and Altruistic Love*, edited by Stephen G. Post et al., 51–64. Oxford: Oxford University Press, 2002.
Post, Stephen G., et al., eds. "General Introduction." In *Altruism and Altruistic Love*, edited by Stephen G. Post et al., 3–12. Oxford: Oxford University Press, 2002.
Prokhorov, Constantine. "'Living as Monks' and Fools for Christ's Sake in the Russian Baptist Brotherhood." *Theological Reflections: Euro-Asian Theological Journal* 11 (2010) 155–74.
———. "Russian Baptists and Orthodoxy, 1960–1990: A Comparative Study of Theology, Liturgy, and Traditions." PhD diss., International Baptist Theological Seminary, Prague, 2011.
Radice, Betty, trans. *The Letters of Abelard and Heloise*. London: Penguin, 2003.
Ramon, Brother. *The Flame of Sacred Love*. Oxford: Bible Reading Fellowship, 1999.

Randall, Ian M. *What a Friend We Have in Jesus: The Evangelical Tradition*. London: Darton, Longman & Todd, 2005.

Reichert, Tom, and Jacqueline Lambiase. "How to Get 'Kissably Close': Examining How Advertisers Appeal to Consumers' Sexual Needs and Desires." *Sexuality and Culture* 7 (2003) 120–36.

Reynolds, Jill. *The Single Woman: A Discursive Investigation*. London: Routledge, 2008.

Ritchhart, Ron. *Intellectual Character: What It Is, Why It Matters, and How to Get It*. San Francisco: Jossey-Bass, 2002.

Roberts, Sam. "51% of Women Are Now Living without Spouse." *New York Times*, January 16, 2007. http://www.nytimes.com/2007/01/16/us/16census.html?pagewanted=all.

———. "It's Official: To Be Married Means to Be Outnumbered." *New York Times*, October 15, 2006. http://www.nytimes.com/2006/10/15/us/15census.html?pagewanted=all&_r=0.

Roby, Douglass. "The Doctrine of the Spiritual Friendship." In *Spiritual Friendship*, by Aelred of Rievaulx, 3–40. Kalamazoo: Cistercian, 1977.

Rokven, Josja, et al. "Family." *Atlas of European Values*. http://www.atlasofeuropeanvalues.eu/new/docsfin/en/Family%20Revision%20EN%20-%20Logo.doc. Document downloaded from the internet.

Rolheiser, Ronald. *Forgotten among the Lilies: Learning to Live beyond Our Fears*. New York: Doubleday, 2005.

Rolston, Holmes, III. "Kenosis and Nature." In *The Work of Love: Creation as Kenosis*, edited by John Polkinghorne, 43–65. London: SPCK, 2001.

Rosen, Christine. "Virtual Friendship and the New Narcissism." *New Atlantis* 17 (2007) 15–31. http://www.thenewatlantis.com/publications/virtual-friendship-and-the-new-narcissism.

Rossi, Philip J. "Sojourners, Guests, and Strangers: The Church as Enactment of the Hospitality of God." *Questions Liturgiques* 90 (2009) 121–31.

Roth, John D. "Family, Community and Discipleship in the Anabaptist-Mennonite Tradition." *Mennonite Quarterly Review* 75 (2001) 147–60.

Rougemont, Denis de. *Love in the Western World*. Translated by Montgomery Belgion. Rev. ed. Princeton: Princeton University Press, 1983.

Rouner, Leroy S., ed. *The Changing Face of Friendship*. Notre Dame: University of Notre Dame Press, 1994.

———. Introduction to *On Community*, edited by Leroy S. Rouner, 1–11. Notre Dame: University of Notre Dame Press, 1991.

Rovna, Lenka. "Women in New Member States vis-à-vis the EU: The Case of the Czech Republic." Gender equality and Europe's future conference, European Commission, 2003. http://ec.europa.eu/education/programmes/llp/jm/more/confgender03/rovna.pdf. Accessed 13 September 2011. Link no longer accessible.

Ruether, Rosemary Radford. *Christianity and the Making of the Modern Family*. London: SCM, 2001.

———. *Sexism and God-Talk*. London: SCM, 1983.

———. *Women-Church: Theology and Practice of Feminist Liturgical Communities*. San Francisco: Harper & Row, 1985.

Ruhland, Catherine von. "All by Ourselves." *Third Way* 32 (2009) 26–29.

Runcorn, David. *Spirituality Workbook: A Guide for Explorers, Pilgrims and Seekers*. London: SPCK, 2006.

Runzo, Joseph and Nancy M. Martin, eds. *The Meaning of Life in the World Religions.* Oxford: Oneworld, 2000.

Russell, Letty M. "Hot-House Ecclesiology: A Feminist Interpretation of the Church." *Ecumenical Review* 53 (2001) 48–56.

Saucier, Catherine. "The Sweet Sound of Sanctity: Sensing St Lambert." *Senses & Society* 5 (2010) 10–27.

Schaeffer, Frank. *Sex, Mom, and God: How the Bible's Strange Take on Sex Led to Crazy Politics.* Cambridge: Da Capo, 2011.

Schmidtz, David. "The Meanings of Life." In *If I Should Die.* Boston University Studies in Philosophy and Religion 22, edited by Leroy S. Rouner, 170–88. Notre Dame: University of Notre Dame Press, 2001.

Schwartz, Matthew B., and Kalman J. Kaplan. *The Fruit of Her Hands: A Psychology of Biblical Woman.* Grand Rapids: Eerdmans, 2007.

Seligman, Martin E. P. *Authentic Happiness: Using the New Positive Psychology to Realise Your Lasting Fulfillment.* New York: Free Press, 2002. Kindle ed.

Sharma, Sonya. "When Young Women Say 'Yes': Exploring the Sexual Selves of Young Canadian Women in Protestant Churches." In *Women and Religion in the West: Challenging Secularization*, edited by Kristin Aune et al., 71–82. Aldershot, UK: Ashgate, 2008.

Shaw, Perry W. H. "Ministry with Singles: An Unrecognized Challenge for the Lebanese Church." *Theological Review* 29 (2008) 115–27.

Sheridan, Jean. *The Unwilling Celibates: A Spirituality for Single Adults.* Mystic, CT: Twenty-Third, 2000.

Shoop, Marcia W. Mount. *Let the Bones Dance: Embodiment and the Body of Christ.* Louisville: Westminster John Knox, 2010.

Simonaitytė, Ieva. *O buvo taip* [It was thus]. In Lithuanian. Vilnius: Vaga, 1977.

Simons, Walter. *Cities of Ladies: Beguine Communities in the Medieval Low Countries, 1200–1565.* Philadelpia: University of Pennsylvania Press, 2003.

"Single-Minded: Single People in the Church." *Administry Resource Paper* 92 (1992) no pages.

Sirgy, M. Joseph, and Jiyun Wu. "The Pleasant Life, the Engaged Life, and the Meaningful Life: What about the Balanced Life?" *Journal of Happiness Studies* 10 (2009) 183–96.

Slee, Nicola. *Faith and Feminism: An Introduction to Christian Feminist Theology.* London: Darton, Longman & Todd, 2003.

Smit, Laura A. *Loves Me, Loves Me Not: The Ethics of Unrequited Love.* Grand Rapids: Baker Academic, 2005.

Soelle, Dorothee. *Suffering.* Translated by Everett R. Kalin. London: Darton, Longman & Todd, 1975.

———. *To Work and To Love: A Theology of Creation.* With Shirley A. Cloyes Philadelphia: Fortress, 1984.

Solomon, Robert C. *Not Passion's Slave: Emotions and Choice.* Oxford: Oxford University Press, 2003.

Soni, Vivasvan. *Mourning Happiness: Narrative and the Politics of Modernity.* Ithaca: Cornell University Press, 2010.

Spalding, Anne. "Being Part of 'Right Relation.'" *Feminist Theology* 22 (1999) 43–65.

———. "'Right Relation' Revisited: Implications of Right Relation in the Practice of Church and Christian Perceptions of God." *Feminist Theology* 28 (2001) 57–68.

Stankūnienė, Vlada, and Aušra Maslauskaitė, eds. "Lietuvos šeima: tarp tradicijos ir naujos realybės" [Lithuanian family: Between tradition and new realities]. In Lithuanian. Vilnius: Socialinių tyrimų institutas, 2009. http://www.demografija.lt/users/www/uploaded/mografijos/tekstai/summary_seima.pdf.

Stark, Rodney. "Physiology and Faith: Addressing the 'Universal' Gender Difference in Religious Commitment." *Journal for the Scientific Study of Religion* 41 (2002) 495–507.

Stassen, Glen H., and David P. Gushee. *Kingdom Ethics: Following Jesus in Contemporary Context.* Downers Grove: InterVarsity, 2003.

Steedman, Ian. "Economic theory and happiness." In *The Practices of Happiness: Political Economy, Religion and Wellbeing,* edited by John Atherton et al., 23–41. London: Routledge, 2011.

Steger, Michael F. "Meaning in Life." In *Oxford Handbook of Positive Psychology,* edited by Shane J. Lopez and C.R. Snyder, 679–87. Oxford: Oxford University Press, 2009.

Steinmann, Pauline. "Singleness and Sexuality." *Vision: A Journal for Church and Theology* 9 (2008). http://www.mennovision.org/Volume9-2.htm.

Stevenson, Betsey, and Justin Wolfers. "The Paradox of Declining Female Happiness." *American Economic Journal: Economic Policy* 1 (2009) 190–225.

Stoeger, William R., and Nancey Murphy, eds. *Evolution and Emergence: Systems, Organisms, Persons.* Oxford: Oxford University Press, 2007.

Stone, Lawrence. "Passionate Attachments in the West in Historical Perspective." In *Perspectives on Marriage: A Reader,* edited by Kieran Scott and Michael Warren, 176–185. 3rd ed. Oxford: Oxford University Press, 2007.

Stoner, Abby. "Sisters Between: Gender and Medieval Beguines." *Ex Post Facto* 4 (1995). http://userwww.sfsu.edu/epf/journal_archive/volume_IV,_no._2_-_sp._1995/stoner_a.pdf.

Suikkanen, Jussi. "An Improved Whole Life Satisfaction Theory of Happiness." *International Journal of Wellbeing* 1.1 (2011) 149–66.

Swenson, Kristin M. *Living through Pain: Psalms and the Search for Wholeness.* Waco, TX: Baylor University Press, 2005.

Taylor, Charles. *Sources of the Self: The Making of the Modern Identity.* Cambridge: Harvard University Press, 1989.

Taylor, Steve. *The Out of Bounds Church? Learning to Create a Community of Faith in a Culture of Change.* Grand Rapids: Zondervan, 2005.

Teilhard de Chardin, Pierre. *On Happiness.* London: Collins, 1973.

———. *On Suffering.* New York: Harper & Row, 1975.

Thatcher, Adrian. "Religion, Family Form and the Question of Happiness." In *The Practices of Happiness: Political Economy, Religion and Wellbeing,* edited by John Atherton et al., 148–56. London: Routledge, 2011.

Tillich, Paul. *Biblical Religion and the Search for Ultimate Reality.* Chicago: University of Chicago Press, 1955.

———. *Dynamics of Faith.* 1957. Reprint, New York: HarperCollins, 2001.

———. *Systematic Theology.* Vol. 2. London: SCM, 1978.

———. *Systematic Theology.* Vol. 3. Chicago: University of Chicago Press, 1963.

Tournier, Paul. *Creative Suffering.* London: SCM, 1985.

Trimberger, E. Kay. *The New Single Woman.* Boston: Beacon, 2005.

Turner, Bryan S. "The Body in Western Society." In *Religion and the Body,* edited by Sarah Coakley, 15–41. Cambridge: Cambridge University Press, 1997.

Turner, Philip. "Sex and the Single Life." *First Things* 33 (1993) 15–21.
United Nations Statistics Division. "Marriage and Divorce." http://unstats.un.org/unsd/demographic/sconcerns/mar/mar2.htm.
Utasi, Ágnes. "Independent, Never Married People in Their Thirties: Remaining Single." Translated by Orsolya Frank. *Demografia* 46 (2003). http://www.demografia.hu/letoltes/kiadvanyok/Dem_angol/2003/Utasi.pdf.
Vanier, Jean. *Becoming Human*. London: Darton, Longman & Todd, 1999.
———. *Man and Woman He Made Them*. London: Darton, Longman & Todd, 2001.
Vardy, Peter. *The Puzzle of Sex*. 2nd ed. London: SCM, 2009
Veenhoven, Ruut. "Arts-of-Living." *Journal of Happiness Studies* 4 (2003) 373–84.
Vershina, Anna. "The Gift I Would Like to Return: Single Baptist Women in Kazakhstan." MTh diss., International Baptist Theological Seminary, Prague, 2011.
Virden, Holly. *If Singleness Is a Gift, What's the Return Policy?* With Michelle McKinney Hammond. Nashville: Thomas Nelson, 2003.
Waal, Frans de. *Good Natured: The Origins of Right and Wrong in Humans and Other Animals*. Cambridge: Harvard University Press, 1996.
Wadell, Paul J. *Becoming Friends: Worship, Justice, and the Practice of Christian Friendship*. Grand Rapids: Brazos, 2002.
———. *Friendship and the Moral Life*. Notre Dame: University of Notre Dame Press, 1989.
Wagner, Henry N., Jr. *Brain Imaging: The Chemistry of Mental Activity*. London: Springer, 2009.
Wallerstein, Judith S., and Sandra Blakeslee. *Second Chances: Men, Women, and Children a Decade after Divorce*. New York: Ticknor & Fields, 1989.
Walter, Tony. "Why Are Most Churchgoers Women? A Literature Review." *Vox Evangelica* 20 (1990) 73–90.
Walzer, Michael. *Obligations: Essays on Disobedience, War, and Citizenship*. Cambridge: Harvard University Press, 1970.
———. *Spheres of Justice: A Defence of Pluralism and Equality*. New York: Basic, 1983.
———. *Thick and Thin: Moral Argument at Home and Abroad*. Notre Dame: University of Notre Dame Press, 1994.
Wanner, Catherine. *Communities of the Converted: Ukrainians and Global Evangelism*. Ithaca: Cornell University Press, 2007.
Ware, Kallistos. "The Body in Greek Christianity." In *Religion and the Body*, edited by Sarah Coakley, 90–110. Cambridge: Cambridge University Press, 1997.
———. *The Orthodox Way*. Rev. ed. New York: St. Vladimir's Seminary Press, 1979.
Watson, Natalie K. "Reconsidering Ecclesiology: Feminist Perspectives." *Theology & Sexuality* 14 (2001) 59–77.
Way-Clark, Roberta. "My Second Life: Single Again!" In *Single Women: Affirming Our Spiritual Journeys*, edited by Mary O'Brien and Clare Christie, 67–76. Westport, CT: Bergin & Garvey, 1993.
Wenham, Gordon J., ed. *Genesis 16–50*. Vol. 2 of *World Biblical Commentary*. Dallas: Word, 1994.
White, Carolinne. *Christian Friendship in the Fourth Century*. Cambridge: Cambridge University Press, 1992.
Whitehead, Evelyn Eaton, and James D. Whitehead. "The Meaning of Marriage." In *Perspectives on Marriage: A Reader*, edited by Kieran Scott and Michael Warren, 124–33. 3rd ed. Oxford: Oxford University Press, 2007.

Wilde, Oscar. *The Importance of Being Earnest*. New York: Dover, 1990.
Wilkinson-Hayes, Anne, and Paul Mortimore, eds. *Belonging: A Resource for the Christian Family*. Baptist Union of Great Britain, 1994.
Williams, Charles. *The Figure of Beatrice: A Study in Dante*. Berkeley: Apocryphile, 2005.
———. *He Came Down from Heaven*. London: Faber & Faber, 1956.
———. *Outlines of Romantic Theology*. Edited by Alice Mary Hadfield. Berkeley: Apocryphile, 2005.
Williams, Daniel Day. *The Spirit and the Forms of Love*. New York/Evanston: Harper & Row, 1968.
———. "Suffering and Being in Empirical Theology." In *The Future of Empirical Theology*, edited by Bernard E. Meland, 175–94. Chicago: University of Chicago Press, 1969.
Williams, Emyr, et al. "Changing Patterns of Religious Affiliation, Church Attendance and Marriage across Five Areas of Europe since the Early 1980s: Trends and Associations." *Journal of Beliefs & Values* 30 (2009) 173–82.
Williams, Kipling D., and Steve A. Nida. "Obliviously Ostracizing Singles." *Psychological Inquiry* 16 (2005) 127–31.
Williams, Rowan. *On Christian Theology*. Oxford: Blackwell, 2000.
Wills, Eduardo. "Spirituality and Subjective Well-Being: Evidences for a New Domain in the Personal Well-Being Index." *Journal of Happiness Studies* 10 (2009) 49–69.
Wilson, Philip B. *Being Single: Insights for Tomorrow's Church*. London: Darton, Longman & Todd, 2005.
Wilson, Robin. "Singular Mistreatment: Unmarried Professors Are Outsiders in the Ozzie and Harriet World of Academe." *Chronicle of Higher Education*, April 23, 2004.
Wink, Walter. *Engaging the Powers: Discernment and Resistance in a World of Domination*. Philadelphia: Fortress, 1992.
———. *Naming the Powers: The Language of Power in the New Testament*. Philadelphia: Fortress, 1984.
———. *Transforming Bible Study: A Leader's Guide*. 2nd ed., rev. and exp. Nashville: Abingdon, 1989.
———. *Unmasking the Powers: The Invisible Forces that Determine Human Existence*. Philadelphia: Fortress, 1986.
Winner, Lauren F. "Solitary Refinement." *Christianity Today*, June 11, 2001, 30–36.
Winter, Sean. "Persuading Friends: Friendship and Testimony in Baptist Interpretative Communities." In *The "Plainly Revealed" Word of God? Baptist Hermeneutics in Theory and Practice*, edited by Helen Dare and Simon Woodman, 253–70. Macon, GA: Mercer University Press, 2011.
Wolterstorff, Nicholas. *Lament for a Son*. Grand Rapids: Eerdmans, 1987.
Woolever, Cynthia, et al. "The Gender Ratio in the Pews: Consequences for Congregational Vitality." *Journal of Beliefs & Values* 27 (2006) 25–38.
World Council of Churches. *Living Letters: A Report of Visits to the Churches during the Ecumenical Decade—Churches in Solidarity with Women*. Geneva: WCC Publications, 1997.
Yoder, John Howard. *Body Politics: Five Practices of the Christian Community Before the Watching World*. Nashville: Discipleship Resources, 1994.
———. *For the Nations: Essays Public and Evangelical*. Grand Rapids: Eerdmans, 1997.

———. *Singleness in Ethical and Pastoral Perspective*. Elkhart: Associated Mennonite Biblical Seminaries, 1980.
Yong, Amos. "Many Tongues, Many Senses: Pentecost, the Body Politic, and the Redemption of Dis/Ability." *Pneuma: The Journal of the Society for Pentecostal Studies* 31 (2009) 167–88.
Zeitzen, Miriam Koktvedgaard. *Polygamy: A Cross-Cultural Analysis*. Oxford: Bert, 2008.
Zhebit, Mariya. "Odin v dome ne voin" [One in the house is not a warrior]. In Russian. *Rossijskaya Gazeta*, October 24, 2010. http://www.rg.ru/2010/10/24/odinochestvo-site.html.
Zimmermann, Anke C., and Richard A. Easterlin. "Happily Ever After? Cohabitation, Marriage, Divorce and Happiness in Germany." *Population and Development Review* 32 (2006) 511–28.
Zolotarevskyi, Sergey. "Nasha propoved' dolzhna proyavlyat'sya v hristianskoy zhyzni" [Our preaching must be expressed in a Christian life]. In Russian. Interview by Igor Popov. http://www.word4you.ru/news/12005/?sphrase_id=3729.
Zorn, Waldemar. "Slovo redaktora. Novosti s fronta" [Editor's word. News from the frontline]. In Russian. *Vera i zhyzn'*, April 2006. http://www.lio.ru/archive/vera/03/02/article06.html.
———. "Slovo redaktora" [Editor's word]. In Russian. *Vera i zhyzn'*, March 2004. http://www.lio.ru/archive/vera/04/03/article01.html.
Zuurdeeg, Willem F. *An Analytical Philosophy of Religion: A Treatment of Religion on the Basis of the Methods of Empirical and Existentialist Philosophy*. London: George Allen & Unwin, 1959.

Index

A

Abelard and Heloise, 104
Aelred of Rievaulx, 208, 220, 221
African-American feminism, 142
Agape, 99–100, 205
Agape and Eros, 99
Allen, Diogenes, 93
    on our need for God, 134
    on romantic love myth, 103–4, 107
Alves, Rubem, on suffering and death, 135
Aristophanes, 105
Aristotle, 206, 207n
    on friendship, 201n, 202n, 203n, 218n
    on happiness, 123n
Asian feminism, 142
Aspiration higher than marriage motif, singleness and, 72
Aucassin and Nicolette, 103
Aune, Kristin, 41n, 137n, 47n, 55n, 137n, 186n
"Authentic happiness," 82
Available woman, 70
Avenue to flourishing motif, singleness and, 72–73

B

Baptist Union of Great Britain, 90
    Consultation on Singleness Recommendations and, 51
Baptistic, defined, 5–7
Barton, Stephen C., 94, 144
    on sexuality, 187
Beatitudes, happiness and, 130–31
Beatrice and Dante, 110, 111
Beguines, 154
Believing community, "nuclear" family and, 98
Biblical family model, 94–99
"Binuclear" family, 88
"Blended" family, 88
Bodiliness, 157, 254
    the church and, 190–98
    sexuality and, 186–90
    theology of, 183–98
Body tenderness, suffering love and, 239–42
Boyce-Tillman, June
    body/mind split, 157–58
    on self perception, 151
Brown, Joanne Carlson, 227
Brown, Malcolm, 135
Bryne, Anne, 67
Business, awareness of singles by, 66

C

Carr, Deborah, 67
Cathars, 103, 104, 112
Celibacy/chastity, 27–28, 48, 51
Charismatic groups, 162
Charter for a Happy Planet, 75
Chastity/Celibacy, 27–28, 48, 51
Children, being single and, 33

Christian dating agencies, 49
Christian feminism, 143, 150
Christian happiness, 127–31
Christian Single, 27, 35
Church/Churches
  bodiliness and the, 190–98
  compared to a political party, 169
  decline in attendance, 89
  divorce and, 30
  gender imbalances in, 20–26
  marriage and, 22
  single women in, 20–22
  traditional family and, 89
  women in, 22–26
Clapp, Rodney, 105n, 135n, 181n
  on family, 89n, 92, 95, 97n
  on friendship, 215n, 217n, 219
Coakley, Sarah, 235–36
Cohabitation, 4
Commitment, as a friendship virtue, 208–9
Communion. *See* Eucharist
Community/Communities
  as emergent structure, 170–75
  suffering love and, 238–39
  underestimated, 169
Connected self, 152–56
Consultation on Singleness Recommendations, Evangelical Alliance, 51
Convictions, 116–19
  friendship and, 215–21
Coupledom, 75
  central role of, 88
  churches and, 89
  meaning of life and, 134
  motherhood and, 78
  standard of, 76–78
    alternatives, 78–83
Coupledom/partnership/family motif, 81, 82
Culture
  happiness and, 73–76
  religion and, 61–62

D

Daly, Mary, 143
  on sisterhood, 154
Dance, liturgical, 196
Dangerous divorcee, 70
Dante and Beatrice, 110, 111
Dating agencies, 49
de Chardin, Pierre Teilhard. *See* Teilhard, Pierre de Chardin
de Rougemont, Dennis. *See* Rougemont, Denis de
Deacon, Terrence W., 174
Death, happiness and, 135
DePaulo, Bella M., 67n, 68n, 69, 77n, 83n
  on family values, 88, 92n
Discrimination, against singles, 67–68
Disillusioned singles, 32
Divorce, 29, 30, 65, 253
  communities of faith and, 89
  counseling and, 52
  Eastern Europe and, 30
  Europe and, 64
  singleness and, 4, 28–29
Divorcee, dangerous, 70

E

Ecofeminism, 142
Ellis, George F. R., 174n, 230
  on kenosis, 231, 233–4, 237–38, 247
Enlightenment, body/mind split, 157
Eros, 99–100
Erotic
  Audre Lorde on the, 159
  language, 160
Eucharist, 182
Evangelical Alliance, 20
  Consultation on Singleness, 51
  recommendations by, 51
Experiential-expressive model of religion, 39

F

Faith and Life, 15, 22
Family
    crisis in, 87–90
        affect of on singleness 89
    helper, 70
    motif, 81
    romantic relationships and, 88–89
    "Family values," 88
    strain on families and, 90
Farley, Wendy, 160
    on communities, 162
    on self perception, 152
"Female sin," Mary Gray on, 147
Feminism
    impressions of, 141–47
        as a curse word, 141
        range of, 142
        sisterhood and, 153
Fiddes, Paul S., 100, 137n, 247n,
Fiorenza, Elisabeth Schussler, "women are church," 143
Freud, Sigmund, 101–2
Friends, 67
Friendship
    assumed inferiority of, 205–7
    being single and, 32
    commitment as a virtue of, 208–9
    convictions and, 215–21
    marriage and, 93
    reconsidered, 202
    reduction of, 202–5
    virtues of, 207–8
        commitment, 208–9
        mutuality, 210–12
        particularity, 209–10
        vulnerability, 212–15
    within the church, 169

G

Gender imbalance, in churches, 20–26
"Generace Singles," 66
Gift, singleness as a, 43–44
Gilliam, Connaly, 26n, 35–36, 170n, 181n, 233n, 242n
Gillis, John, 92
    on marriage, 88n, 91n
    on motherhood, 79n, 80
God's realm, witnessing to, 179–83
God's will
    happiness and, 53–57
    alternative views, 57–59
Graham, Billy, 129–31
Grant, Collin, 230
Green, Joel, 187, 188n
Grey, Mary, 149, 151, 159, 160, 161–2
    on communities, 144n, 162–63
    on connected self, 152n, 153
    on "female sin," 148
    on motherhood, 57
    on sisterhood, 155–56
Guder, Darrell L., 117
Gushee, David P., 118, 130 n, 131, 218n, 235, 237n

H

Happiness, 82–84
    beatitudes and, 130–31
    Christian, 127–31
    culture and, 73–76
    gift of, 136
    God's will and, 53–57
        alternative views, 57–59
    perceptions of, 82, 89
    polymorphous character of, 122
    stereotypes, 126
    suffering and death and, 135
    synonym of meaning of life, 131–38
    triple beatitude of, 129

Happiness-in-motherhood motif, 79–80
The Happy Planet Index, 74–75
Hauerwas, Stanley, 97, 98n
    on friendship, 200, 212n, 215n, 221n
    on our identity, 239
    sexuality and, 185
    on suffering-love, 226n, 240n, 246
Heloise and Abelard, 104
Hillis, Marjorie, 73
Holism, 174–75
Hospitality, as a virtue, 181–82
House Church movement, 162
Hsu, Albert, 32, 41, 44n, 54

I

Ignatian Exercises, 190–91
Ignored singles, 41–43
Immaturity, singleness viewed as, 52
Industrial Revolution, 91
Intentional community, 36
International Congregational Life Survey, 20
Internet dating agencies, 49
Involuntary singleness, 2, 5
    letters on, 15–19
    responses to, 16–18
    temporary, 26–28
    see also Single women; Singleness; Women
Isolde and Tristan, 103

J

Jesus, marriage and, 95–96
Jones, Keith, 194n, 218–19
Judah, Genesis 38 story of, 1–3
Juliet and Romeo, 103

K

Keay, Kathy, 31n, 33n, 34n, 49, 56n, 57n, 185n
Kekes, John, 123–24
Kenosis, 233–49
    bodily tenderness, 239–42
    persons, communities, visions, 238–39
    social setting of, 242–45
    vision of, 245–49

L

Lack of experience, singleness viewed as, 52
Language, erotic, 160
Latin American feminism, 142
Layard, Richard, 77n, 81, 82n
Libido, 100–103
    defined, 101
Licht im Osten, 15
Life, metaphor on, 133–34
Lindbeck, George, 38–40
Listening, 192
Liturgical dance, 196
Loneliness, 15
Lorde, Audre, 159
Lord's Supper. *See* Eucharist
Love, myths of, 99–113

M

MacIntyre, Alasdair, 119n, 122, 208, 217
    practice described by, 176–79
Marguerite of Oingt, 191–92
Marriage/Marriages
    absent in heaven, 47
    advantages of, 54–55
    central role of, 88
    changing role of wife in, 91–92
    church attendance and, 22
    declining number of, 64, 87–88, 253

Marriage/Marriages (*cont.*)
  divorce, 29
  eagerness for, 76
  elitism, 55
  friendship and, 93
  Jesus and, 95–96
  re-Christianising, 180–81
Marriage/sex/kids triad, 55
Marital status, 65–66
Mary Magdalene, 45, 197
McClendon James Wm., 10, 144, 179, 214
  on culture, 62
  on ethics, 137–38, 254
  on family, 95n
  on happiness, 137–38
  on love, 100, 112n, 224n
  on kenosis, 235
  on baptistic identity, 5–6, 94n, 129n, 235n
  on theology and convictions, 116, 117–18
  of culture, 62
McFague, Sally, 159, 181n, 207n, 235
Meaning of life. *See* Happiness
Media, awareness of singles by, 66
Meilaender, Gilbert, on friendship, 202n, 203, 209n, 210–11, 214, 216
Mental health, unexpected singleness and, 31
Meaning of life, happiness as synonym of, 131–38
Metaphysical holism, 170, 254
Moltmann, Jürgen
  resurrection hope and, 137
  on seeing, 193
  sensoriness and, 191
Monroe, Kristen, 228, 229n
Moravians, bodiliness and, 190
Morris, Wendy L., 67n, 68n, 69, 77n, 83n
  on family values, 88, 92n

Mother, single, 33
Mother Mary Francis, on friendship, 200, 207, 209, 210n, 212n, 217, 218n
Motherhood, 33–34
  being a true woman and, 57
  coupledom and, 78
  motif of happiness in, 79–80
  price of, 79–80
Murphy, Nancey, 170n, 179, 198n, 224, 231
  on holism, 174–75
  on kenosis, 230–31, 233–34, 247
Mutuality, as a friendship virtue, 210–12

N

Naugle, David K., 53, 58n
Neglected singles, 41–43
Nelson, James B., on sexuality, 189
New Economics Foundation, 74–75
New Testament, single women in, 45
Nicolette and Aucassin, 103
Nicomachean Ethics, 123n, 206
Nouwen, Henri, 233n, 240–41
Nuclear family, x, 87n, 88, 113
  church and, 22, 89, 98
Nygren, Anders, 99–100

O

Organic development, happiness and, 127
Osiek, Carolyn, 94, 95n, 96n, 98n
Overlooked singles, 41–43

P

Pain
  happiness and, 135
  moral universe and, 228–32
Parker, Rebecca, 227
Particularity, as a friendship virtue, 209–10

286 Index

Parushev, Parush, 116n, 138n, 175n, 217n, 218, 235
Patterson, Sheron, 42n, 51n, 55
Paus, Ole, 226
Pentecostalist groups, 162
Perceptions of self, 147–52
Personal development, 80–81
Phaedrus, 62
Philia, 100, 202
Pinches, Charles R., 200, 212n, 246
Plato, *Symposium*, 62n, 105
Poètová, Jana, 66
Polygyny, 167–68
Practice
    Alasdair MacIntyre on, 176
    discussed, 176–79
    of witnessing, 179–83

Q

Quakers, 217

R

Radical Reformation, 5
Religion
    culture and, 61–62
    experiential-expressive model of, 39
    represents, 38–39
Religiosity, of women, 25
Ruether, Rosemary Radford, 143, 147n
Reynolds, Jill, 4n, 63n, 69n, 70–71, 77n, 140n
Rolheiser, Ronald, 54, 99n, 189n, 211
Romantic love myth, 103–9
Romantic relationships, family crisis and, 88–89
Romantic theology, 110
Romeo and Juliet, 103
Rolston III, Holmes, 229n, 232
Rougemont, Denis de, 100, 103–10, 112

S

Schmidtz, David
    meaning of life as a gift, 135n, 136
    metaphor on life, 133–34
Scriptures, formative role of, 39
The Secret of Happiness, 129–30
Secular world, 121–26
Self
    connected, 152–56
    finding, 147–52
    as organic relationality, 156–63
    perceptions of, 147–52
Senses, using, 190–95
Sermon on the Mount, happiness and, 130–31
Service sector, awareness of singles by, 66
Sex and the City, 67
Sexual chastity, 27–28
Sexuality
    bodiliness and, 186–90
    defined, 189
    dimensions of, 186
    minus sexual acts, 186–90
    scripture and, 184
    as viewed by the church, 183–86
Shunning, 30
Sight, using, 193
Silence, employing, 192
Simonaitytė, Ieva, 147
Single/Singles, 33
    awareness of, 66
    being identified as, 49–50
    defined, 4–5
    discrimination against, 67–68
    households, 65–66
    ignored/overlooked, 41–43
    intentional community and, 36
    mothers, 33, 69
    stereotyping of, 69
    taught, 43–50
    temporary, 26–28
    unexpectedly being, 28–31

Single/Singles (*cont.*)
  welcomed, 50–53
Single women
  childless, 33
  by choice, 34–36
  in churches, 20–22
  disillusioned, 32
  in the New Testament, 45
  see also Involuntary singleness; Single/Singles; Singleness; Women
Singleness
  advantages of, 47
  effect of family crisis on, 89
  aspiration higher than marriage motif, 72
  avenue to flourishing motif, 72–73
  definitions of, 63–66
  as a gift, 43–44
  motifs concerning, 71–73
  numbers, 63–66
  professed theologies of, 40–53
  as suffering, 137
  themes concerning, 71
  in theologies of culture, 66–76
  unfair world motif, 71–72
  see also Involuntary singleness
"Singularly Significant," 20, 23
Sisterhood, community of, 153–55
Smell, using, 194
Smit, Laura, 27n, 56n, 77n, 111
Socrates, 62
Soelle, Dorothee, 125n, 236, 243, 244n
Solomon, Robert C., 106
Song of Songs, 160
Soni, Vivasvan, 76
Soul, 188–89
Spalding, Anne, on sisterhood, 146n, 155
"Spinster," 69–70, 227
St. John of the Cross, 224
Stark, Rodney, 25

Stassen, Glen Harold, 46n, 118, 130n, 131, 218n, 235, 237n
"Step" families, 88
Stereotyping, of singles, 69
Suffering
  happiness and, 135
  moral universe and, 228–32
Suffering-love
  body and, 239–42
  central to Christian practices, 224
  delineating, 225–27
  persons, communities, visions, 238–9
  social setting of, 242–45
  vision of, 245–49
Suikkanen, Jussi, 121
Symeon the New Theologian, bodiliness and, 190

T

Tamar, Genesis 38 story, 1–2
Taste, use of, 193–94
Teaching, on singleness, 43–50
Teilhard, Pierre de Chardin, 127–29, 135, 231n, 246, 248
Temporarily single, 26–28
Theology, tasks of, 116
Theology of culture, 62–63, 117
  singleness in, 66–76
Tillich, Paul, 61–62, 118, 233
Touching, 194–95
"Traditional" families, 88
  believing community and, 98
  church and, 89
Transforming initiatives, 131
Trimberger, E. Kay, 65–66, 73n, 84
Tristan and Isolde, 103
Turner, Philip, 51, 158n

U

"Ultimate loyalty," 118
"Ultimate reality," 62

288   *Index*

Unexpected singleness, 28–31
Unfair world motif, singleness and, 71–72
Ursulines, 153–54

V

Vardy, Peter, 62
Vera i Zhyzn, 15
Virtue
 described, 178
 hospitality as a, 181–82
 witnessing as a, 179–83
Vulnerability, as a friendship virtue, 212–15

W

Wadell, Paul J., 206, 207n, 213n, 214n, 219n, 222
Website, dating agencies, 49
West, Angela, 145
Widows, 29, 69
Williams, Charles, 110–12
Williams, Daniel Day, 109n, 113, 238n
 on kenosis, 236, 239, 243, 247n, 248n
Williams, Rowan, 115
Willimon, William, 20n, 24n, 41n, 48n, 49n, 97
Wilson, Philip B., 98, 169

Wink, Walter, 195n, 248
Witnessing
 practice of, 179–83
 to vision and virtues, 175–79
Wives, changing perception of role of, 91–92
Woman-as-mother, price of, 79–80
Womanism, 142
Women
 changing role as wife, 91–92
 childless, 33
 in church, 22–26
  single, 22–26
 religiosity of, 25
 single
  by choice, 34–36
  disillusioned, 32
  temporary, 26–28
  unexpected, 28–31
 see also Single women

Y

Yoder, John Howard, 43, 179, 256

Z

Zuurdeeg, Willem, 116–18

www.ingramcontent.com/pod-product-compliance
Lightning Source LLC
Chambersburg PA
CBHW071237230426
43668CB00011B/1477